BACKSLIDERS

Printed in the United States of America.

Copyright © 2018 by Victor McGlothin
ISBN: 978-0-9667243-2-5

Victor McGlothin
3700 Mapleshade Ln.
Suite 2085
Plano, TX. 75075

www.VictorMcGlothin.com

BACKSLIDERS

A NOVEL

VICTOR McGLOTHIN
National Best-Selling Author

ALSO BY VICTOR McGLOTHIN

Autumn Leaves: A Novel

Borrow Trouble

Down on My Knees

Every Sistah Wants It

Indecent Exposure

Ms. Etta's Fast House

Schemers

Sinful

Sinful Too

Sleep Don't Come Easy

The Secrets of Newberry

What's a Woman to Do?

Whispers Between the Sheets

---

*How to Win in Inner-City Classrooms:
Champion Mentoring Curriculum*

The Writing Coach: How to Start Fast and Finish

ACKNOWLEDGMENTS

I am humbled and thankful for an amazing professional writing career which has spanned 20 Years. I am grateful for the chance to have lived out my dreams, met thousands of very loyal fans, and sat down with nearly 100 book clubs to discuss my novels. I've had a blast and wouldn't trade a second of it for the world.

To my beautiful wife, Terre - thank you for relinquishing your time, for months on end, while I sat in the other room or my other office (Denny's) creating characters with very interesting lives of their own. You have given up a lot and I really appreciate that.

To Ebony EyeCU Evans and EyeCU Reading & Social Network group on Facebook. You offered a freestyle writing challenge about Church Drama and I accepted it, along with many others. BACKSLIDERS is what resulted from a short 250-word scene that I crafted in less than thirty minutes. Thanks for the challenge and platform to push it out. Keep it up!

What God has for you, no one can keep from you. Hallelujah!

"McGlothin's rugged prose captures the sultry locale, and the suspenseful edge is a nice complement to the story's social conscience."

—*Publishers Weekly*

"Victor McGlothin has written an amazing story of spiritual and emotional redemption. DOWN ON MY KNEES is a welcome addition to Christian fiction."

—Victoria Christopher Murray
#1 *Essence* Bestselling author of *Grown Folks Business*

"McGlothin unravels at a relentless pace a sexy and twisted story of marital and spiritual unfaithfulness, culminating in a shocker of a conclusion. Eric Jerome Dickey, watch out."

—*Publishers Weekly* on *Sinful Too*

"I found myself lost in the story, living the moment with the characters and feeling their emotions. I recommend this book to those who love post-civil war era stories and romance."

—APOO Bookclub

"The last few chapters had me furiously turning pages to find out what happens."

—Laura L. Hutchison, *The Free Lance-Star*

"A talented storyteller with a knack for telling a convincing story, McGlothin manages to weave an entertaining story that may indeed ring true to many readers… *What's a Woman to Do* will introduce readers to yet another new and refreshing voice in the world of contemporary African-American fiction."

—*QBR* on *What's a Woman to Do*

"The twists and surprises are both plausible and unbelievable, the novel both engrossing and entertaining."

—*Booklist* on *What's a Woman to Do*

"4 Stars… Victor McGlothin has written a superb, true-to-life book. With a masterfully created plot, it explores the turbulent lives of three courageous women. This book offers a gripping, emotional glimpse into the dark world of the unknown."

—*Romantic Times BookClub* on *What's a Woman to Do*

"A fast-paced, soulful, dramatic story."

—*The Sunday Oklahoman* on *What's a Woman to Do*

"An absolute page-turner...intriguing and thought-provoking"

— Kimberla Lawson Roby, *New York Times* Bestselling Author, on *Autumn Leaves*

"Credible, honest." —*Kirkus Reviews* on *Autumn Leaves*

"The pacing of the story and the storyline itself ought to keep the reader interested until the last page is turned since there's plenty of drama and secrets to keep you wondering and guessing until the end. Victor McGlothin has told a story that is sure to satisfy fans of his first novel, AUTUMN LEAVES, as well as new readers."

—Book-remarks.com on *Autumn Leaves*

"McGlothin creates a sizzling slice of life in 1947. McGlothin weaves convincing historical elements into a fast-moving caper, and Baltimore Floyd is a delightful scoundrel."

—*Publishers Weekly* on *Ms. Etta's Fast House*

1

WHAT'S DONE IN THE DARK

The air was crisp for an April night in Texas. It was common for Dallas to experience extreme swings in temperature without notice, subjecting the city to all four seasons during the same week. Orlando Clay didn't seem to mind as he strolled out of the private exit of the pastor's office, with a firm grip on a brown leather satchel stuffed with large bills. When he entered the church parking garage, he surveyed his surroundings carefully. Not another person in sight so he continued toward the spaces reserved for church leadership. Orlando's lean frame moved with confidence, accentuated by a perfectly tailored navy blue two-button suit with golden clover-shaped cuff links. His movie star swagger, buttery complexion, and sharp features were merely three of his coveted assets. He was also a dynamic mega church preacher.

As Orlando drew near a four-door car, he glanced over his shoulder before placing the bag into the trunk of his new toy. Fresh off the showroom floor, the exquisite custom-ordered Bentley Flying Spur idled quietly against the curb. Orlando opened the car door then eased into the ivory-colored passenger seat.

He leaned back against the quilted leather then took a measured nip from a silver-plated flask to help collect his thoughts.

"Maybe this thing we're trying to pull off will buck. Maybe not. Either way," he said to the driver, "this is going to be a night to remember. Let's ride Mosley."

The Bentley pulled away from the church parking garage. Midnight blue with metallic flakes and crafted from the world's most luxurious line of automobiles, the hand-built engine purred as it zoomed west on Northwest Highway. There was only the muted hum of the heater until Orlando remembered something that made him smile.

"What do you do when your woman isn't home by four o'clock in the morning?"

Steven Mosley, with perfect white teeth, was dark as chimney soot and built like he'd been put together on a Buick assembly line. He heard the question but didn't give it much thought.

"Don't think I like that situation, pastor."

"You put her belongings out on the porch so she don't disturb your sleep, when she finally does come to her senses," he said, behind a soft chuckle. "I had a girlfriend once, she always treated me so doggone mean."

"Yeah?" Mosley asked.

"I stayed with her for ten years because she convinced me I liked it. I even tried to quit her once but she wouldn't let me. I had to set her house on fire to get away," he mused. "Then I married her, twice."

"Oomph," Mosley grunted, in place of a laugh. "Ain't that something?"

The driver was a man of very few words. His measured response brought a satisfying grin to Orlando's lips.

"I figured you'd like that one Mosley. I think I'll tell it at Bishop's next week."

The Bentley glided along the back streets toward the west end of town for twenty minutes then turned south onto Harry Hines Boulevard. It passed a row of pink and yellow neon signs with painted lips and curvy women's hips on the marquees. When the car stopped at a topless bar called Twisted Kisses, two young attendants raced to park the luxury vehicle. Orlando peered out of the raised window, looking over the full parking lot.

"You don't have to come in, you know," he said frankly. "Wives don't tend to appreciate their men coming home with flakes of glitter on their faces and the scent of other women on everything else."

Mosley eyed the young men wrestling to get the car door open. "Who you telling?" he said, eventually. "I'll stay here to watch the car and the money. Can't trust all of this with no part-time knuckle heads."

"I'll run in to see what's what. Maybe put an order in for later," Orlando said, as he opened the car door. "Bring you back anything?"

"Nothing I can't take home to the wife."

"Wise man."

Just inside the peach-colored building made of stucco, booming R&B music drowned out all of the private conversations about lap dances and numerous lewd comments. A doorman pointed a metal detecting wand at Orlando, motioning for a stop and frisk. Posha Holywater waved the security detail off.

"It's okay. He's with me."

Orlando's eyes danced when they found the club owner and former stripper, sauntering towards him. After retiring from a twenty-year career on the pole, Posha still had a killer body and the majority of her good looks. There wasn't a single line or wrinkle on her face, a flawless dark brown complexion framed by shoulder length hair. Orlando tastefully inventoried her purple mid-thigh camisole with low cleavage and shiny patent-leather five inch heels.

"Nice to see you Posha. You haven't changed a bit."

"Good thing black don't crack," she joked, then leaned in to kiss Orlando on the cheek. "Didn't think you'd show up. It's been a whole year."

A young hostess showed them to a tall round top table behind a five foot wall of frosted glass separating them from the main stage. Orlando noticed Posha had installed new wall-to-wall carpeting, an impressive light show, a much better deejay, and a number of upgrades in the level of adult entertainers she employed. Posha also owned the swanky nail salon just across the street. She had a head for business and her heart still sped up whenever the one man she couldn't get over came around. It had been several years since they found themselves tangled up in bed together and Orlando was fine with that. Posha, on the other hand, still longed for what they once had, a hot and heavy romance that lasted almost twenty months. She remembered how his passionate moves made her forget about bills, troubles, and both parents dying of lung cancer.

"The parking lot is full. Bartenders are hustling double time." Orlando noted. "I see you've done some things to the place. It's really nice Posha."

"Business is good. I can't complain. I've learned a few things about marketing. You taught me how to handle people so my staff knows I'm a boss who cares about them."

"You always did have an eye for décor. I liked that place you had on Royal Lane. You painted the walls these different colors and transformed that two bedroom into a *Better Homes & Gardens* photo spread."

"That was like a million years ago. I wanted so much more than that. You convinced me that I deserved better. I won't ever forget that." Posha realized Orlando wasn't paying attention any longer. He'd noticed a middle-aged customer grabbing one of the dancers by the wrist and refusing to let go.

"Girl, where you live?" the groper asked, as if he was thinking of dropping by her place. "Nah, never mind that. A body like yours makes a man want to change zip codes."

The petite dancer, who was all dolled up in a revealing private schoolgirl uniform, rolled her eyes then snatched her hand away. "Let me go, fool! I've been on stage all night and my feet hurt. Come and see me in the VIP lounge. You can even pretend to be my creepy teacher if that's your thing. Just bring plenty of money if you want to touch what's under this skirt." She left him standing near a table of college frat boys laughing their heads off.

"Wow, she can take care of herself to be so small," Orlando said, obviously just as amazed by the size of her DDs.

"Pastor Orlando Clay," Posha hissed, disapprovingly. "If you don't put that tongue back in your mouth."

"What? I was only complimenting those…uh," he said, sorely pleading his case. "…I admire her grit."

"And tits. Geeezus, you don't recognize Bonita do you? She goes by Boojie Queen now but that's my kid sis who had that ridiculous crush on you."

"That's your little sister Bonita? Hell, how long has it been since I… we… you know."

"Almost three years. I sent her away to live with some kinfolk in Arkansas when our mom and dad got sick. Couldn't see after them and chase her butt around town too."

"She grew up fast. Got a mouth on her."

"Can't keep her out of trouble. Maybe St. Nick can help straighten her out."

"Who?"

"My new business partner, a Cajun dude named Nickolas."

"Boudreaux?" Orlando asked, hoping he was wrong.

"Yeah, he's comes in here most every night to ask Bonita out. She won't have nothing to do with him yet but it looks like he's wearing her down."

"I can't believe St. Nick is in Dallas."

"Why you asking about him? You know him?"

"I used to. Said he'd kill me if he ever got the chance."

Orlando stood up from the table, he planted a kiss on Posha's forehead. "Excuse me. Gotta go. I'll be in touch." He turned to head toward the exit then bumped into someone. "Sorry pal," he said, looking up to find a fair-skinned albino, who was purposely standing in his way.

"What you want to go and do that for?" the large man said, grinning at Orlando.

"I apologized. That's all you'll get from me. *Nickolas*."

"Watch where you're going," he hissed, like a snake contemplating a better time to strike. Nick cast his eyes on Bonita, who was grinding the pole on stage. "I saw the way you looked at her. Boojie is spoken for."

"Bonita? She's got nothing to do with me. Didn't know you were out of lock up or in my town."

"I'm doing my own thing. Minding my own business, Orlando."

"I can't say where you go or what you do but be careful to watch *your* step."

St. Nickolas scoffed back. "Right now, you're in my step."

The men stood nose to nose, neither interested in backing down.

Posha eased in between them to break it up. "Hold up a minute gentlemen. This is my place, a drama-free zone. So squash it," she added, while pulling on Orlando's hand. He complied and followed her to the front door.

"Don't look now but *Boojie* is drunk on her main stage and I don't trust St. Nickolas as far as I can dropkick his fat pink ass." He pulled out a cell phone quickly typed in a text message. "Posha, how long did you say he's been coming around?"

"Nick showed up a few months ago with a lot of money and some new ideas about running my club."

Orlando watched the dancer take another drunken spill as she exited the stage. "And her?"

"You don't want none of that drama, Orlando. If Boojie Queen wasn't my little sister, I'd toss her out of here myself." She placed her hand in his, kissed his lips and then backed away slowly. "Bonita used to whoop you in checkers back in the day. She's grown now, moved up to chess and is still undefeated. She can handle anything St. Nick throws at her. She's tough like me. Soon enough, she'll have him drowning on dry land like every other man who thinks he can control her."

"Guess I'd better head out. Got a long night planned. I texted Lynn at the Snooty Booty, he's expecting me to stop by, meet his new girls and spread some money around. As long as you and Nick are throwing in together, I'll spend my time on the other side of town. Watch your back and your business Posha."

She watched Orlando walk out of her bar and hoped he wasn't out of her life altogether.

2

MONEY TO BLOW

Thin streams of smoke rose from the lit end of Raymundo 'Big Ray' Williams' menthol cigarette. He'd let it burn half the way down before pulling a long drag from the filtered tip while keeping a watchful eye on the reinforced steel door. The illegal gaming room was packed. Money was pouring in. Rows of senior citizens slapped at the spin buttons on eight used slot machines but the serious betting was taking place in the back end of the shotgun shaped building.

Big Ray was a heart attack waiting to happen. He stood five feet, ten inches and tipped the scales at 316 pounds. Back-to-back gastric sleeve bypass procedures couldn't compete with Big Ray's steady diet of cigarettes, fried food and imported beer. His daily uniform of loosely fitting jeans and oversized polo shirts matched his easygoing spirit. Even after serving two tough stretches in a Texas state penitentiary for drug possession, Big Ray never lost his sense of humor. A strong biracial mix of African American and Latino was evident in the way he wore his hair, short on the top and sides with long curls hanging down the back of his neck. He called it a Mexican Mullet and more than his share of women fell hard for that sort of thing.

When three women dressed in tight leggings and high heels flirted from across the room, calling him Chubby Cakes, he bit on their hook.

"What up ladies? Most of this is baby fat," Big Ray hollered back, much to the women's delight. "Don't let these round angles fool you. I can still twist it up and break it off." They giggled and Ray smiled then he nodded for the bartender to pour the girls another round on him.

He blew a dense cloud of smoke from his nostrils like a carnival act then smashed the cigarette butt out on a plastic black ashtray. He tossed a glance at the metal door again then motioned for two of his goons to take their seats on either side of it. The last time his establishment was robbed, four club jackers got in, made off with thirty-six thousand dollars and made it out without a hitch. Afterwards, Big Ray paid five grand to keep potential threats out and his eager guests feeling safe inside. High rollers felt at home in his back room where money piled high and everyone played for keeps.

Three hard knocks on the middle door got it to open from the other side. Big Ray stepped in and locked the door behind him. He disappeared into the loud, crowded room filled with local gamblers mostly and high hopes. Foggy cigar and cigarette smoke hung over the well-lit gaming table covered with a thin green felt. Expensive suits, silk ties, designer t-shirts, heavily starched jeans and several piles of money all aligned on the rectangular gaming surface.

Slim Woody stood at the head of the table like a big shot. Dapper in a gold colored suit and matching fedora hat, the retired postal worker turned pimp was hogging the dice.

"Ten gets you twenty all day baby," Slim cackled to his audience. "Put your money down on my next point, kinfolk, and catch this money train." Slim Woody was over fifty-five, quite a bit heavier than he was when he delivered mail for two decades. Suffering through a midlife crisis, Slim recently took his wife of nineteen years on an anniversary cruise, then quickly divorced her and sold their home within a month of leaving his government job. Running from his old life, his new lifestyle involved hustling women in the flesh trade. From a three bedroom apartment on Westmoreland Road, Slim provided safety and a clothing allowance for three women who in return treated men to "adult entertainment." He referred to them as one-hour 'bitch and moan' sessions. His girls worked Monday through Friday, from nine to five, catering to a select clientele of doctors, dentists, lawyers, principals, teachers and high school coaches who tipped away from their jobs for a selection of raunchy lap dances to more intimate undertakings. At two hundred dollars an hour, it was a booming business. Slim split the revenue with his staff right down the middle and even offered short-term disability and dental coverage. There was a line of women agreeable to Slim Woody's employment arrangement and a long list of regulars looking for a payday soirée as often as they could afford it.

"Get them bets down on my next point," Slim howled. "I'm hot as hell in this funky joint."

A younger man with long dreaded locks, oily brown complexion, and white gold covering his top front teeth raised his oversized white tee shirt. In a slow southern drawl he said, "I'll fade you shooter for two-hunnid."

He whipped out a thick wad of money that barely fit in his hand then peeled off ten twenty-dollar bills. Sonny Boyette, who was known as Dreadlocks, nodded assuredly then tossed his money on the table.

Several gamblers made side bets on whether Slim Woody would come up on a winning roll during his turn or crap out. Slim looked at his opponent's two-hundred dollar wager and smiled at it like an old friend.

"I could show you a better way to blow two Benjamins. Make it worth your while *and* get you blown real good in the process."

"Nah, I'm good pimpin'. Just agitate them rocks. I ain't got all night to be bumping gums with you."

Slim shot him a friendly smirk then shook the red dice in his right hand. Everyone looked on as he blew on the plastic cubes for good luck.

"Come on doozie. Come on girl." He tossed the dice onto the table. One of them landed on six and the other on two. "Eights the point. I can hit eights all day."

The dice rolled down the long table then banked on the right side before showing a three and two. "I'll take that five. And a few more to get me where I need to be. "

"I'll bet another two hunnid you bust out before that eight bites," Sonny Dreadlocks, said assuredly. He reeled off another stack of twenties and doubled down his two-hundred dollar bet.

When Slim sucked his teeth and matched the man's stack with an assortment of crumpled tens from his mounting pile, both men eyed each other a bit more seriously then.

"I like the way you step right up and give your money away."

Slim threw the dice out and they fell in five and three. His celebration was short lived, realizing that Dreadlocks waved his hand over the dice before they stopped rolling, thereby nullifying the results.

"Not so fast Old School. I caught them rocks. Roll 'em again."

Slim Woody sucked on his dry lips nervously. His chances of hitting another eight before crapping out were greatly diminished.

"Oh I ain't scared. Come on doozie and do yo thang girl. Hit that eight!"

He shook the dice fast then blew on them again. When they flew from his hand, Slim winced. Gamblers watched as the dice bounded down the table towards the other end. When they stopped, everyone howled in their disbelief. The same numbers showed again. Five and three reappeared just like Slim bet they would have.

"Ain't that a doozie!" he cheered. "Atta-girl!!!"

Those who won on the bet collected their winnings. Losers licked their wounds. Bystanders swilled beers and stiff drinks while soaking in the excitement. After Slim hit another six points in a row, Sonny Dreadlocks grew angry.

"You cheating, rat bastard! Ain't nobody that got-dammed lucky."

A hush fell over the room. The claim carried a heavy burden of proof and wielded a wicked insinuation that the game was crooked.

Big Ray pushed his way towards the table. He stood directly across from Dreadlocks, who had lost three grand in just under thirteen minutes, each time raising his bets and enduring uncomfortable ribbing from Slim. "Who the hell is saying my dice game is fixed," Big Ray huffed. Mickey Bombay, a six-foot-seven inch former NFL defense tackle, stood behind the owner with a regulation-sized baseball bat resting on his broad shoulder. His gargantuan build made the bat look like a child's toy.

When all eyes turned on Sonny Dreadlocks, he tilted his head back with a great deal of reluctance. Realizing the mess he stepped in, Dreadlocks grimaced. "Look mane, I didn't mean no disrespect. Just that this dude took thee racks off me and I ain't even touched the dice yet."

Ray nodded and gritted his teeth. He couldn't let the insinuation go without disputing it. "You call my gambling house janky again and I'll have Bombay shove that Louisville Slugger all the way up your ass." He held his hand out in a serious manner. "Slim, hand me those dice."

The former mail carrier dropped them into Ray's mitt. Once Big Ray had them, he held both red cubes up to the light to inspect each one. "Yeah, these are the house rocks I handed out this evening." He shot a stinging glare at the man who brought the erroneous charges. "You've been warned Dreadlocks but just so you don't feel like a total asshole, I'm-ma let you take these dice and crap your sorry ass on up out of here."

Laughter poured into the previously stagnant room. Slim protested harshly. "Come on now Big Ray, this ain't fair to me and who's been betting on my lucky streak. You know the rules. If Sonny Dreadlocks wants my turn to shoot, he's got to pay me for the honor."

Sonny Dreadlocks smiled. "Hell yeah. How much it cost for me to drive this train?"

"Thousand dollars," Big Ray said, hoping that would be the end of it.

Sonny eased his hand underneath his white t-shirt again. As a precaution, Mickey Bombay tighten the grip on his bat. Dreadlocks slowly pulled out another thick roll of bills from his front pocket. It was completely layered with one-hundred dollars bills, fastened together by two thick rubber bands. He methodically shelled out ten Ben Franklins to Slim Woody, who wasn't sure what to do next. He'd been riding the dice and they were smoking hot. Now he was a bystander with the option to bet on or against the next shooter's points. Uncomfortable with upsetting the natural order of the gamblers around the table, Slim collected his winnings then stuffed the loot into his felt hat.

The mood shifted around the table as much as the people did around the room. No one had ever paid a thousand dollars to take over someone else's turn on the dice. Big Ray and Mickey Bombay stood firm.

"You bought the dice. You own the next roll. Make a move."

Someone in the crowd decided to push the issue with Dreadlocks.

"What you going to do now, genius?" he asked nonchalantly.

Ray recognized the man's voice and couldn't help but smile when he heard it. "That's what I want to know, pastor," he said, while keeping his eyes trained on Dreadlocks, the man who brought his dice game to a grinding halt.

Orlando Clay took a long swig from a silver-plated flask then strode up beside Big Ray with a casual saunter like he owned the place. His polished style and charm caused women in the room to take notice. A few of them inched toward the table to get a closer look at the dreamy mega-church minister with thick wavy hair.

Orlando considered the players, the way the game had been going before the pause in action, and how things might play out if he were lucky enough to pull off something amazing and if things fell in his favor. Figuring it was as good a time as any to insert himself into the game which had taken an interesting turn, he cleared his throat.

"It appears we have an unusual set of circumstances. Hot dice in cold hands. Now, I usually don't get involved in things that don't concern me but I could not let this opportunity pass me by." Orlando smiled at Big Ray, as if to ask his consent to continue. Once he received the go ahead, the pastor cast a questioning leer at Dreadlocks. "You do know you went and committed a sin against this situation when you cooled off the dice?"

With two raised fingers, he summoned someone to emerge from the crowd.

Orlando's driver saddled up next to him. He opened the brown leather satchel and waited on instructions.

"Yes, pastor?"

"Mosley. Let's start with six thousand."

Mosley reached inside of the bag to retrieve three neat stacks of twenties, each bound together by a bank currency strap. He handed them over to Orlando one at a time.

"Big Ray, you ain't gon' count those?" Dreadlocks argued. "How we know those straps are marked right? Guess I'm supposed to take his word for it?"

Ray smiled knowingly. "Nah. I'll vouch for the stacks. Take *my* word for it."

"Okay. This is what's going to happen. I'm betting the shooter craps on the first roll. That's right," Orlando announced.

"I'm betting on a snake eyes or an ace-deuce, the snaggletooth. And the best part is... ," he said, pausing for effect, "I'm giving two to one odds. Who wants some, come get some!" Orlando harkened, like a carnival barker.

Everyone bunched around the table at once. Big Ray, Mickey Bombay and Mosley formed a semi-circle around Orlando. Big Ray growled, "Back up man!"

"Move!" Bombay ordered, stretching out his beefy arm and extending the bat with the other hand to stave off an onslaught of people wanting in on a curious bet with excellent odds.

Slim Woody pulled a handful of bills out of his hat. "Put me down for a grand. Ain't no way that dude is rolling a two or three, straight out the gate."

He laid a thousand dollars on top of the first stack Orlando had put down on the table.

Two gamblers standing on the far side of it anted up a thousand dollars each to get a piece of the action. "This is a sucker's bet," the older man laughed. "Easy money."

Orlando invited everyone else to jump in if they had at least five-hundred dollars to stake against his stake. In less time than it took to think, seven other men had laid their money down atop of the pastor's offer.

"I hope it ain't church money," someone yelled, jokingly.

"Least not my church," another person howled, resulting in thunderous laughs.

Orlando surveyed the money, lined up nice and neat on the table. Two thousand per stack. Three stacks altogether. Standing to lose six thousand dollars, he took another swig from his flask then gave Big Ray a nervous chuckle.

Ray shook his head and pushed out a sigh. "You know this is crazy, right?"

Chants of *roll, roll, roll* rang throughout the highly charged room. Orlando sucked in a deep breath then nodded he was ready. "Go ahead. Let's see how this turns out."

"Finally!" Sonny Dreadlock huffed, as he began to shake the dice in his right hand. "Leeet's get this mooooney!" he yelled, then let the red dice fly down the table.

People jumped and lunged, shouting at the dice as they tumbled along the green felt. The first die spun on its corner until resting on two. The other banked off the side then stopped on one.

Cheers of celebration and screams of disbelief bounded off the walls. Dreadlocks slammed his fist down on the table rail. Other gamblers who lost a thousand dollars each appeared more entertained than undone. Big Ray helped to collect all of the money. He and Mosley mounted it in three tall piles.

Slim stared at the money he'd just donated to Orlando's whimsical gaming proposition.

"This some bull crap," he chided. "This is messed up."

"Give me another shot Reverend," Dreadlocks pleaded. "Come on mane. I'll give you two to one this time. It can't happen again."

"Who's willing to put up two to one?" Big Ray said, exuberance dripping off his words. "Nobody? How about even money that the pastor breaks all of y'all off."

Several of the men backed away from the table to huddle and consort with one another. At Big Ray's biding, two different groups stepped up with five thousand dollars each. They agreed to put up ten grand against the same amount from Orlando. When Mosley stacked piles of money on the table, matching the wager already in place, Ray wished he had scheduled more guards for the night. Things could easily have gotten out of hand if the pastor won another boat load of money from gamblers who hadn't seen anything like him before. Not all of them would be willing to take it lying down.

Orlando sipped from his container with "0415" engraved on the side. "Tell you what. Fair is fair. Everybody gets a chance to win their money back but only if *I* get to handle the dice this time." There was a murmuring among the crowd then eventually a consensus to let the pastor roll. "I get one roll… but! I'm shooting for seven *or* eleven."

"Man, you're on some whole other type stuff," Slim said, with a side-eye expression. "My momma didn't raise no fool." He slurped from a long neck beer bottle, wiped his top lip with the ridge of his index finger then gave it a second thought. "However, I am a sporting man. I'll jump on this here wild ride." He dug back into his hat for more cash then placed it on the table, directly in front of him. "Put me down for three grand."

Pastor Orlando Clay was at the tail end of a bender, eighteen straight hours of debauchery and devilment. It was an itch that needed to be scratched. With all eyes on him, Orlando glanced at his diamond-studded Rolex to be sure of the time which was fleeting. The minister's congregation was well aware of his scandalous indulgences but still held him in high regard, esteemed above all other leaders of the prosperous 8,000 member mega-church. This pastor was special. He moved mountains and made miracles happen for his congregation but they also revered him because he was a first rate storyteller who could preach the sin off of Satan.

27

Once all the bets were made, cheers and enthusiasm poured back into the narrow musty room. A monogrammed handkerchief dangled from the minister's long manicured fingers as he wiped sweat from his moistened brow. He was nervous now and couldn't hide his concerns. There was the slightest of chances he could actually win. Orlando knew that going in, but winning didn't matter much. It just occurred to him that there would likely be a problem getting out alive if he actually found a way to pull it off.

As anticipation mounted, the minister raised his left arm. He held the dice like precious gems then began to shake them hard in a loose fist. His hand went back and forth until he felt the moment had arrived. "Oomph," he groaned, as the red cubes shot out of his hand onto the table. They tumbled half way down then rolled to a complete stop.

"OH MY GOD!" Big Ray shouted, when his eyes landed on the dice. "Oh my, oh my God!"

People screamed, waved their hands frantically, and squealed excitedly. "I'll be got-dammed," Slim Woody said, staring at the dots on the dice. "This lucky sucka done rolled a five and six at the same damn time."

In the middle of the rowdy room spilling over with resentment and regret, the minister smiled to himself while he kept an eye on Mosley, his muscular bodyguard and trusted friend who was always mere inches away from his semi-automatic handgun.

"Come on deacon," Orlando said to Mosley, as they gathered a mountainous stack of well-handled ten's, twenty's and hundred dollar bills off of the dice table.

Mosley swallowed hard when he noticed several men in the after-hours gambling establishment looking on with envy, watching their money disappear into that leather satchel. As a precaution, Mosley drew his weapon while Orlando backed slowly towards the door.

Sonny Dreadlocks looked demoralized after losing three thousand dollars. Watching it go so fast didn't sit well with him.

"How'd he get that gun in here, Big Ray? You said, no straps."

Big Ray smiled. "He's a holy man, a church deacon who wouldn't think of pulling a rod after losing his re-up money." Ray's charm was spent when he added, "But some people get desperate when they lose, especially if that grip belonged to St. Nick."

Dreadlocks wasn't ashamed to admit he had in fact gambled away a stack of money that was owed to a ruthless dealer.

"Man, you got to let me out of here," he spat, moving away from the table. Mickey Bombay cut him off with a bat raised to swing. Sonny Dreadlocks threw up both hands in a defensive manner. "Hey! Chill out, Mane."

"Where you going? Huh?" Big Ray huffed suspiciously. "You think you can run to the car and get your piece? Pull a jack move in my parking lot then take your money back?"

He winced at the menacing way Bombay glared at him. "Nah, Ray. I'm just gon' stand right here and mind my own business 'til you say I can go."

Orlando drew their attention from the rear door by clearing his throat. "I want to thank you gentlemen for your hospitality *and* your honor. No need in getting unruly over bad luck. It's God's will that it landed like it did," the minister said, with reverence dripping from his words. "I would give y'all bible, book, chapter, and verse but I'm running late at the moment. Eight o'clock church service starts in a few hours and I promised to make it rain at the Snooty Booty before all of my favorite darlings go home."

Mosley stood guard as Orlando stumbled to the Bentley parked against the curb. The minister's nerves were steadied after he took a healthy nip of cognac from the flask. "Whew-wee! That was fun. Hurry up, Mosley. I'm gonna bless a few of those fine young things at the shake shack with rent money. Its times like these I need more than one bed to lay my head."

3

ABOUT LAST NIGHT

Morning came too soon. Bursts of annoying sun rays pushed in between the gaps of partially closed drapes in Room 818 at the W Hotel. The digital clock on the nightstand read 6:05. Orlando squinted at small black box, hoping the time was wrong. It wasn't. He yawned so hard that his arms trembled, then he threw his legs over the side of the king size bed which smelled of expensive cologne and sweetly scented body lotions. After his feet hit the floor, a soft hand reached around his waist from behind. Orlando casually brushed it away.

"Party's over," he announced quietly. "Please call the front desk and tell Enrique to send for your ride."

Orlando stood up, naked as the day he was born, and surveyed the mine field he'd played in just a few hours ago. Two exotic dancers from the strip club laid sprawled on top of the bed. They were determined to show their gratitude after receiving one-thousand dollar tips for their spectacular girl on girl private show. When Orlando settled his bill with Lenny, the club manager, the dancers asked for a ride in the Bentley. He happily obliged.

Their thrill ride continued upstairs in Room 818 until each of them were sexed, satisfied, and sound asleep.

Three hours later, a golden brown twenty-five-year old Puerto Rican, working her way through college, watched Orlando walk to the closet and unzip a long cloth garment bag. She liked the way his butt muscles flexed when he shifted his weight to fluff out a dark gray suit coat.

"Ooh, that's bigger than I thought it was," she cooed, with her eyes trained on his back. "What's with that giant cross? You super religious or something?"

"Something," he answered, hesitantly. "Don't be here when I come out of the shower. And if you're thinking about taking anything that doesn't belong to you, don't."

Suddenly the covers stirred. Nestling into a spooning position was a nearly six-foot bronzed Floridian. A former starting point guard who had actually graduated from college. She wore a close buzz cut on one side and a whole foot of hair swung over her other shoulder. As Orlando entered the bathroom and closed the door behind him, the former lady hoopster opened her eyes.

"You talk too much," she said, behind a sleepy yawn.

"What'd I say?"

"He's a minister, dummy, and you just had to go and ask about that cross tattooed on his back."

"Oh, that. I didn't know he would get offended," she said, with a puzzled expression. "I'll go in there and apologize. Try to fix it."

"Too late now, he's got somewhere else to be. And I really gotta pee."

When Orlando emerged from the steam filled restroom, the girls were gone. He looked at the nightstand next to the bed. His Rolex watch and wallet were just where he'd left them. He grinned after noticing three empty gold-foil condom wrappers on the floor but the box with the remaining nine was missing. Better safe than sorry, he thought.

Pastor Orlando Clay was in lobby within the hour enjoying breakfast when he received a text. *You didn't come home, again.*

He sighed before wiping his mouth with a black cloth napkin. Not sure how to respond, Orlando typed – *See you at church.* Then pressed send. He peered out of the window when his car pulled into the valet lane. He left a couple of twenty's on the table for his meal then walked out of the exit with a dark garment bag over his arm. He climbed into the back seat of the Bentley, leaving last night and a trail of sins behind, or so he thought.

Several of the executive church parking spaces were taken when Mosley pulled into the first slot, facing a sign which read: *Reserved for the Pastor.* 7:47 AM, Orlando followed his friend and bodyguard inside of the building through the garage. Methodist Episcopal Greater Apostolic (M.E.G.A.) church started as a small A.M.E. congregation on Metropolitan Avenue in the early 1960's. After it endured several names changes, church membership splits and relocations, M.E.G.A. was constructed off of Interstate 20 near the state college.

Where cattle ranches and hay fields once painted the land-scape, stood a massive facility built for praise, pomp and certainly circumstance. M.E.G.A., designed to resemble a palace, was made of buff-colored stone with a circular driveway in front and a number of tall spires that reached towards the heavens. The 5,200 seat auditorium was routinely booked for high school graduations, weddings, theatrical plays and gospel concerts. Churches in Dallas, affectionately known as the buckle of the bible-belt, devised a plan to make religion extremely lucrative. The Republican controlled state legislature granted tax-exempt status to congregations with over 4,700 annual members, which orchestrated a legal license for church leaders to print money and enough loopholes to keep it all. Problems and personality conflicts usually became an issue when some of the senior stakeholders didn't feel like they were getting their share.

None of that mattered during the worship hour at the M.E.G.A. church as the forty-member mixed adult choir belted out a rousing rendition of "Standing on the Promises of Christ My King." Their white robes were trimmed in a thick crimson piping. The singers rocked from side to side, hitting every note with perfect pitch. Harold Bennet, the long-time choir director, was in his early 60's. He was thin and as limber as a college drum major. He bobbed his head to the rhythm of the organ and stepped with high-knee precision to the percussionist's syncopated beat of the base.

"Hands clapping!" he demanded. "Up, up, up, and now."

Sarah Wilcox grabbed the microphone and broke into captivating run up the scale, singing, "Standing on the promises of Christ my King. Through eternal ages let His praises ring. Glory in the highest I will shout and sing— Standing on the promises of God."

The talented choir chanted, "Standing on the promises! Yes, standing on the promises! Standing on the promises! I'm standing on the promises!"

A single mother of three girls, Sarah had a difficult week with disciplinary problem from her oldest child but you couldn't tell she'd lost sleep over it while leaning her head back and moving the audience to stand on their feet.

"I'm standing. I'm standing. I'm standing. I'm standing on the promises of God!"

Someone handed her a towel as sweat streamed down her forehead.

"Glory Hallelujah!" she screamed. "I am standing on His promises. Standing on all He's done for me."

"Glory. Glory," Orlando said, as he walked toward the lectern in the center of the stage. He held a cordless microphone in one hand and a red leather-bound bible in the other. "If you truly believe that you are standing on the promises of God today, say Yeah!"

"YEAH!!!"

"SAY YEAH!!!"

"YEAH!

"Now have a seat and get your swords out. If you brought your sword today raise it up."

Orlando looked out into the vast sea of faces. He saw thousands of men, women and children with bibles lifted above their heads.

"Yes, we have some dragons to slay today. Lower your swords and meet me at Genesis, chapter two and verse seven."

While pages flipped and choir members settled in, Orlando raised his bible towards the crowd.

"People often ask me why I carry around this red bible. Most bibles are covered in black or brown. No I don't have anything against those colors but when I was a small boy, getting into this and

that like little boys tend to do, my momma told me to stop embar-
rassing her and act like my bible was read." Laughter rang out in
the audience. "Heck, I thought she meant R-E-D," he added, then
another wave of laughs ensued after others finally caught on to the
joke.

"I like that one pastor," someone said, in the front row. "That's
a good one."

"Okay, the dragon we're going after today is Living Below the
Promise you're supposed to be standing on. Can I get and amen?"

"Amen!"

"Alright then, we see that God had done all of these wonderful
things like back in chapter three when he hung the sun and said let
there be light." Orlando snapped his finger. "And just like that, the
sun burst with millions of rays that still light up the world today.
Next, God dug rivers and filled them with water and brought in all
of the beasts and birds which was really cool because what good
is a free zoo, without any animals?" There was a faint amount of
snickering in the audience. "Ah-huh, so there in verse seven, He
scooped up some dirt off the ground and formed a man. It didn't
say how but if I had to guess, God formed man with his hands. And
that makes a ton of sense because God has had his hands in our lives
ever since. Can I get an amen?"

Orlando glanced up from his notes when a commotion at the
main entrance caught his attention. Mosley marched up a side aisle
to address the noise.

There was a man standing in the middle aisle demanding to be
seated. He was black, dressed in jeans, tennis shoes and a heavy
jacket. His hair was nappy and void of any style. He pulled away

from the female usher who tried to show him to the balcony.

"Then there in verse fifteen of the good book," Orlando continued. "God put man into the Garden of Eden with all of that beauty, gold and onyx, and rivers running all through it then told the man not to mess nothing up," he added, to maintain the crowd's attention.

Orlando saw two other deacons approach the man, who was so disruptive. They tried to speak to him and explain there was already a message being delivered so he couldn't interrupt by taking a seat in the lower bowl. When the guy kept shaking his head defiantly, Mosley gave the pastor a troubled look.

"Now we get to the good part. Well, since all of the good book is good, maybe we're getting to the good-er part." Another round of laughter spilled into the auditorium. "Children, don't take that word to school and try it out on your teacher." More laughter poured out as people stayed locked onto the preacher. "In verse eighteen, the Lord said, 'It is not good for man to be alone.' Since God wasn't talking to himself, there was someone or something there with him to witness this undertaking." Orlando lost sight of the visitor and assumed the disturbance was over. "God also said, I will make a helper suitable for him."

Mosley approached the lectern and passed Orlando a note. *"Possible threat. Strongly advise you leave the stage now!"*

Mosley looked over his shoulder, to see if the other men had the individual calmed down or removed. Orlando shrugged it off and went back to his message.

"That's a lesson within itself y'all. Brothers and sisters listen closely. God wants you to have someone suitable for you, that's right. None of us are without flaw so remind yourselves of that when the Mr. or Ms. Perfect you want so bad don't want you back."

Mosley shook his head regretfully then started back up the aisle towards the trouble again. This time people started to wonder what was going on.

"Suitable for you means made to fit your lifestyle, imperfections, hang ups and paycheck." The audience chuckled when they heard paycheck put into the mix. Men, if you can't afford a woman who needs her hair did and nails done on a weekly basis even when you can't keep the light on, she ain't for you!"

"Amen," an older women heckled. "Tell him again, reverend."

"And ladies," Orlando said, stepping onto the side of the lectern. "Ladies, my sisters, I hope you're listening today. Your man's rock hard abs, swagger, and sparkling teeth can't do you any good if he keeps landing behind bars. I believe in jail house ministries too but some of y'all women take that *good* Samaritan thing too far." The concerned expression on Orlando's face caused several people in the front rows to turn around. "My brothers, this might sting a bit but I got to ask. If you are over thirty five and single, what's wrong with you?"

A thunderous applause shot through the congregation. Women howled, laughed, and co-signed openly.

"I know that's right, pastor."

"Preach! I'd like to know what's the matter with them, too!" a single woman shouted seriously.

"Men, don't you want to be a part of God's plan?" He tried to preach over the loud commotion brewing in the back. "The bible says a man who finds a wife finds a good thing. That means you live longer when married, a better life with a good wife, sure 'nuff better food, less stress and better sex." Orlando watched and the visitor pushed his way down the center aisle with Mosley trying to corral him from the front. "And ladies, a man can't find you if you're always trying to prove you don't need no man because your new Lexus already came with a GPS. Take my word for it ladies, there is an art to looking lost. Not lonely but lost. And, lots of married women in here have practiced and passed with flying colors."

"I'm sorry, pastor," Mosley huffed, wishing he'd still packed the pistol from the night before. This man said he was gonna talk to you one way or another. Wouldn't take no for an answer."

With the church shooting in the news, Mosley tackled the divisive visitor to the ground when he reached into his jacket.

"STOP!" Orlando demanded, into the microphone. "If he doesn't have a weapon, hand him a microphone so everyone can hear what he has to say to me." Mosley patted the intruder down but only found a worn bible tucked into the man's ratty belt.

"Just this, preacher man," the intruder said, then raised it high like the others did earlier. "*This* is my weapon, my sword, and you are a false profit!"

A deep murmuring swept throughout the auditorium. Mosley looked helpless when he handed the intruder a hot microphone. The pastor slid both hands in his pant pockets at the same time.

"Sorry, but I don't recognize you and if I've wronged you somehow, please come and see me after service. This isn't the place if you have a quarrel with me."

A number of men were standing, ready to assault the intruder if necessary. "Man, go sit your tail down!" one of them hollered.

"Nahhh, nah. We're all friends here," Orlando suggested to

everyone, hoping to calm the waters. "Hebrews thirteen, verses one and two says, 'Continue in brotherly love. Do not neglect to show hospitality to strangers. For by doing so, some people have entertained angels without knowing it.' "

"How would you know? You're nothing but the devil standing up here in your fine clothes, driving a brand new Bentley and sucking all of the money out of this church."

"Shut up fool!" Mosley said, leaning close to the man's face and threatening to do him bodily harm. "Don't make me stomp you in front of all these people."

Orlando knew the man wanted something but didn't know what it was. He needed to find out before someone got hurt.

"Are you an angel, Sir?"

"I'm a troubled man. One who's seen the truth. I saw you last night at the gambling room shooting dice, pastor."

A number of people in the audience gasped.

"Now I dare you stand there, lie and tell your *fans* you weren't dranking while tricking pimps and drug dealers into going up against you in a game of dice."

Orlando nodded slowly. "All that is true. Over 2,000 years ago, Jesus turned water into wine and I can't find anything wrong with me enjoying libations in moderation now."

"Tell them, pastor," said Mosley. "Tell them why you went there."

"I did go to gamble and had a fine time," he answered. "Yes, it was a den of thieves, pimps, gang bangers and grifters."

"He left with luggage full of money too," the disrupter scoffed, gesturing proudly around like a politician on a campaign stump.

"I won over twenty thousand dollars in about five minutes. This morning I gave nearly all of it to the church treasurer as a donation to the Building Enhancement fund. Make no mistake, I had a ball with some of my winnings before handing over a big bag of money."

Suddenly, groups of people started clapping and cheering.

"Go ahead on pastor. After winning all that money, I probably would have partied some too," Sarah said, from the choir stand.

Orlando turned and smiled at Sarah the soloist. "Thank you, Sister Wilcox."

He turned back to address the audience and the man who had thrown a wrench into the morning worship service. "I am sorry for this disturbance y'all. We came to worship God. I suggest we get back to it. Brother, you're welcome to stay but the lower seating area is full. If you don't mind, please join our members in the balcony or come back *on time* next week."

He grimaced and backed away slowly. "I'm not your brother. And this isn't over. You're a hypocrite and a thief."

Mosley had seen and heard enough. He reached under the man's jacket, grabbed a fistful of skin and clawed it. "That's it man! You're done!"

There were cheers and celebration as Deacon Mosley paraded the fish on his hook up the middle aisle and out of the auditorium. When they reached the side exit, Mosley walked him outside where a white plumbing van awaited with the back door open.

"You're right about one thing *brother*, this ain't even close to being over."

"Who you supposed to be, some kind of tough guy?"

"You're about to find out," Mosley answered angrily. "Meet Duke and Grunt."

A muscular chocolate-covered man with a shaved head, neatly-trimmed black goatee and dimples, jumped out of the van, on the driver's side. Dressed in baggy jeans and a tight wife-beater t-shirt, Duke looked harmless until he punched the visitor in the face with a stiff left- handed jab, knocking him out cold.

A smaller man, who went by the street name of Grunt, was partial to his perfectly manicured beard. He was two shades lighter than his co-worker and had light brown eyes. He preferred to wear sweat pants, always wore a navy blue work shirt, muscles like an athlete and a full afro. Grunt dragged the church visitor's limp body into the back of the van. He collected several feet of brown bungee cord and duct tape then closed the door.

"Hey deacon, I was on my way to fix a drainpipe when I got your call," Duke informed him. "I'll look into this dude though, see why he stunted on y'all like that and get back to you. Tell Unca' Lando I need him to get at me about them washin' machines."

"Thanks Duke. I got you covered."

The white panel van rolled out of the parking lot slowly. With their hostage sound asleep, bound and gagged, there was no hurry to begin the tactical interrogation sure to follow.

After church service, Orlando sat in the pastor's office. He leaned forward on the broad mahogany desk, reading over bank deposit receipts from the day's tithes. One hundred and sixteen thousand dollars was a twenty percent increase over the normal congregation offering. Theatrics from a seemingly deranged visitor inspired members to dig a lot deeper in their purses and pockets when the baskets came around. He found himself wondering what the angry man wanted bad enough to disrupt a worship service and how long it would take Duke to get the truth out of him. Before Orlando could give it another thought, someone was standing in his doorway.

Carolyn Drew leaned against the door frame of Orlando's office wearing a fitted red skirt, black three-inch heels and a long sleeve eggshell colored blouse with French cuffs. Her oval-shaped face was the color of desert sand. High cheek bones and generous lips caused even the most devout of men to take a second look when she walked by. Her round light-brown eyes twinkled when they looked at Orlando although she rather they didn't. Stopping by to get a number of construction plans initialed, Carolyn paused when she saw the concerned expression on Orlando's face.

"May I come in, pastor, or it this a bad time?"

"Good afternoon Sister Carolyn. Of course. Come in and have a seat," he said, rising to his feet. "This is still Pastor Drew's space until the leadership hands it over permanently to another shepherd. Your husband gave his life to this church."

"Thank you," she replied, "But I just came for you to sign these."

Carolyn laid the stack of papers on the desk then strolled over to the book shelf, where a photo of the previous pastor sat in bronze 5X7 frame. It was still prominently placed where it always had been, on the third shelf. "It's kind of you to leave everything just as it was when…"

"Don't," he interrupted. "It's okay. I'm not in any hurry to change a thing."

Her husband of twelve years passed away less than a year ago. He literally had a heart attack in the pulpit. Carolyn was in mourning but still very much a woman.

"Please don't feel like you have to keep all of Thomas' things on my account," she said, choosing her words carefully whenever around Orlando.

He observed her casual sway as she walked across the room to doctor an ivy plant suffering from dehydration. Orlando enjoyed the way she moved, never in a hurry and seemingly comfortable in her own skin. He liked her confidence, intelligence, and the hair bun she wore like the hot librarian in every teen aged boy's sexual fantasy.

"Feel free to drop by any time you like," he replied eventually. "Whether I'm in or not."

Orlando walked towards Carolyn and reached across her to pick up a few dried leaves that had fallen on the window ledge.

"It gets warm in here Sister Carolyn. I'll bet this plant is really thirsty. I know it doesn't get watered enough."

She moistened her lips with her tongue as she nervously shifted her weight away from him.

Thirty-six years old, Carolyn was determined to maintain two things, her position as the church chief financial officer (CFO) and her sterling reputation as a lady of honor. She rubbed her hands down the sides of her shirt when they suddenly felt sweaty.

"Uhh, I think it might be a lot cooler over there," she said, blowing out a stream of pent up anxiety. "I have to keep my distance from potentially precarious situations Brother Pastor. I haven't been married in a while but I still have sense enough to stay away from men like you."

"See that's where you're wrong Carolyn," he whispered. "There are no men like me left."

He watched her adjust her skirt, which fit tighter than she liked but it was perfect according to Orlando. "I see you're uncomfortable. I'll stay in my lane."

Her eyes fell towards the floor. "Thank you, Sir. I'll come back when you've had a chance to look over the construction bids and initial each page."

"If I've offended you. I apologize."

She turned to leave then stopped, closed the door, and leaned against it. "I'm a big girl, better yet, a grown woman who can shut a man down if I feel he's putting me in an unfair position. Present company included."

He smiled and nodded softly. "Point taken."

"Then, can I ask you something personal that I've been wanting to know all day?"

Orlando didn't realized she'd had been wearing rimless glasses until she pulled them off and folded them into her hand.

"Go ahead. I'm an open book," he replied.

"That man who leveled those accusations at you during the sermon, was everything he said about you true? The gambling, carousing, and drinking?"

"Yes, all true, I'm afraid. However, he didn't know that my escapades continued long after I left Big Ray's joint. I also had a wild night of entertainment with two women I met at an upscale strip club," he added, to see her reaction.

"Oh," she said quietly, searching for words to convey her surprise. "Very interesting. Is that how you've gotten over losing your wife?"

There was a knock on the door.

"Who says I have?" he answered, breaking eye contact.

"One minute please," he said, loud enough to be heard outside of the door. He wisely handed the documents back to Carolyn, unsigned. "It would look better if you leave here with something in your hands."

"I'll get these copied and distributed by tomorrow," she said, while opening the door. "Thanks for looking them over, pastor."

Standing outside of the door was the church leadership, three old fogies who helped to build the organization and sustain its success.

"That's Interim Pastor," the Church Mother announced. "Please excuse us, Sister Drew. We need to speak with Brother Clay immediately."

Sister Betty Burlington had been the first lady of the congregation since her husband founded it in a small house over fifty years ago. She was large woman, round in the middle mostly, a dull shade of brown and she rarely smiled. Her job was being the queen of everything M.E.G.A. and she made sure everyone knew it.

Orlando waved goodbye to Carolyn then immediately regretted not being prepared to address his biggest critics.

"Talk to you later, Sister."

Sister Burlington, pushed her way into his office, wearing thick green dress with big ruffles circling the bottom. With one hand parked on her sturdy hip, she snapped her fingers two times.

"Come on in brothers." On cue, two old men in their late seventies strolled in with their hands pushed deeply into their pockets. "Brother Langston and Brother Simons here have something to tell you and it's urgent. You already know how I feel about you pastoring this congregation. I didn't think you were the right fit as Interim Pastor when Reverend Drew passed on. And after that spectacle in the auditorium this morning, I am convinced that we need to initiate a search for someone more... how do I say this, in good taste? *More decent and upright.*"

"More mainstream," Brother Langston answered, begrudgingly.

"Less polarizing," said Brother Simons, without making eye contact.

"You mean, more respectable?" Orlando offered, with a straight face.

"Yes!" the older men answered in unison.

Sister Burlington pointed her index finger at Orlando then waved it at him. "You heard what I said."

A young bi-racial woman walked into the office wearing black flats and a Tiffany blue dress that hit her just above the knee.

Jessika Parker, medium build, shoulder-length black hair, hazel eyes and an innocent smile, seemed to have stumbled directly into the middle of the volatile vortex.

"I'm sorry, didn't know you were in a meeting Uncle Orlando," Jessika said, matter-of-factly. "I've waited as long as I could but I'm likely to faint if I don't eat right now."

She gave Orlando a look, strongly suggesting he play along if he wanted off of Sister Burlington's firing line.

"Oh. Ohhhh. I'm very sorry Jessika," Orlando said, after he caught on. "Sister Burlington, Brothers, I fully understand about your wanting to go in another direction. Please keep in mind that down is also another direction. Regardless, I'll do everything I can to make it a smooth transition once a *respectable* replacement is found."

47

Orlando left the office with his conscience clear and church leadership on a mission. They had big plans for Methodist Episcopal Greater Apostolic but none of them included Interim Pastor Orlando Clay. In less than a year, he stood in the gap as a provisional minister, thrilled the congregation every time he preached, and managed to wear out his welcome.

4

SOUTH BOULEVARD

Sun blanketed the city in beautiful yellow arrays. Mosley pulled the pastor's Bentley in front of a magnificent six-bedroom home, wrapped in rust-colored brick and accented with white stone masonry around the windows. The six-inch tall brickwork that walled in the flowerbeds, spread across the front of the house, from one corner to the other. Together, the design and decor made for attractive curb appeal.

Orlando bought the home on South Boulevard in foreclosure for a quarter million dollars then spent the next year pouring in another five-hundred thousand of repairs and custom designs to make it special.

Once the luxury sedan stopped out front, Orlando asked Jessika if she liked their lunch at the Sweetcake Factory.

"I love that place. Everything on the menu is tasty. Although, I don't think it's fair that we never have to wait in the lobby when they're busy. I feel some type of way about zooming right past all of the other people standing in line."

"It pays to know people who make decisions. Lines are for people who don't know any," Orlando answered.

"It's not fair but it's life. Maybe next time we'll eat at Thibodeaux's Cajun Cookin' in Duncanville. That's *my* favorite."

Orlando asked Jessika to step out of the car for a minute while he passed on some private information to Mosley. After she obliged and headed toward the front door, Orlando handed his driver an envelope. It contained a three-thousand dollar bonus and a note suggesting his friend spend every dime on sweet apologies to his wife.

"I know Paula doesn't care much for me but she deserves to be made up to regularly for all the time I take you away from her and the kids. Maybe take her shopping or something. Let her buy anything she wants and don't put up a fuss. New refrigerator, some of those red bottom shoes all the women scream about or a whole new collection of church hats." He looked out of the tinted car window at a house directly across the street. "It doesn't matter what she buys as long as she keeps letting you pal around with me every now and then."

"Thank you, pastor," Mosley said, proud of their friendship and Orlando's appreciation.

Actually, Paula could hardly stand the amount of time her husband was required to be a personal confidante, chauffeur, and personal advisor. Mosley considered that when he placed the envelope inside the pocket of his suit coat. "This here quiets a whole lot of arguing."

Orlando grabbed the door handle. "Leave the car here for now. Go be with your family. I'll put it away later."

He climbed out and headed for the front door, noticing Jessika was looking on from the window in her upstairs bedroom. She was concerned and had reason to be. Jessika was nineteen now, more of a grownup than a girl, she displayed signs of petty jealously just like any loving woman would.

"Don't forget about garaging the car, pastor," Mosley shouted, from the cement porch of a four-bedroom salmon-colored brick house on the other side of the street. He waved goodbye then stepped into his home.

After spying on their exchange through a crease in drapes, Jessika raced down the stairs in a hurry. She hit the first floor then ran into Orlando's arms as soon as he closed the front door.

"Oh Uncle, I thought that man was going to shoot you this morning!" she whined. "God, what was the matter with him? I was so scared but you didn't even flinch. Aren't you afraid of dying? What if he comes back? What if he comes here?"

"Whoa, whoa. So many questions." He kissed her on the top of her head then tried to appease her fears. "Come over here and sit down."

She followed him into the formal living room, which was a masterpiece decorated in silver, white, and aqua shades of blue. The baby grand piano anchored the great room on the far right side. A contemporary sofa and love seat bordered a light distressed wood coffee table with thick tempered glass. Artwork from the Harlem Renaissance accentuated the walls, covered with a swarthy faux finish.

Jessika took a seat on the leather sofa that Orlando special-ordered in a dark turquoise then she crossed her legs like a debutante.

"No one is going to shoot me, at least not if I can help it. I don't know what was wrong with that man but I am going to find out."

Orlando sat down beside her, leaned in, and held her hand. "Listen Jessika. You know I've been distracted lately. I'm going through something but I don't believe in bringing children into adult business."

She shifted on the sofa, taking her eyes away from his.

"You think I'm still a child? I know what's going on with you. This time every year, you get to acting out and staying gone at all times of the night and chasing women like a man fresh out of jail."

"Wait a minute," Orlando said, with a raised brow. "Who do you think you're talking to?"

"A man who's grieving the death of his wife and children that happened five years ago but hasn't quite healed yet."

Orlando was befuddled by Jessika's brazen bluntness and mature perspective. His mouth fell open but nothing came out.

"I'm not a child anymore. I know just about everything that goes on in this house. I know what you need."

"I think you need to go off to college," he said jokingly. "I'll run up and pack your bags right now."

Jessika had been taking college courses online but was not comfortable being away from Orlando for long periods of time so college living was out of the question. Her father's name didn't appear on the birth certificate because he denied having an extramarital affair with her mother, a former Miss Texas pageant winner. After falling on hard times Jessika's mother, Sabrina, fell into the bottle and drug addiction. She never could beat either one. Sabrina was killed in a cheap motel while Jessika hid under the bed. Orlando's aunt Theresa took Jessika into her foster home in central Texas when she was found dirty and wandering the streets of Waco. Jessika dealt with abandonment issues and kept to herself as much as possible. Aunt Theresa passed away three years ago so Orlando complied with her dying wish to look after the girl until she could do it for herself.

A knock at the door.

"I'm not done with you young lady."

"Good. I'm not done with your either," she shot back.

"What the hell..." he mouthed, like a proud father. "Girl, you went and grew up while I wasn't looking."

When Orlando heard a car door close outside, he peeked out of the window. There was a familiar silver Mercedes wagon parked out front. Orlando opened the door and smiled. A thin willowy-built man wearing a fashionable three-piece cream suit smiled softly as he nodded hello.

"Pierre, I forgot you were coming today. I'm not ready to be fitted yet."

"Should I reschedule Mr. Clay?"

"No, come on in and bring your things."

Pierre lifted a hard rectangular case off of the porch then proceeded inside. "Is it alright if I set up in the formal sitting room like the last time?"

"No, let's do it in my office. I have some multi-tasking to do."

Pierre made a makeshift showroom in the pastor's office then unfastened the wooden box and took out a felt garment bag. He handed one of the suits for Orlando to put on.

"This is the material and cut you wanted to try," he said. "It's a higher lapel and high-waisted trousers."

"You say this is the newest style from across the pond, huh?" Orlando asked, somewhat skeptical.

"It plays very well in London. New York will catch on soon."

Orlando held up the brown pants, with thin pinstripes then he cut his eyes at Pierre.

"Will trousers like this ever make it to Dallas? That's the question."

"In about a year, sad to say. This is as far south and as slow as fashion will travel."

Jessika was sitting in Orlando's leather wingback desk chair when he returned from the restroom down the hall decked out in a new suit. "Heyyy now! Look at you uncle. The fancy dresser," she complimented.

"You truly like this style, Jess?" he asked, squirming in the pants and fitted suit coat.

"Yeah…" she replied.

"Yes," he corrected her.

"Yes, it looks like the clothes that male English models wear in those fashion magazines."

Pierre smiled smartly, with a yellow tape measurer hanging around his neck. "As I told you Mr. Clay. Very dandy in deed."

Looking himself over in the tall floor mirror, Orlando liked what he saw. "I look rather respectable if you ask me," he said, with a British accent. "I could get used to the smaller lapels on the jacket but the trousers fit kinda bunchy."

"I can loosen the inseam if that's the issue."

Orlando winked at the tailor to confirm he'd nailed the issue exactly. "I'll need a little extra room for my…"

"Ewwww!" Jessika said, cringing.

"I was talking about my *cell phone*," Orlando lied, then tossed Pierre a knowing expression.

While he stepped into the other two slacks Pierre brought with him, Jessika thumbed through the mail in a shallow decorative box on Orlando's desk. "You're up for jury duty in two weeks."

"Yes, I know," he replied.

"Did you know you're being audited by the IRS?"

Orlando saw the tailor fussing with shirt fabrics on the love seat, trying hard to act as if he hadn't been listening. Orlando knew better. "Maybe we should discuss *my* personal and financial matters after *my* company is gone."

"No worries. I'm about to be out of your hair for this fitting," Pierre said, sorting out several different cotton swatch designs on his lap.

"What'd I say?" Jessika asked, unaware of the implications that IRS audits suggested.

"Isn't she simply a doll?" Pierre said, fawning over her innocence.

"Oh yeah, she's something alright," Orlando replied, with a sharp eye on Jessika.

"You said *yeah*," she scoffed. "Why do I have to say *yes*?"

"I have two college degrees," Orlando quipped evenly. "When you have proven yourself dedicated enough to grind out two degrees and you *still* want to go around saying *yeah*, then you've earned the right. Got it?"

"Yeeessss," she sang sweetly. "I got it."

"I just love coming here and seeing the father-daughter exchanges between you two."

"She's my niece but thank you Pierre. Write up the invoice and Jessika will settle my account."

Jessika looked at the price written on the invoice. The total was $1,700. She went directly to the top desk drawer pulled out a $1,500 bank card and two $100 bills. Orlando noticed that Jessika seemed bothered by something he didn't dare inquire about in front of Pierre, after he'd just grilled her about discussing his personal business. Instead Orlando thanked the tailor and saw him to the door. "Same time next month Pierre. I'd like suspender buttons inside of all my pants from now on."

"Very good, sir. I'll see to it and bring your order of custom shirts. Three with French cuffs and three with standard sleeves."

When Orlando wandered back to his office, Jessika was no longer there. He found her reading a magazine in the den.

"Hey Super Jess, I noticed it looked like you swallowed a bug before the tailor left. Did I say something wrong?"

She hesitated, flipped several pages then stopped when she was ready to answer. "It's not that you said something wrong actually. But, you were so quick to tell Mr. Pierre that I wasn't your daughter. He didn't know any different and it would have been kinda cool to pretend. Maybe."

He tried to see things from her point of view. Never knowing her father and previously being taken advantage of by all of the men in her life, Jessika had a rough go of it. Orlando was the first positive role model in her life and he promised himself to remember that going forward.

"You're right Jessika. I'm sorry. Guess that I'm so ready to protect our relationship, I over reacted."

"If I was your daughter, would that be so bad? I mean, I know I'm biracial and that would mean you were in love with a white woman. Would that be so bad?"

"No, no, no, no. There is nothing wrong with being biracial or loving someone of another race. Please don't think that. You're a beautiful young lady. Who your parents were don't matter anymore."

"I wish I believed that. Black girls have always said I'm not black enough to hang with them. White girls act like I don't exist. But when their boyfriends start asking for my phone number, it's on. Oh yes, they realized pretty damn quick I got some black in me then."

Orlando was at a loss for words. "Jessika! I...uh."

"It's okay. You're out all day, and lately half the night, fixing the world's problems Uncle Orlando. You can't know or fix everything. Only Jesus can do that." She wiped a tear from her cheek.

"Can I have a hug? I could really use a hug right now," he said, feeling awfully fatherly at the moment. She fell into his arms, wrapping hers around his waist and smushing her face against his chest.

He wiped her tears away with a plaid cotton handkerchief from his back pocket. "Hey, let's get out of here. Take a trip to Hawaii. I've been reading up on these Hylaeus Bees. Listen, they've been on the islands for millions of years and now they face extinction."

"That's a shame, Uncle. Yes, I'd like to go. I've never been to a beach before."

"Don't forget those yellow-faced bees, we have to see them before they're gone like the Xerces Blue Butterflies, dinosaurs and unicorns."

Jessika gave him an adorable side-eye smirk. "You do know unicorns don't really exist?"

"Well, not anymore they don't."

She laughed until all of her straightened teeth showed between her thin lips. "You almost got me. That was a good one."

"Yeah?"

"Yes."

Night fell on South Boulevard. All was quiet as usual in the upscale block of refurbished houses, bordered on all sides by run down apartments, and dilapidated homes in desperate need of repair. It was understood that South Boulevard started the process of reclaiming prime real estate once owned by the city's richest Jewish families but was later worn down to the bone by African Americans who lacked the finances or foresight to return the community to its former prominence. Orlando purchased three houses on the street when he caught wind that it was destined to become the newest block to receive a prestigious charter from the Dallas Historical and Preservation Society. That meant tax breaks for the owners and funding from the city. Things were about to change for the better. Some of Dallas' black elites wanted to stake their claims to it, from the inside out.

Around eleven o'clock that night, three young black men circled the block in a black Escalade SUV. When they came across the Bentley, still parked against the curb in the front of Orlando's home, they slowed down and took a good look from a lowered window. The car- thieves couldn't believe their good fortune. Orlando had forgotten to store it in the garage like he told Mosley he would.

"Okay, this right here is what we're gonna do," one of the men said, as he drove off to the far end of the street. "I'll drop y'all here and you double back to the Bentley on foot. Don't want nobody tryin' to track this heist back to my whip."

As agreed, two of them hopped out of the long vehicle in the shadows then casually strolled back towards the Bentley as if on a nightly stroll. As soon as they drew nearer to the car, one of them crept up to it and jiggled on the front passenger side door handle.

"Hey mane. Get that Slim-Jim down in there and pop it before somebody sees us," one of them said, looking up at the street light shining down on the car.

"I know how to do this," the other one replied, while forcing the thin flat metal tool down into the window well. He fished it around but couldn't locate the wire to trip the switch.

"Mane, what you doin' over there?" the larger one whispered. "You takin' too long." Concerned with being caught, he scooted around the driver's side. "If you can't pop it we got to beat it out of here."

"I got this. I got it," the smaller one complained, anxiously shaking the door opening tool.

"Screw this Son, I'm out." He pulled on the door handle to steady himself as he stood from a crouching position. He almost fell backwards onto the sidewalk when the door opened.

"What the hell dude? It was already popped?"

"Stupid ass, it was unlocked. Get in! Get in!" the larger man, known as Hollywood Harris, squawked.

They climbed inside after discovering the $215,000 vehicle was out in the open, unprotected from the elements, and unlocked.

"Hollywood. We's getting crazy paid tonight. Crazy paid," he added, slicing the ignition wiring beneath the steering column.

"Sonny, twist them wires and jump it off. I'm gettin' them new Jordans. Some diamond earrings. And some super fine freaks who do anythang for a piece of change."

The ignition turned over and the car started.

"Oh hell yeah. We 'bout to come up."

"Hit it Sonny. Let's be out."

The one called Sonny mashed the gas pedal. They turned on the stereo and cheered as the Bentley surged ahead. Their celebration was short lived. With rap music blaring inside the luxury vehicle, it sputtered to a complete stop in the middle of the well-lit street.

"What happened?"

"Hell if I know why it stopped."

"Get it crunk again, Sonny."

He attempted to start the car in the same way that worked earlier but the starter didn't make a sound. "It won't do nothin'."

Suddenly the anti-theft alarm began to clamor loudly. It was maddening inside of the car.

"Mane, let's get out of here before the cops come," Hollywood said, working feverishly to open the car door. He began to pant nervously when the handle wouldn't release the unlock switch.

"Dammit it won't open. Try the back doors."

The other man dove into the back seat, frantically pulling on the door latch.

"This devil car locked us in here. Kick them windows out!"

They kicked and threw their shoulders at the bullet proof windows until both of them realized they were trapped.

"Mane, call Criss-Cross. Tell him to send the SUV back and get us out of here."

Hollywood pulled out his cell phone and press the send button.

"Hey, dude. Where's Criss-Cross? What you mean you ain't seen him? Look, look dude. Y'all gotta send somebody. Where we at? Trapped in a possessed Bentley over here on South Street."

"Tell him South *Boulevard*," Sonny corrected him.

Porch lights flicked on in several houses on the street. Men with guns, lead pipes and baseball bats walked out onto the sidewalks then poured into the streets. Neither of the men inside of the Bentley noticed initially. They were crouched down in the seats, hiding.

"I'm telling you that we're stuck in a car and it won't let us out. Hurry up! Oh, Sonny said it's not South Street but South Boulevard. Wait! Hello? Hello?"

"They coming to save us, right?"

"Naw, they hung up in my face. Nobody's seen Criss-Cross all day," he answered, like a man who had seen a ghost. "Way'ment. Look. Who all those people coming over here?"

They finally realized the group of men were not only coming down the street towards them but also encircling the car. Doctors, lawyers, teachers, auto shop owners and executives recently bought homes on the famous boulevard. They took it back from drug pushers and prostitutes who chased off decent home owners years ago. This time around, the residents vowed to stick together regardless of who threatened their safety zone.

Mosley walked toward the car then stood beside it and looked inside. He pressed the key fob to cut off the loud alarm sirens. When the thieves fought to get out of the car again Mosley tapped the business end of his semi-automatic pistol against the driver's side window. He wanted to make sure he had their undivided attention.

Orlando came out of his house last, wearing long silk pajamas, a thick striped robe and leather house slippers. He took measured steps while keeping a stern eye on his car.

"Go ahead. Let the fish out of that jar," he said to Mosley.

Mosley pressed a fob again. All of the doors unlocked at once. Mosley opened the driver's door and yanked Sonny out of the car by his dreadlocks. Two of Orlando's neighbors brought their pit bulls out on thick chains. They held the dogs back as the other carjacker hustled around the vehicle quickly to join his partner in crime. Besides, he wanted to put some distance between himself and those menacing canines.

Orlando slid both hands inside of his housecoat. He looked the men over carefully then squinted at the one who seemed familiar.

"This block is untouchable," he said evenly. "Mosley take their phones," he added.

Mosley instructed two other men to confiscate their cell phones then he went a step further.

"And take their IDs too."

Once they were collected and handed to the deacon, Mosley inspected them. "Louisiana boys, both of them from Baton Rouge. Only one has a phone though." He took a closer look at one of the men's faces. "Look at this, pastor. It's Dreadlocks from the gambling shack last night."

"Yeah, I noticed that was him in that nightgown looking tee-shirt."

All of the neighbors laughed.

"Well, we're not standing out here all night so...," Orlando said, with a pregnant pause. "Who are y'all affiliated with in Dallas?"

Orlando pulled his hands out of his housecoat pockets when neither of them spoke up. He took a calculated step closer to Dreadlocks. "I asked who y'all working for?"

Sensing he was about to be assaulted, Sonny Dreadlocks flinched. "Nobody mane. We just took this here car because it was parked on the street. And because it's a Bentley. You know how much it would go for at a chop shop?"

Orlando felt Mosley toss him a look for failing to garage the expensive car but he didn't acknowledge it. "No chop shop in the city would pay you for this car, if you did find one fool enough to accept it. It has a state-of-the-art tracker, bullet proof windows, a kill switch and the most important thing... it belongs to me."

"Sir, we're so sorry," Hollywood said. "We didn't know about this street being off the board or believe me, we would have gone somewhere else."

"Don't you punk out, Hollywood. This preacher ain't gonna do nothing," Dreadlocks warned. "Too many witnesses."

Mosley laughed when Orlando held out his hand to the side.

"You done messed up now."

Orlando received the cell phone and driver licenses. "Oh, I see. You think you know me and what I'm capable of. These aren't witnesses. They're alibis," he said, with a broad wave of his hand, like a circus ring master.

Mosley nodded assuredly. "Yep. The pastor's been in bed all night. If y'all come up missing, he was never here."

"Now that you have disturbed these good people's sleep and violated our block, how do you propose we set it straight?" Orlando asked.

"I say we let Duke handle this," said one of the neighbors, with two hands on a taut dog chain.

"Naaaah, nah," Orlando replied slowly. "That's bound to get nasty. Duke can't always control himself."

Hollywood's right knee began to shake. He was frightened when Mosley took pictures of their driver's licenses and their faces, then showed the photos to the pit bulls. Sonny Dreadlocks started whimpering when the biggest dog snarled and tried to bite a chunk out of him.

"Good doggie. Good Duke," Dreadlock cooed, when the dog lunged violently at him. "That's a good doggie."

The dog sensed his fear and growled at him even more intensely.

"That ain't Duke," Mosley said, with a cunning smile.

"Sit down bitch!" Orlando snapped sharply.

Both of the carjackers immediately flopped down Indian-style on the hard concrete. The bigger dog sat down too.

"I was talking to the animal but I understand how you fellas feel. See, Tiger Belle gets a little feisty every now and then. She doesn't like strangers coming around here unannounced and you've already worn out your welcome."

"That means it's time to leave," Mosley announced, his voice was strong and mellow. "Get up and get gone."

Both men stood up and took off running down the boulevard.

Orlando saw a puddle of urine on the spot where Sonny sat.

"He pissed himself. I hate it when bad men piss themselves. Better let the dogs out."

Tiger Belle and her little brother shot out after them, growling and barking. The residents watched and laughed when they heard grown men screaming in the darkness.

"Head on down there and save those idiots," Orlando ordered. "I'll go in and call Duke."

5

FAMILY AFFAIRS

Duke Milton owned a thriving plumbing company. LaDuke was his given name although few people called him that to his face because he thought it sounded queer. When he wasn't doing snatch-and-grabs for Orlando and friends, Duke was thinking of ways to increase his profits and collecting rent payments from reluctant tenants on the first of each month. Operating out of a former convenience store in West Dallas, Duke listened well and watched Orlando's every move. In the past three years, he purchased the old 7-Eleven building with cash then started squirreling money away for a major transition that paid much better dividends than unclogging toilets and greasing pipes. He had dreams of becoming a first-rate fixer for wealthy people who didn't want to get their hands dirty.

Grunt Gibson was Duke's sidekick, almost a foot shorter and often more diabolical than his boss. Grunt didn't possess high-level business savvy or keen interest in making sound financial decisions, but he thoroughly enjoyed technology and making people scream.

With a firm directive to pry information out of the stranger who disrupted the church service, Grunt was tired, sweaty, and running out of ideas.

All that he managed to get out of the captive was his name, Christopher Crossman. On the street, they called him Criss-Cross.

On the cement floor of the once refrigerated room used to keep cases of beer and soda cold, Grunt leaned against a metal cabinet digging skin out of a meat grinder then picking his teeth with the same sharp metal screw. He stared at the church visitor who had a cloth sack over his head. He had been tied to a chair with rope for 18 hours, sitting in blood stained clothes and soiled pants.

"I beat him and burned him but I still didn't break him," Grunt said to himself, in a disappointed tone.

Duke came in through the back door with two carjackers blindfolded and bound by their wrists with tire chains. They had rips and tears in their clothing. One of them smelled of urine.

"Hey Grunt, I got two more!" he shouted, with his large hands around the backs of their necks.

At six-foot three, Duke towered over the thieves. Two-hundred-fifty pounds of solid muscle and shoulders like a moose, he was more than man enough to clang their heads together anytime they complained about being held against their wills. "Clear out some space right over there by the table," Duke Ordered.

Grunt jumped to it in a hurry, eagerly throwing all sorts of objects, most of them used to inflict pain, onto the floor. He grabbed two folding chairs and sat them side by side, directly in front of their first prisoner.

"Why are their clothes already torn and tattered Duke? I hope you didn't start without me this time," he protested.

"The dogs had them before I showed up. Tiger Belle was about to eat this homeboy alive," Duke explained.

He slammed the men down into the chairs so hard their heads bobbled.

"Hey mane, you didn't have to do that," Sonny Dreadlocks said, sniffing the air. "Hollywood, you smell something?"

"Yeah man. Something stinks like a gorilla's ass."

Duke ripped the blind folds and ropes off of them then warned the men not to get any ideas about escaping. Both of the thieves covered their mouths and noses when the pungent odor of feces and dried blood rifled up their nostrils. When their eyes focused on the slumping man sitting in front of them, head still bowed and covered, they started to panic.

Sonny stood up and looked around the room nervously.

"Hey lil' man, what's that smell?" he asked, with one eye on Grunt. "Y'all got it stanking like a zoo up in here."

Grunt put on two leather weightlifting gloves. He casually stepped in front of Sonny and gut punched him until he doubled over in pain.

"Lil' man, huh? Now I'm looking down on you, podner."

When it was clear that Grunt sent the right message, Dreadlocks waved him off. "No need because I don't have a thing to say about nothing or nobody else."

"Good. Then sit right there and behave until it's time to tell us who sent y'all to take that Bentley from the pastor."

He tied each of them to a chair then removed the sack off of the battered church intruder. As the new arrivals leaned in to see if he was still breathing, the man coughed and spit up blood. The jackers recognized him, then nervously exchanged knowing glances.

Criss-Cross worked for St. Nick as a middle man who set up the routes for car thefts then paid the street crews when they delivered high-priced vehicles. With Criss-Cross out of commission, the new arrivals to the plumbing shop knew that no one would be coming to rescue them.

Duke pulled off his poorly-made polyester shirt then walked over to Grunt and the men yet to be interrogated. "Grunt, I'm hungry. What you want to do with them? And, make it fast so I can order takeout."

Grunt placed the cloth sack back over the severely beaten man's head then he slugged the other two in their faces. When they came to their senses, both of the men's hands were retied with leather straps.

Grunt stood over them holding a small cage, covered with a dark drape. The men squirmed in their seats, wondering what Grunt had up his sleeves.

"Don't do nothin' crazy now," Hollywood whined. "All we did was take a car and didn't even get away."

"Y'all went and pissed off my Unca' Lando," Duke said, while reading over a Hoagies & Heroes Sandwich menu. "Somebody's got to pay."

Grunt pulled the drape off of the cage, revealing two big black rats with long tails. They were standing on their hind legs, looking out of the cage.

"What you gonna do with them huge rats, mane?" asked Sonny Dreadlocks.

"I'll slap you around a while then strip you down to your socks. That's when we dip your nuts in melted cheese. Rats go crazy for melting cheese."

When hearing Grunt's immediate plans for them, Dreadlocks peed his pants again.

"Uh-uh, we ain't doing that," Duke objected. "I will not be involved in handling another man's dick. Besides, this one keeps pissing his self. I ain't cool with none of that."

Grunt snapped his fingers like a big idea had just popped into his head and he couldn't wait to share it. "Okay, I got it! We'll drip a gallon of scalding hot cheese on their balls and then bring in the rats."

"Let's just snap off their pinky fingers like we did them other dudes," Duke debated. "Teach 'em we mean business."

Dreadlocks winced and squirmed in his chair. "Hey Mane, none of this is called for. We made a mistake. We so-so-so sorry and won't do it no more. Nobody sent us after that Bentley. We just saw it sitting outside on the curb and tried to boost it."

After disregarding the man's plea for leniency, Duke studied the menu harder. "Hey Grunt. I'm goin' to call in a blackened-chicken foot long on toasted white bread. What you want to eat?"

"A Philly Cheesesteak," Grunt answered, as he pulled a rat from the cage by its long black tail. "Yeah, make mine with *extra* cheese."

The following morning, Orlando received a calming field report from Duke. The carjackers weren't sent to deliver a message but instead stumbled into the wrong neighborhood when they came across the brand new Bentley Silver Spur sitting on the street, just asking to be snatched. Since it was merely a mistake, Duke figured he'd let them go but only after having them put through the wringer first.

On his way out of the door, Orlando stepped into his home office to finish up on some old business. He saw Jessika writing out checks to pay the monthly household expenses.

"Thanks for taking care of that," he said, while opening the wall safe next to the desk.

Jessika pretended she didn't already know the combination as Orlando opened the wall safe. It was hidden behind the picture of Toussaint L'Ouverture, leader of the Haitian Revolution who defeated Napoleon and freed his country. Orlando admired the ex-slave who didn't have any military training but managed to embarrass large French regimens and ultimately drove them back to the Caribbean Sea.

"You're very welcome," she said, pleasantly, then threw a know-it-all smirk at her uncle. "However, you do know this would be so much faster if *somebody* let me set up electronic bill pay? I could settle all of these accounts with one simple click."

Orlando took out some cash and handed Jessika a few twenties. "Here, stop by the grocery store and pick up that salad dressing I like. The Asian Fusion."

Orlando also took out a small black case then opened it. There was a short stack of shiny blue bank cards, labeled with their pre-loaded amounts on them in gold writing. The set of cards he slid back into the case included one for $1,000, two for $500, and three more in the amount of $250 each.

As his home phone rang, Orlando handed Jessika a $250 bank card. "Jessika, please don't hang out all day at the mall."

"I won't go close to a mall today. I have to study for a test."

"Can you get the phone?" he asked.

"It's not for me. Besides, who has a LAN line these days anyway?" she added playfully.

Orlando picked up the phone and pretended to wrestle the bank card away from Jessika.

"Can't even get you to answer the phone. Maybe I should cancel that card so you can't shop."

"Maybe you should say hello to whoever called you on the phone," she quipped.

"That's some fresh mouth on you lately," he said, raising the phone to his ear. "Sister Carolyn Drew, how are you?"

Jessika laughed and quickly shoved the card in her pocket.

"Is this a good time?" Carolyn asked.

"Yes, I can talk. What's going on?"

"I listened to the message you left but I'm not sure why you want me to look at your taxes."

"I received a 'kick in the pants' letter from the IRS. I want you to consider advising me on this audit threat. I need someone I can trust," Orlando explained.

"I'm flattered but there might be a conflict," she said. "I am the CFO of record at the church. You're the pastor of record."

"I understand where you're coming from. Embezzlement, entanglements and whatnot. Still, I don't see a conflict of interest," he debated. "This would be totally separate from your CFO duties at MEGA. Please tell me you will at least think about it? I'll call you later to beg you some more. I know you women like for the fellas to beg."

Jessika rolled her eyes after hearing his comment. Orlando disregarded Jessika's embarrassed expression with a dismissive wave.

"Alright now Brother Pastor," Carolyn warned, with a whole lot of smile in her voice.

"Huh? You know I'm just playing around right? Please don't get out there on Twitter and go all "hash-tag me too" on Pastor Clay.

I don't need any more trouble. *I* can do bad all by myself. Ha-ha-ha. That's right, you heard me."

Orlando heard the doorbell chime. He gave Jessika a look to go and attend to it but her face was buried in her cell phone.

"Okay, I've crossed the line with you enough for today."

"Yes, you have," Jessika whispered, in his direction.

"Yeah we'll talk again soon, Sister Carolyn. Goodbye." Orlando put the phone down on his desk then sneered at Jessika.

"So you can hear all of my conversation but you couldn't hear the doorbell chiming?"

"Oh, I thought that was my phone," she answered, cleverly.

"Don't you leave that spot until I get back."

Orlando walked down the hall then peeked out of the window to see who was visiting. He opened the door wearing an inviting smile. Detective Vera Miles, his on-again, off-again love thing, smiled back. It had been a number of months since he shared her bed but by the way he gazed at her thick hips and full lips, Orlando still missed her being in his life. Vera's naturally curly hair, cut in a Betty Boop style, her even brown skin, and almond-shaped eyes caused perpetrators and other policemen to discount her grit.

As an officer, she was as tough as they came and smarter than the hordes of criminals she put behind bars. Vera felt his eyes all over her when she walked into the broad foyer.

"Vera. You look amazing as usual. Nice semi-auto, by the way," he said, noting the black slender handgun holstered on her side.

"Thank you," she said softly.

Vera allowed his eyes to follow her around the room as she admired the new turquoise leather sofa and loveseat.

"Looks like you've changed some things in here. It's nice. I saw some of these paintings at an art show once, classy."

"Thanks. So, to what do I owe this honor?" he said, eventually. "It's been a minute since you stopped by."

"Unfortunately, this is a business call. You've probably heard about the rash of murders in the southern sector, two last night in your neck of the woods." Vera read the concerned look on Orlando's face and knew it was real.

"Who?" he asked, as if wondering whether she was going to name the thugs who tried to steal his car the night before.

"Two black females. Both sliced up pretty good, doused with gasoline, and burned beyond recognition."

"Women?' he said, obviously caught off guard.

"Why does their gender come as a surprise?" she asked, in a probing manner.

Orlando wrinkled his brown purposely, because he knew the detective was interested in his reaction.

"I've seen reports on the news and thought the victims were all male. Maybe a gang turf thing."

Vera didn't buy his explanation. She handed him a slip of paper with two names on it. "You know these two small time hustlers?"

Jessika stepped off the stairs wearing fitted jeans and tennis shoes. It was obvious she had been listening curiously when Vera passed behind Orlando and headed toward the kitchen. The detective caught a casual glance of Jessika, who threw it back like the woman of the house sizing up the competition.

After Orlando looked at the familiar names, he shrugged. "Are they members of my congregation? If they are, I need to preach and pray a lot harder. Maybe help them see the error of their ways."

"I doubt that. These men haven't been here long enough from Louisiana to set foot in a church much less find a church home."

Detective Miles headed towards the door, surveying the furniture and custom molding then she suddenly stopped. The detective pivoted on the spot then turned to face Orlando.

"They've filed complaints about being taken hostage on South Boulevard last night."

"Really?" he asked, though not surprised in the least.

"Yeah, they showed up this morning at the station all bruised, beaten, and each missing a pinky finger.

"You don't say," he replied, feigning utter disbelief.

He knew Duke had gone too far but couldn't have guessed those carjackers would go running to the police. "Well isn't that something?"

The detective smiled, knowingly. "That's exactly what I said."

"I'll see you out," Orlando offered, as he opened the door then following the attractive detective out onto the broad brick porch.

"I gotta run but been meaning to tell you that I saw Jessika the other day at the dry cleaners. Didn't even recognize her. Girl's got more curves than I do," she said, while swinging her hip toward him. "You have a grown woman in your house now."

Orlando was over it and getting peeved. "I know that," he responded, with hints of agitation. "Get around to making your point, Vera."

"I'm just wondering how long a young woman, who isn't related to you gets to parade around like she owns the place?"

"I know where this is coming from so I'll address it head on and leave no doubts as to how I feel about this situation," he said,

74

assuredly. "You're right, Jessika isn't my blood but she's the closest thing to family I have left."

"She's a woman," Detective Miles insisted.

"She's had more than her share of heartache, ups and downs. She's got a heart bigger than Texas and if you knew what she's been through, you'd be ashamed of those suspicious things running through that pretty head of yours." Orlando took a calculated step towards Vera and kissed her on the cheek. "There's no reason to be jealous of that girl in there. She can't do for me what you do and you can't mean to me what she does. By the time Jessika's fully grown, her life will be the kind of story people write books about. She's smart as a whip and tougher than she looks, only she doesn't know it yet. Deep down inside, she's still a girl. "

"I'm sorry if I was out of line," Vera said, almost repentant. "I know you know what you're doing."

"Always."

Vera wanted to say more, maybe press her lips against his, but the detective understood her special time in his life had come and gone.

Orlando, arriving at the same conclusion, tried to shake the memories of that dark gray Dodge Charger parked behind his garage overnight, too many times to count, but there was no use. Vera had solidified a place in his past. Unfortunately for her, that's where Orlando decided she belonged.

A few minutes after the detective left, Orlando walked across the street from his house then rang the doorbell at Deacon Mosley's home.

"It's me. The paper boy," he said, when someone asked who was at the door.

Paula Mosley opened the door, brown-skinned and straight faced. She wore a red sweater dress and matching leggings. Once she saw it was Orlando, Paula gave him an unimpressed once over from head to toe. "Oomph," she said, tossing a look back over her shoulder. "Steven's getting dressed so I guess it's okay if you came in a second and waited."

She was a full-size woman with smallish legs, a full trunk and round breasts. Paula had the kind of build that made men wonder how everything might have stacked up fifteen or twenty years earlier.

Orlando followed her back into the house. "Thank you, Paula," he answered, with a crooked smile.

He knew the pretty mocha colored woman was rather indifferent to him and standoffish when he came around. Keeping his church congregation safe often required dirty deeds being done in the middle of the night. Paula understood but that didn't mean she had to like it.

"Where are the boys?" he asked.

"Stay here, I'll get them," she said, with a slight eye roll, then she started off in the other direction. "Noble! Honor! Yawl's Uncle *Orlando* is here." Paula was out of the pastor's presence as soon as possible.

Orlando's face lit up like a neon sign as two nine-year-old twin boys came sprinting out of the den. They met him in the formal living room, decorated with modern furnishings and a gray micro-fiber sofa that gave it a suede-like finish.

"There they are, Larry and Harry," he mused.

76

"Hi Uncle Orlando!!!" they cheered in tandem. "We're not Larry and Harry."

"I know that. You're Eric and Derrick, my favorite nephews," Orlando teased, as their Grandma Gigi came around to look on.

She was an older version of Paula, only thinner and possessed an epic fondness for Orlando. At seventy, she still had a vivid sexual imagination and a lot of wiggle left in her wagon.

"No, that's not it either. You've forgotten our names again," one of the twins laughed aloud.

"Try again," the other boy said, with a mouthful of teeth showing. "One more guess."

Orlando winked at Grandma Gigi, who turned into butter on the spot. Then, he rubbed his hands together as if he had it figured out.

"I got it. You're Beans and Cornbread. I love beans and cornbread." The boys fell over laughing and hugging Orlando around his waist. "Now I remember, Noble and Honor. How could I ever forget?" He passed them twenty dollars bills then put a finger up to his mouth. "Shush, don't tell your mommy where you got it unless she ask you."

"Okay. I hope she doesn't ask," Honor mumbled quietly to his brother.

"Me neither," the other twin cosigned. They shoved the money into their pockets and dashed off to watch cartoons.

"They love them some Uncle Orlando," Gigi said, flirting with her eyes. She smiled while giving him the same once over her daughter had but for a different reason altogether. "When are you going to let your pretty niece babysit for the twins again? She's the sweetest thing. Never will take a dime for her troubles."

"She won't? I need to talk to her about that. Looking after these rambunctious boys for free? Huh, must be good home training or something."

"Everyone can see you're doing a great job with Jessika. Don't you think you could add a woman's touch? Every girl needs a momma?" she quipped.

"Oh where has the time gone?" he laughed. "Grandma Gigi, I'm half your age. I would have to move out if I let you tip across the street to play step-momma at my house."

"If you don't open your mouth, run and tell your business, ain't nobody got to know."

"Ha-ha! Woman, you're going to get me into trouble with Paula over joking about this.

"Who's joking?"

"I know you'd better be. I don't know CPR."

"Well I do and I'm *good* at it too."

"Ok. I don't think that means what you think it means."

"That's where I get to straddle you, spread my hands on your chest and blow kisses into your mouth til you start to kissing back," she answered, with both hands parked on her narrow hips. "I'll keep at it until somebody comes around to pull me off. You'll be satisfied alright."

"You mean resuscitated?"

"Same thang in my book. I might be older, pastor, but I'm not old. Keep that in mind when the winds gets to blowing too hard on your side of the street."

"PAULA!" Orlando hollered for help, and staggered backward. "Paula! Where did those adorable kids go?"

"Don't get scared now," Grandma Gigi whispered.

Paula brought the boys back into the foyer, wielding them by their arms. "What you two got to say for yourselves," she asked, looking down on them.

"Thank you?" Noble said, hunching his shoulders.

Honor gave his twin a defeated look. "We're sorry Uncle Orlando but my Mom won't let us keep the money."

"Boys this age don't need that much money," Paula said, a little peeved. "They'll only use it on something foolish because they didn't earn it."

"I can earn it," Grandma Gigi said suggestively, much to her daughter's dismay.

"Mama don't. Not right now," Paula chided.

The boys held the twenty-dollar bills out for Orlando to take back.

Grandma Gigi took them instead.

"I'll see that Mr. Orlando gets them," she told the boys, then tucked the money into her bra for safe keeping as soon as they were ushered out of the room.

"Everybody can't be bought," Paula hissed, then stomped out annoyed.

"*I* can be bought, paid for or rented," Grandma Gigi offered. "For the right price and a handsome man, I'll do all sorts of..."

"Deacon Mosley, we need to go now," Orlando hollered, loud enough to be heard from anywhere in the two story house.

Mosley came down stairs buttoning a brown vest with a satin-finish backing. "What's going on down here?"

Paula stepped back in to add her two cents. "Wanna guess?"

He took one look at Orlando, uncomfortable and avoiding eye

contact with the mother-in-law but he dared not say what was on his mind. When Mosley looked at his sons, peeking at him from each side of their mother's wide hips, he knew.

"Pastor trying to spoil the twins again by handing out five and tens?" Mosley asked.

"Twenty dollars apiece this time. He keeps getting worse," Paula smirked. "What's it going to me next month, hundred dollars?"

Grandma Gigi pursed her lips then cleared her throat. Orlando tried to pretend he didn't see it.

"Can't I bless them with a little walking around money?" he asked. "Wish I had some spending change when I was their age."

Paula shook her head disapprovingly and stood her ground.

"They are not you, that's the difference Mr. Clay."

Both boys groaned and walked away. Knowing where this was headed and refusing to be caught in the middle, Mosley nudged Orlando towards the door.

"Come on pastor before Paula climbs onto *her* pulpit."

They got out the door as quickly as possible. Orlando gave Mosley a panicked look.

"Man, your mother-in-law almost raped me."

"Sorry about that pastor. She says you're cute."

"But she is too old Mosley. Too damned old to be trying to date rape me every time I come over."

"I know that," he answered, "but she don't know that. Grandma Gigi thinks she can still put it down."

"Man, let's get in this car," Orlando huffed, joking. "We have some corners to turn and I need to forget about what happened in there."

"Might be wise for you to stay away from Gigi for a while. She's onto your scent."

"You think."

As soon as they were sitting in Orlando's car, he reached over and locked the door. "Come on Mosley, let's get out of here man."

The Bentley pulled away from the curb, carrying the pastor far from a woman who still thought of herself as a worthy sexual companion for a much younger man. Grandma Gigi was an old woman but she was still all woman.

Paula stood in the window with her arm folded across her chest, still fuming. Gigi idled up beside her with a cup of coffee.

"Not every man has the kind of friendship those two get to enjoy Paula. They're like brothers. That pretty pastor needs someone like Steven to be there when doing all of the great things he has to for his congregation. Men like Steven need close friends to even out everything else they have going on, like this family. Don't be jealous. It's a balancing act. Every relationship is important. Every one of them is necessary."

"You sure about that Momma?" Paula asked, fearful that her husband was in over his head.

"As long as your man keeps bringing his money home and giving you all the attention you need. Yes, let everything else go by the way side because it don't matter. You'll thank me later. Now let's get in there and see what Whoopi is up to on The View."

"I hope you're right," Paula responded, softly. "I sure hope you're right."

6

IN THE HOOD

South Dallas was once considered the eastern border of downtown that backed up to the Trinity River and many believed it included north-eastern parts of Oak Cliff, which was once a small city to the south of Dallas. Incorporated as a Dallas borough in the early 1900's, Oak Cliff managed to sustain a strong and distinctive neighborhood identity. With over 250,000 residents, ten high schools, home to once famous blues greats, Aaron T-Bone Walker and Stevie Ray Vaughn, the sprawling area was also notable for its most infamous inhabitant, Lee Harvey Oswald. After assassinating President John F. Kennedy, Oswald ducked into the local Texas Theater to hide out. It took more than thirty years to wash that sinister stain off the city's reputation. Although some will always charge it to the debt Oak Cliff owes in apologies to the rest of Dallas, people old enough to remember the bitter taste of pain spewed over the old neighborhood from outsiders, calling it the *City of Hate*.

Local attitudes regarding fidelity to family remained steadfast, firm, and unyielding. Suspicious of outsiders, the neighborhood became ultra-protective of its own if trouble started. Right, wrong or indifferent they stood and fell together.

"Something isn't right Mosley. I can feel things tightening around me, the church, and the neighborhood," Orlando said, while cruising down I-67 towards Camp Wisdom Road. "They keep saying crime is down although there's been less of a police presence than I can remember."

Mosley agreed as he guided the Bentley into the exit lane.

"I read in the paper somebody is burning young girls alive."

"I saw that article and it's all over the TV News too. Since when did we start treating our daughters this way? What's happened to us? The hood isn't what it used to be."

"No sir. It sure ain't," was Mosley's quiet reply.

The car stopped in front of Grace's Dry Cleaners. It was owned by Orlando, through a shell corporation that allowed him to buy up several businesses along the Camp Wisdom corridor between I-67 and Westmoreland Road without anyone taking notice. Named after Orlando's mother, the dry cleaners was refurbished and prided itself on offering the best customer service on that side of town. Within the first year, business tripled. Orlando considered adding another location but hadn't made any moves yet.

"Better let me handle this one, pastor. Too close to home," Mosley suggested.

"Okay. I'll stay put but I want this lecture you're about to give to send the right message."

Mosley walked in through the front door. He had a short discussion with the manager as to the reason for a surprise visit and then proceeded into the busy pressing room near the back door.

Several of the Hispanic and Black employees ended their friendly discussions when Mosley crept through rows of plastic-covered clothing hanging from the tall motorized conveyor machine. Everyone saw what was destined to happen except for the man it was going to happen to. The employees went back to work as if trouble wasn't seconds away from spilling over, Mosley snatched the ear buds off the head of the new delivery driver.

"Hey man, what the hell?" the slender built twenty-one year old, complained.

"You the one they call Hatch?" Mosley asked, a few inches from the employee's face.

"What's it to you? *Old School.*" he said, before a left-handed uppercut smashed into his chin. Hatch's eyes crossed as he shook off the stinging blow from the seat of his pants. It was plain to see that he had underestimated the older man.

"You just *had* to get assy with me, didn'tcha?" Mosley had slapped the taste out of his mouth then urged him to take it like a man. "Get yo punk butt up! You're gonna deal with this right here. Right now."

"Man, who are you and what you think I done?" Hatch asked, after he climbed to his feet.

"Don't matter who I am or who I represent. You've been talking nasty to the female customers, following them back out to their cars and cussing them out when they don't give up their phone number."

"Whatever bitch said that, is a damn lie!"

That response upset Mosley even more. He socked Hatch in the stomach then punched him straight in the nose. Down the trouble maker went again. His attitude was incorrigible and it had him looking up at the ceiling from his sore behind for a second time.

"Uhhhhh-huh, uhhhhh-huh," he breathed in and out frantically, after having the wind knocked out of him. Why you keep hitting me?" he cried, struggling to stand back up.

"Because you keep missing my point, so let me make this clear," Mosley growled, as he yanked the employee to his feet by his shirt.

"You ever say anything other than '*hello*' and '*have a nice day*' to the women doing business here, I will pay you another visit and won't *nobody* see you again until Jesus comes back. You hear me?"

Hatch sniveled as blood streamed down his chin from a split lip.

"Yeah-yeah, mister. You won't ever have to come back, sir."

"We'll see," Mosley said, staring into the man's frightened eyes.

"Oh and if you happen to see Jessika again, turn and go the other way."

"Wait, how will I know which one she is?"

"For your sake, man, I sure hope you figure it out."

Mosley walked back through the steam and press room to find many of Hatch's co-workers smiling agreeably.

"Thank you sir, have a nice day," a petite Latina said, as the deacon passed by.

When he climbed back into the car and put it in reverse without as much as a word, Orlando gave him a look.

"You think he understood the error of his ways from grabbing women and calling them 'stuck up hoes' when they refuse his advances?"

"He'll straighten up now," Mosley assured him. "If only I could have the very same lecture with that fake President Trump."

Orlando smiled at the mere thought of it. "He'll get what's coming to him either here or on the other side."

"Won't we all."

"Amen."

Less than a block away, Orlando walked into a laundromat with Mosley on his heels. Duke was replacing a tumbler in the last commercial dryer on the end. He performed all of the repair work on the secondhand machines in Orlando's biggest money making establishment. Quarters quickly became dollars when he installed security cameras and armed guards from 6:00 PM until closing at 10:00. Once Orlando learned he could net over $100,000 a year without a dime of traceable income, he purchased the *Soapy Suds* then immediately remodeled the seating area with laptop docking stations and USB charging ports to lure in millennials who couldn't afford washers and dryers in their one bedroom apartments. His newest venture was paying off and keeping Duke's idle hands busy with business matters.

Orlando found Duke reaching into a wall unit, tightening down the expensive piece of machinery. "LaDuke," he said, knowing that would get a rise.

Backing out of the hole in the wall, where the panel was removed, Duke whipped his head around angrily.

"Who's calling me that? Oh, Unca" Lando. I didn't know that was you," he said, wiping his greasy hands on a red shop rag. "What it do deacon?"

Mosley nodded hello but remained silent. Taking in the man's swollen arms, rounded shoulder and thick check, Orlando shook his head at the thin tank tops Duke wore, regardless of the temperature.

"Why you dress like that Nephew? You make good money. Long sleeve shirts are a thing. They're sold everywhere you get those skimpy tanks."

"I don't like clothes. Only wear them cause I got to," he answered, sorely. "I'd work every day in my draws if I could. You can believe that."

Mosley looked at Orlando, who slapped the plumber on the shoulder. "Nah, don't do that Duke. Wouldn't be fair to us normal-size men," he joked.

"Been gettin' customer complaints about these machines goin' on the blink more than usual. Like somebody's messin' with them."

"We have video surveillance. I'll look in that. You just keep these money makers running. I'll get to the bottom of it. Call me if something else stands out, as unusual."

"Will do. When you gonna come by my office and see about that other thang? Grunt's sittin' on that situation but it's about to expire."

"I'll come through there after I swing by Bishops' for a cut."

Duke raised his brow but didn't see any point in arguing. Orlando was the boss and their relationship worked when the younger man did what he was told. It's been that way since Duke showed up at Orlando's Aunt Theresa's foster home five years earlier. He was almost seventeen, undernourished and mad at the world. Abused by family members and ready to strike out at anything that remotely felt like authority, Duke presented a problem for Orlando, who was dealing with numerous problems of his own. Eventually, both men learned to count on one another to rebuild their lives. Orlando adopted Duke, sent him to plumbing school then made him the sole repairman for all sixteen of his rental properties and commercial investments when he graduated with honors. Their bond was thick, deeper than blood, and unbreakable. Loyalty was first, last, and always.

Bishop's Barbershop was next on their list of stops to make. It was an iconic hub to meet and match wits for neighborhood residents and miscreants who left their disagreements outside on the streets. Regardless of strife between rivals, inside was a haven where mutual respect was guaranteed.

Orlando had a standing appointment on Mondays at two in the afternoon. The shop was closed to the general public and only serving a very exclusive clientele. A three-foot orange construction cone held the parking space until he arrived. Numbers, a mentally challenged man well known and tolerated in the neighborhood, hustled off of the sidewalk to remove the cone when he saw the luxury car swoop into the parking lot.

Numbers was always dressed in slacks, church shoes and a white button-down shirt. He often walked the avenue talking nonsense or politics with people at the car wash, grocery store and of course the barbershop. His IQ was off the charts. It was rumored that Numbers passed up a full scholarship to MIT because he would have had to get on a plane to attend their prestigious math program. He was always up on current events, the latest right-wing conspiracy theories on President Obama's success and never forgot a single word he ever heard. He could factor numbers faster than a calculator but could not rationalize how an airplane weighing thousands of tons actually lifts off of the ground to fly. He understood the physics, algebra, and aerodynamics involved but something inside of him refused to set foot on a plane. In an amazing turn of events, the flight Numbers was supposed to catch to MIT crashed in the Boston Harbor, killing all 276 people aboard the plane that day. The last twenty years of his life has been marred by finger pointing and poking fun at him. Oblivious to the taunts and poor treatment, Numbers was as clueless and carefree as a child.

"Let me hold the keys Mr. Clay. You know, I like fine automobiles like this Mr. Clay. Bentley four seater. Silver Spur. Cost one-hundred and ninety-thousand off the showroom floor. 12 cylinders, hand crafted and hand made. It's a panty dropper... Mr. Clay."

"Hiya doing Numbers? This car is all that and more my friend. I bought a lot of custom extras," said Orlando, knowing that the fellow couldn't help being compulsive. "You got any tips for me? What stocks should I buy today?" was Orlando's normal greeting.

"You should have bought Bitcoin last year before it crashed and burned like that airplane I was supposed to be riding on. Apple is a good stock but too much competition in wireless phones. Today would have been a good day to get you some Amazon. It's down nine percent and ready to rebound as soon as the world finds out they building five one-million square foot warehouses in South Dallas under another name."

"How you know that?" Mosley asked, with a face full of interest.

"Because-I-read," he answered in one breath. Then, he lowered his head toward the ground. Numbers actually did read everything that other people left at the bus stop, on park benches or handed him so he'd go away.

Orlando knew the man was a bundle of knowledge but most people didn't talk to him long enough to realize or utilize it.

"I appreciate that tip Numbers but I don't think Mr. Mosley is in the mood to let you hold the car keys this afternoon but maybe you can work on him some."

Mosley lagged behind to discuss stocks and options with Numbers but Orlando couldn't wait to get inside the barbershop. It changed ownership a couple of times over the past thirty years but somehow Bishop's name stayed on the window and his signature on the deed.

A long padded bench hugged the wall just below the large plate glass window with the owner's name stenciled on it in thick white cursive writing. Parallel to that sat a row of vintage barber chairs, upholstered with red leather rounded seats, matching armrests, and sturdy silver foot rails. Five caramel colored leather chairs aligned the rear wall of the shop, giving it a gentlemen's lounge appeal. The floor was laid in wall to wall black-and-white checkerboard from beginning to end. A tall, sickly looking, potted cactus anchored the floor near the door. Other than the wooden coat rack posted up at the front, that cactus was the only thing allowed to stay on the floor longer than a few minutes before being swept away by one of the barbers who didn't have a client in the chair. Bishop, a retired military sergeant among other things, believed in keeping a floor tidy enough to eat off. He often told his staff, "If you got time to lean, you got time to clean."

Orlando walked into the spotless man cave wearing an impish grin that shamed the devil. "Afternoon, 'gents, today is a good day for it is one that God has made," he announced boldly.

"And it wasn't two seconds after God made it all beautiful and lovely before a woman come along and pissed on it all," Bishop snapped back, with a black seersucker cape over his arm. "Might as well sit right down in the chair Pastor Clay," he said, as an afterthought.

After Orlando sat down, he noticed the barber had quite a bit less hair than when they met a few years ago and that Bishop's movement seemed slower and more deliberate than normal. The owner was getting old but that didn't stop Orlando from starting right back where he left off the last time he came in. Riling up the clever storyteller, strictly for amusement purposes, was the highlight of his appointment and everyone got a kick out of it.

"What you talking about Bishop? Can't no woman in her right mind get over you," Orlando teased, to get the retired Army veteran going.

"That don't stop 'em from trying to put things over on me though. Smelling all sweet and good enough to eat," he added, for affect.

Orlando sat down in the head barber's chair and howled with laughter. "Bishop, man you're something else. What has any woman ever done to make you feel about them that way?"

"I had this woman once. She stole my dreams and my Cutlass Supreme. When I found out what she done, the sweet young thang pulled a knife. She ran out on me and split the money with my wife," he said, like a politician on a stump. "Twenty years later they're still shacked up in a duplex near Kiest and Polk. Now that's a dog gone shame. But it ain't no joke."

Two customers who just walked in seemed to enjoy the quick-witted stylist. Slim Woody had some chubby guy with him, who wasn't much of a body guard if that was the role he played.

Byron, the newest barber, chuckled. He was barely twenty-one and fresh out of clip-and-cut school. He'd wandered in a year ago, begging to sweep up the place for lunch money so Bishop took him in and taught him the trade. The young man stuck around like a shop mascot ever since.

Mosley walked in wearing a frown as he took a seat by the door. He could tell the jive talking had already commenced and that he'd missed something to laugh at.

"Awe hell," he mouthed to himself, hoping he'd remember to ask Orlando about it later on.

Numbers came into the barbershop offering to watch Orlando's car. "It's been sixty-three seconds Mr. Clay. Can I watch the car for you now?"

"What's all this Mosley?" Orlando asked, figuring he had something to do with it.

"Uh, Mr. Mosley said I could come in and see if you wanted your Silver Spur watched in a minute. Its sixty-eight seconds now. Am I too late?"

Bishop's protégé Byron looked at Numbers and tried to run him off. "Get out of here fool. I done told you once today," he barked.

Orlando raised his hand to stop everything when it appeared that Byron was going to chase Numbers away with a broom.

"Let him work," Orlando said, more insistent that he meant to be. "Numbers, what day of the week did Dr. Martin Luther King Jr. come to Dallas, to beg these spineless ministers to get involved in the civil rights struggle?"

"It was a Tuesday," he said, as everyone laughed. "Tuesday, March 24th. The Year of Our Lord 1961." Numbers had recalled the event then immediately the year, corresponding month, and day.

"How he know?" Byron asked, still bothered by Orlando's directive to stand down.

"Tell this young man how you can be so certain of the year, month, and date."

Numbers looked at Orlando as if he'd asked a trick question. "Because it was 20,845 days ago."

"Ahhh hell to the yeah," Slim Woody cackled. "Somebody pay that man." He went into his pocket and pulled out a few singles but Orlando wagged a finger.

"No hard feelings Slim but I got this one." Orlando held up a hundred dollar bill. "Numbers, come on over here and get this money. You deserve it."

The timid math whiz hurried to retrieve the single bill from Orlando. When he took it, Numbers also gladly accepted the three dollars offer from Slim then walked out of the shop mumbling to himself. "It could have been a Wednesday."

It was well known that several of Dallas' Black leading ministers declined to organize at Martin Luther King Jr.'s behest after weighing their options. They thought they had it better than most blacks around the country and decided the trouble wasn't worth the trials. Highly disappointed, Dr. King stepped back onto a TWA flight and never set foot in Dallas again.

Slim Woody looked at his empty hand then at Orlando suspiciously. "That fella Numbers is a helluva lot smarter than he looks. You didn't use that dude as a voodoo dice whisperer when you took down that crap game the other night, did you?"

"Didn't need no voodoo. The Holy Spirit backed me all the way," Orlando answered.

"Well next time lemme use the dummy to win back some of the money I lost to you."

Orlando held still as Bishop clipped away at the top of his hair. "He's no dummy. What you might call an idiot savant."

"A which?"

"His brain works seven times the normal speed when he's calculating figures. He's a good man to know even if his mind isn't quite right."

Bishop ran a comb through Orlando's thick wavy hair and crooned as if a Negro spiritual had washed over him.

"Mmmm… mmmm mmm… mmm… mmm. A man like Numbers is probably as loyal as a good dog," he said, as he continued to comb. "If only I was lucky enough to have one loyal woman like that."

Slim sat up on the padded bench seat, poised for more barbershop shenanigans. "Oh yeah. Here we go."

"What you get yourself into Bishop?" Orlando said, to poke at him.

"Well, a number of years ago I was in love with a girl and spreading myself a little thin. I got caught spending too much time with this little thing I had stashed away on the other side of town."

Slim leaned in like he had a reason to be alarmed.

"You used to live down the street from me, Bishop. Which side of town did you stash your sidepiece?"

"Which side of town? Oh, way-way, wayyyy on the other side, over yonder," he explained, while feigning nervousness. "She lived near this hole-in-the-wall where they serve whiskey and chicken wings until the wee hours of the morning. But see, eventually I stumbled on my way home and found another man's drawers on the floor in my bedroom. Then, I found the toilet seat left up."

"But you were out catting around too," Bryon said, then immediately went back to sweeping the floor, with his mouth closed.

"What the youngster wants to know is, did your conscience ever bother you enough to stop all that tipping around?" Orlando said, on Byron's behalf. This brought a thank you smile from the protégé.

Bishop tilted his head down like he was giving it some serious thought then laughed. "Me and my conscience made a deal a long time ago. I stay out of my conscience's way and it keeps the hell out of mine." He saw Mosley still sitting by the door with traces of a smile on his face but Bishop wanted more of an outpour. "If I only just had one good woman I'd change. I swear I'd change," he howled, with his left hand placed over his heart. That move caused Mosley to signify right on along with him.

"Amen, Brother Bishop," he said. "Amen."

"I need me a warm-hearted and wrong-doing women to ease my troubled mind too," said Orlando, playing along. "You know where I can get me one Bishop?"

"Yeah but I'm doing my best to keep her busy for a few more days," he answered loudly. "She's right outside if you want to meet her."

When Byron craned his neck to look out front of the shop, everyone fell over laughing. Orlando was gasping for breath.

"That's right, son. If I tell you that a flea can pull a train, what do you do?"

"Hook it up, I guess," the boy answered, to even more merriment among the men.

Numbers heard the laughs so he stuck his head inside of the door. "I'm still watching this car Mr. Clay. Is my time up yet?"

"Yes it is Numbers. You've done a fine job. I'll catch up with you and stay out of that bakery. The lady said you take out the trash too much."

Numbers nodded like a child who had been reprimanded then disappeared back outside.

"Don't take no wooden nickels and stay your simple behind away from dice games!" Slim Woody hollered after him.

Slim's hired man was listening attentively then he stood up suddenly. "So this here is the slickster who cheated you out of four grand? He don't look like much."

Slim yanked on the man's cuff, bidding for him to let it go but he wouldn't.

"I'll bet you and that idiot whatchamacallit cheated with him." Mosley wrapped his long fingers around the pistol grip hang-ing out of his waistband and he kept an eye on the bodyguard, who was woefully out of his league. Bishop turned towards the top drawer where he kept the shaving tools, combs, brushes and a .44 caliber nickel-plated revolver. As the big mouth carefully sized up Orlando, the barber eased the drawer out in a slow and mater-of-fact manner like he'd done a million times.

"Slim Woody. I'm only tolerating this man because he's with you and he has no idea what he's up against," Orlando said calmly, with his gaze locked onto the agitator's eyes.

"He's hot headed, Mr. Preacher," Slim answered plainly, like he didn't care either way. Deep inside, he kind of wanted to see how his buffer would handle himself. "Can't make no grown man do nothing he don't want to."

"Mister, please sit down and forget you ever got up," Bishop told him. "We don't allow none of that arguing and fronting up in here."

"I'll sit down old man, when this slickster pays Slim back half of the money he stole in that rigged dice game."

When Orlando felt the firearm that Bishop passed to him underneath the black shiny cape, he smiled.

That angered the guard even more.

"What you laughing at nigga?" he scoffed, as his butterfly knife came out of nowhere. "I got half a mind to stomp that money out yo ass right here then carve you up for being a cheat."

Orlando measured the distance between him and the man now holding a knife. "Son, go on and move clear away from this wild dog," he ordered Byron.

Once the young man backed up several feet and clear of danger, Orlando shook his head at Mosley, who had no idea about the secret weapon pointed straight ahead.

"Why you in such a hurry to end your life, man. Don't you like breathing?" Orlando questioned him.

In a huff, the bodyguard took a step towards Orlando's chair with his knife raised high.

His eyes popped out of his head when the cape was thrown aside to reveal a hand canon poised to rip a big hole through him.

"Ever hear the old saying, never bring a knife to a gunfight?" Orlando asked, angrily. "I ought to blow your head clean off, fool!"

"I was-was-was just... talking loud," the man stammered nervously.

Orlando sighed with both nostrils flared. "And saying nothing. Mosley, you think I ought to shoot him?"

"Naw. Naw, pastor," the deacon answered, assuredly. "Let me do it." Everyone except Orlando stared at the pistol that Mosley was aiming at the foolish man.

"Clearly you did not think this through, did you?" Orlando asked. "Give that pig sticker to Bishop then sit back down like your boss told you." The bodyguard complied then slowly returned to his seat. "If I hear another word out of you today, this will not end well."

When the fearful guard sat down on the chair, brooding like a small child, Slim Woody gave him a disappointed stare.

"You fired. Big ole scary ass," Slim said, sullenly and dejected. "All that money I done paid you."

"You buy a Bentley and then everybody wants to try you," Orlando joked. "Like they haven't heard about me."

Byron was amazed at how Orlando handled himself in the midst of danger. He didn't blink. Not once. Bishop had a run in with some loan sharks a few years back. Orlando went to negotiate with them and he had to tune up one of the money-lender's thugs then, too. Bishop was there to witness Orlando's toughness, so he knew what was coming. It didn't faze the old man, one bit.

Moments later, he was brushing the clippings off of Orlando's collar when he heard the door open and close. Bishop stepped back onto the three-by-five foot double-sponge floor mat.

"We closed," he said, in that general direction. "Come back tomorrow."

However, the stranger continued to stand there, surveying everyone in the room calmly. Orlando sat still with the gun perched on his lap.

"Well I'm here today so..." the white man responded. He swaggered in an off white custom-fitted suit, tanned skin, a hundred dollar haircut and walked towards a group of men he didn't know, like his *give-a-damn* was broken. When the white man, with soft blue eyes, stood five feet away from Orlando, he stopped to broaden his stance evenly atop expensive brown ostrich boots. Then, the smooth stranger unfastened his jacket to show everyone he was strapped with a weapon holstered on his hip.

Slim Woody's guard looked up at the man's black gun then at the barber's cape laying across Orlando's lap. He shook his head sorrowfully like he wanted to be anywhere else in the world other than caught in the middle of a gun fight. In the blink of an eye, he was off of that bench and sprinting towards the door.

"You look like a man who's got business with me." Orlando said frankly, not shaken at the sight of the man in pricey clothes and thousand dollar footwear. "You got something to say, best get to it."

"Alright then. I was in love a long time ago, to a woman I thought I'd spend the rest of my life with, until she met a guy who came between us. Her loving was so sweet, I couldn't do nothing but what she said to do. One day she caught me misbehaving and said, 'git over there and stand in the corner'."

Orlando swallowed hard and adjusted his finger on the gun handle. "So what you do then?"

"Hell, I thought about being stepped on and played the fool. But then I thought about all that good loving she put on me there was only one thing left to do. Stand in the corner? Shiiiiiid, which one?"

Mosley looked at the man like he'd lost his mind. Orlando pulled the cape off, stood up and handed the gun to Bishop, whose cheeks jiggled as light laughter came from deep down inside. He watched Orlando shake hands with the smooth jokester then hugged him like a long lost brother.

"Y'all this is Nelson Rockefeller Brown. He was my old partner when I did some government work a while back."

Bishop gave him a dismissive look then. "Rockefeller? As in Nelson Rockefeller, the Vice President to Gerald Ford's goofy ass?"

"My mother was a Republican."

"Evidently! Well, in this here barbershop, we don't allow no cussing, lying or drinking." He took a healthy swig from a half pint of bourbon he kept on hand for medicinal purposes. "Shit, I probably shouldn't lie in front of company," he said, smacking his moistened lips. "Oh, it's Republican's we don't allow in here. Cussing, lying and dranking is strongly encouraged."

"I heard a lot about your shop Bishop," Nelson said, with a firm handshake. "People said you love spinning tales about good women gone wrong and such."

"I tell a good one every now and then," the old man replied.

Nelson turned to Orlando's right hand man, who wasn't a bit impressed by Nelson's fancy clothes or grand entrance.

"And you must be Deacon Mosley."

"Yeah, I am," he answered, as if it was a dare.

When Orlando saw where this was headed, he pulled Mosley aside. "Me and Nelson got some things to settle up on. Take the car on home. I'll check with you later."

"You know you can't trust him. That man dogged you out. Left you for dead," Mosley said, in a low hushed tone. "Or did you forget?"

"No, I ain't forgot."

7

PARTNERS IN CRIME

Nelson leaned against a black Cadillac outside of Bishop's. He looked around the strip center which was showing signs of a comeback in the making. A fresh coat of sand colored paint covered the buildings, making them look newer and uniform. He had no idea that his former partner and special agent in the Office of Inspector General owned more than half of them.

Orlando exited the barbershop with a close shave and a fresh shallow fade. He wasn't in any hurry to get things straight between them if at all possible since Nelson showed up out of the blue. Besides, Orlando had a lot of business to take care of and he didn't want to spend any of it barking directions.

"You in town a while or just passing through?"

"I got time."

"Then give me the keys and buckle up," Orlando demanded.

Nelson gave him a look of disbelief. "You're serious?"

"Always wanted a Caddy but couldn't afford the up keep."

"Says the guy with a new Bentley, and a driver."

"Mosley is not a driver, he's a deacon. And my friend," he said, as if that would be the final word on the subject.

The Cadillac tore out of the strip center with Orlando behind the wheel and heading east on Camp Wisdom.

"Sure does drive nice," he said, checking the rear view mirror.

"I know. That's why *I* rented it."

"You sound a bit testy for a man who dropped out of the sky today and showed up without warning to a place that very few people know I'd be." Orlando looked over at his passenger, who was trying to find the right words.

"I am sorry for the way things went down Orlando. You had to know I couldn't chance getting mixed up in none of that. You can't blame me for staying out of it."

Suddenly the car swerved onto the shoulder, leading off of the highway, then skidded to an abrupt stop.

"*You* don't get to tell me about how my life got pulled inside out when the Feds threw me to the wolves over a Louisiana drug boss," Orlando growled. "*You* were my partner in the OIG. *You* were supposed to have my back, help me clear my name. *You* had better be glad I am working on my anger issues or *you* would be eating that sissy pistol you got strapped on your hip.

Orlando glanced up at the rear view mirror again.

"We're not being tailed," Nelson replied, adamantly.

He watched dozens of cars zoom by them on the road. "Well, if your *coworkers* were following us, they're not anymore."

He pulled back onto the road quietly. Neither of them said a word until they walked into the M.E.G.A. church building.

Nelson walked a few paces behind Orlando to take in the grandeur of red carpeting, cathedral ceilings, polished wood molding and frosted glass office doors.

"How does a country boy from central Texas end up with all this?" he asked, really wanting to know.

As they entered the pastor's office, Nelson sat down in one of the black leather chairs opposite the broad mahogany desk.

"When I was inside, they locked me away in solitary confinement. Said that segregating a federal agent from the other prisoners was for my own good." Orlando let that sink in while he took a seat behind his desk. "That's two years and seven days of being alone, dying inside every day after my family was killed, and trying to figure out what was left for me on the outside *if* I ever made it out alive."

Nelson was smart enough to keep his mouth closed and listen, so that's exactly what he did. "How did I end up in the ministry?" Orlando asked, with a soft smile. "When it was clear to the guards and my jack-leg lawyer that I was coming unglued, they gave me a better cell with more sunlight and let me read every day." Orlando leaned back in his chair as if that took him back to the worse days of his life. "I read the good book from sun up to sun down with the voracity of a starving man who hadn't eaten in years," he explained, with an air of showmanship used at the pulpit.

Nelson sat up straight in the chair and nodded agreeably. "Are you preaching right now, cause I can't tell?"

"It was during those weeping hours of my life that I found God and discovered who my Savior was. Jesus came into my heart. Jesus flowed into my veins. Jeeeeesus told me it would be alright. Jeeeeeesus helped me sleep at night. My God is alive and He lives in me. I found myself broken and He put me back together and sent me on my way," Orlando said, as he stood up and shouted.

"Nothing! Nothing but the blood of the Lamb could have saved me because I was broken, lied on and abused. I was contemplating the quickest way to take my own life. I had given up on all things that mattered in this world. I was finished, tired, and through but then God! God! God sent the Holy Spirit to my room at the gray bar motel and said, stand up! Stand up! Stand up and take your rightful place as a child of God."

Nelson wiped his mouth then anxiously rubbed his fingers against his palms. "Hot-damn Hallelujah!"

Orlando exhaled mightily then took a seat. "That is what God gave me when I promised to take up my cross and follow Him. He remade me, Nelson. God gave me my life back but it was better than when I was a fraud dawg for the Office of the Inspector General and more peaceful than I ever thought possible after Shonda and my kids were brutally taken from me."

"I should have been there when you got arrested," Nelson lamented, "I know that better than anybody Orlando. That whole thing was foul. From the day they pulled you in for questioning and all of the drugs and illegal guns they found in your garage."

"It was a set up and you know it!"

"Yes, of course it was. I knew you couldn't have been dirty. Hell, the whole department knew it," Nelson confirmed.

"Yet not one of y'all stepped up in my defense. Not one of you true believers in Orlando Clay's innocence came by to say a damned thing when they brought me into that courtroom chained up like a runaway slave!" he hollered.

"Pastor!" Carolyn shouted, from the half opened door. "Is everything in here alright?"

That inquiry was meant to question his relationship with the good looking visitor whose face was reddish and flushed.

"I'm sorry Carolyn. I must have been quite loud," Orlando apologized.

"It sounded like a fire and brimstone sermon for the last days," she said, still visibly shaken.

Sister Burlington stormed into the office, pushing Carolyn aside. "Sounded more like an exorcism!" she argued. "I suggest you save all of that hollering for your Sunday speeches and not to disrupt the entire office complex of M. E. G. A."

She gave Orlando and Nelson a look that suggested she didn't care for either of them. "Interim Pastor Clay, please stop by my office before you leave today. We still have some unfinished business to discuss."

"Yes, Sister Burlington," was his humble reply. Orlando had no intentions whatsoever to be brow beat into helping the leadership selection committee find his replacement in the pulpit. "I'll be along directly ma'am," he lied, as she walked out of the room.

Carolyn stood just inside the doorway with her eye dancing back and forth between Nelson and Orlando. When she cleared her throat, the pastor got the message. "Oh, Sister Carolyn Drew, please meet my former partner with the OIG, Nelson Brown."

Carolyn nodded hello while still unsure what relevance any of that had on the shouting and testifying going on inside the pastor's office. "Nice to meet you," she said, not certain if Nelson was friend or foe.

Nelson stood up to shake her hand but Carolyn was reserved, she clasped her hands together instead.

"Good meeting you too… Miss."

Suddenly feeling like a third wheel, Nelson excused himself from the room that was still spinning. "I'm sure y'all got a pile of men's rooms around here. I'll go find one."

He backed away from the twosome then threw a questioning look at Orlando as he exited the office.

"What was that all about?" Carolyn asked, with a level of concern that she regretted immediately.

"Old wounds. Me and Nelson have some things to get over."

"More like unresolved issues of the worse kind to me and you know Sister Burlington is out for your scalp."

"Don't I know it," he agreed, as his face tightened. "She's even expecting me to help feel out the men they've selected to interview for my job. I don't have time for that."

Carolyn walked a little closer and lowered her voice. "Your day is about to get busier. There's a pretty lady detective waiting *right outside*."

"Vera?" he asked, with a softer expression.

"Funny. Somehow I guessed you *already* knew her name." Carolyn walked away with a long, slow confident stride. She wasn't ready to admit her intimate thoughts and deepening interests in Orlando but she'd certainly been sleeping on them.

Orlando walked to the doorway as Vera Miles came in. "Hello detective. You keep showing up like this and it'll be hard to fight off the rumors," he kidded.

"Like I'd ever care what church folk thought about me."

Orlando smiled then folded his arms. "Yep. That would be difficult to imagine," he agreed, as a few of her favorite sexual positions zigzagged through the recesses of his brain.

106

"So, what I am accused of doing this time unless this is a friendly visit?"

"I wish it was but only more bad news I'm afraid. Three more dead bodies discovered down by the university. The pot is brewing closer to this church community, Orlando."

Nelson returned to find a different woman standing near Orlando than when he left. "Oh, I'll go wait outside," he said, about to back-pedal out of the room.

"No, stick around Nelson. This is Detective Vera Miles, one of Dallas' finest homicide officers."

"Always nice to meet one of Dallas' *finest*," Nelson flirted.

Orlando was embarrassed for his old friend for chasing up the wrong tree. "Vera, Nelson Brown is with the OIG. He used to be my partner."

"Oh, I heard of you. How long have you been busting white-collar deadbeats and federal tax cheats?"

"Better part of twelve years," he said, inching closer to her with his words. "I've snagged my share of corporate giants."

"Uhhh-uhh. Don't waste your time Special Agent Brown. Unless Orlando is suddenly into sharing his women, you have no shot at snagging this."

"Oh," said Nelson, with egg on his face. "I don't know how I missed that." What he didn't know was Orlando had thrown in the towel in their relationship but Vera wasn't about to give up.

"Now that everyone is on the same page, Vera can get back to telling me about some bodies discovered over on University Hills. College kids?" Orlando asked, hoping it wasn't. Getting local high school students to attend the budding University of Texas

Consolidated – Dallas campus was a challenge. Several generations of residents in the southern sector of Dallas never considered institutions of higher learning as an option and their descendants had yet to realize the new educational jewel in their own back yard.

"No, none of the UTC-Dallas students have been reported missing. More than likely, these victims were casualties of the new gang tensions brewing on the south end. Three of them, burnt to a crisp."

"I just came from Monroe, Louisiana," Nelson chimed in. "Dousing victims of crime is one of the ways they're destroying evidence. Turf wars in small towns is all the rage now. They're setting fire to homeboys, rednecks, hood rats, and trailer-park hoes. Pardon my French, Reverend."

"And lady," Orlando added, in an attempt to defend Vera's honor.

"Whatever!" she retorted, suggesting that she didn't need defending. "It's going to be hard getting any prints or DNA to identify them," she said, with a steam of irritability.

"Teeth," Nelson suggested. "Teeth are the only way."

Orlando shook his head when he saw what was coming next.

Vera leaned on her right hip to get his attention. "Since I've been solving homicides for the *better part of twelve years myself*, I have a few pretty good ideas on how to proceed." After Vera checked Nelson on the spot, she planted her eyes on Orlando. This time they were deadly serious. "Downtown HQ asked us to warn churches to be on the lookout for people who don't belong."

"I'll pass it on. Thank you," he said, knowing there was more to it than Vera was divulging. She wasn't familiar enough with Nelson or she just didn't like him.

Both men watched her walk out of the room. One, wondering what it might be like to lay her down. The other, knowing all too well that it was worth the trouble every time.

"Let's get out of here, while the coast is clear," Orlando said, with Nelson by his side.

"Yeah, that office of yours was starting to become a revolving door for women wanting face time with The Illustrious Pastor, High Potentate and Grand Poohbah all rolled into one."

"Being a shepherd for a flock this big does come with its drawbacks."

"Pastor Clay! Don't you take another step!" Sister Burlington was marching towards them as the men headed for the side door leading to the parking garage.

"I'm just going to the car Sister Betty," he hollered back. "Then I'm going to get in it and drive away," he whispered to Nelson. "See you in a second Sister BB. I'll be right back," he lied, again.

As soon as they exited the building, Carolyn fished around in her trunk then came away with a box of colored folders. She walked past the men as if she had never seen them before then entered the same door they walked out of.

"What did you do to piss her off?" Nelson asked.

"Maybe nothing. Too much perhaps. Heck if I know, she's a woman. Can't figure them out and better not stop trying. Get in the car."

"I'm driving this time, Orlando," said Nelson.

"The hell you are. Either I can call and tell you where to pick it up after I'm finished with it or you can get in and see some of the duties a High Potentate has to endure first hand."

After they were in the Cadillac and on the road, Orlando made a call. He put it on the speaker phone then turned it up loud.

"Speaking of hands, watch this Nelson."

As the phone rang, Orlando began to whistle the way he had when he was still a special agent about to go after one of the bad guys.

"Ohhh, I do remember that? You'd go to whistling when you were about to climb all up in somebody's colon. Anybody I know?"

"Yeah," said a voice on the phone.

"Yeah? *St. Nickolas*, you fat puss ball, I got your *yeah* in my pocket," Orlando said. "I also got your number from a snitch working for you. One of the punks who tried to steal my car."

"Who dis?" St. Nick answered.

"Dis... Pastor Orlando Clay, you piece of crap wanna-be gangster," he teased.

"Why in hell you calling my phone and what do you *think* you're talking about?"

While Orlando berated the gangster who recently moved to town with a crew of neophyte hustlers, Nelson listened uncomfortably to every word exchanged between them. Orlando noticed but pretended he hadn't.

"Listen Dumbo, a lady cop stopped by my house and told me two of your top dogs came to the police station whimpering like abandoned puppies."

"I'm guessing it was the two bitch-made homies whose paws got clipped? I'll handle that. You got my word it wasn't supposed to go down and they won't come back around to bother you anymore," St. Nick said, adamantly.

"Send them back to South Boulevard if you want to. That'll be the last time they do any dirt, to anybody, anywhere," Orlando answered.

"Don't be threatening my people. I done told you it was a mistake," Nick added. "If I wanted to hurt you, you'd still be feeling it now."

"Listen to me, St. Nick. I have a feeling we're not finished with our former lives, me and you."

"Man, don't bother yourself about that. Soon as I catch them, it's done."

"Get your house in order, *Nickolas*. I'd hate to be the tornado that tears down everything you build in Dallas but I will," Orlando threatened.

"You always did like to hear yourself talk. My reach is longer than you think," St. Nick assured him, like he knew something Orlando didn't. "I got people everywhere now. Funny how money makes that possible."

Orlando was thinking of something to say when the line went dead.

"Something ain't right," he said as the phone rang. "What!" he yelled, into the phone. "Oh, I'm sorry Sister Burlington, something came up. "No I didn't. No I don't but I can."

He wedged the phone between his jaw and shoulder then pushed a stick of gum in his mouth. "Mmm hmmm. I know where it is."

He put the phone down on the console and kept quiet all the way to the Omni Hotel. For the first time, he'd had a grip on everything is his life and he felt uneasy about the vibes buzzing around him. Something was definitely off.

"I hope this hotel has a bar," Nelson said, with a bothered expression. "I could use a tall cold beer."

"We're not staying that long. I've got to pick up a gentleman who just might be my replacement," Orlando told him.

"As the church pastor?"

"No, as the stunt double in this movie I just landed. Yes, as the church pastor."

"Why you getting assy, Orlando? Huh? Did I do something to you?"

Orlando didn't have time to answer. A middle-aged man with impeccable style walked out of the front door, as he was saying goodbye to a man wearing a dress and heels.

"What in hell?" Orlando said, shocked and surprised.

"Dallas done changed on me," said Nelson, eying the skinny man, who appeared to be a trans gender reassignment participant. "There was a time when man-ladies kept to their own. Things were a whole lot simpler then."

"Hush, I think this is the preacher I'm supposed to ride around."

"On what?" Nelson joked.

"Shut up and be on your best behavior," Orlando reprimanded. "I might be working for this fellow when it's all said and done."

Nelson objected harshly. "This is my rental car and I'll do what I damn well please in it."

When Orlando looked at him with a look of desperation, Nelson threw his hands up. "Okay, I promise not to make your ministerial guest cry before he becomes your boss."

"Thank you." Orlando got out of the car and waved at the man, who was looking at all of the cars pulling in front of the hotel.

"Minister Howard T. Breedlove?"

"The third," the man answered, then sauntered toward the Cadillac.

"Oh brother," Nelson cackled. "This is gonna be harder than I thought."

8

DUKE AND GRUNT

"How was your flight in Brother Breedlove?" Orlando asked, to feel out the applicant for himself.

"It was okay, I guess. Not much turbulence. However I did not expect to travel in coach. I was just meeting with my publicist who specifically asked for first-class accommodations."

"Publicist?" Nelson mouthed, as he looked at Orlando.

The pastor was not having it.

"I would take that up with Sister Burlington and the church leadership. I believe it was a simply misunderstanding. We're glad you're interested in shepherding the flock and leading the church into the next chapter of its divined existence."

"I was going to ask you about that Minister Clay seeing as how the current position is yours to lose."

"Nah, I was merely holding onto it until the right man comes along." Nelson choked down a laugh, thinking that's probably what Brother Breedlove does on the regular. "I have a passion for spreading the word but sometimes the business of protecting the flock from ravenous wolves gets to be extremely time consuming.

It's moments like this that compensation feels like it's stored up in heaven with the mansion, robe, and crown we all aspire to receive."

"A congregation that size would come with a certain level of commitment and over time," Brother Breedlove added.

"You have no idea how much it takes to keep the motor running."

"There are some sensitive questions I would like to ask, if you're agreeable to that with present company included."

There was a deadening silence until Orlando looked in the rear view mirror to see Brother Breedlove motioning toward the front-seat passenger.

"Oh, I see," Orlando said, in ah-ha fashion. "This is Nelson. He's a lawman who comes along when I need an extra pair of hands."

Brother Breedlove looked confused. "I don't think I understand."

"You will shortly," Orlando reassured him. "Nelson is also pretty handy with a pistol if it comes to that."

"Really?" the visiting minister asked, with a raised brow. "I was hoping to sit down with you before my meeting with the MEGA leadership to discuss some potential pitfalls." Orlando was thinking about his *man-lady* publicist being one of them. "I don't like to discuss compensation until the second round of visits but I am curious about your agreement."

"What agreement is that?" Orlando asked, for his and Nelson's edification.

"Well, it has been widely reported in the brotherhood that you recently purchased a new Bentley Silver Spur and that your salary is based on a percentage of the weekly tithing."

"Can't eat if I don't put butts in the seat, right?"

"I would not have used those exact words but I do get your point."

"I do make a percentage of what the sermons bring in but I don't accept any of it," Orlando answered, much to Nelson's surprise. "There are far more needful things around Methodist Episcopal Greater Apostolic church than stuffing my pockets. I donate every penny to the college scholarship fund."

Nelson and Brother Breedlove both listened up a little harder when they heard it.

"I don't expect everyone to follow my lead but I've been blessed financially. My salary donations have put six of our member's kids through school, debt free. Three at Prairie View A&M, two at UNT Dallas and one at UT Consolidated. I've made some good stock purchases and hit it big. Big enough to make a difference for people around me."

Brother Breedlove was contemplating his next line of questioning but kept his cards close to his vest. "Blessing on blessings on blessings, as the young people say."

"Big dreams take big piles of dough but it's the little things that can tear a congregation apart," Orlando reasoned.

"I'm sure there are battles to be won to keep the peace in a church that size," Breedlove queried.

Orlando looked in the rear view mirror again. This time to see if any suspicious cars were traveling the same road behind them for too long. "At times fighting isn't enough Brother. Every now and then, you have to cut the head clean off."

Nelson knew Orlando was up to something. He looked up from his cellphone screen when realizing he had no idea where they were headed. Brother Breedlove peered out of the window with a hint of concern when the car traveled into West Dallas, near an industrial district.

"Where are we going, exactly? If you don't mind my asking."

"To see some subcontractors that do work for the church. Duke and Grunt."

"Oh my," Brother Breedlove replied, with a pretentious sneer. "Duke and Grunt sounds like something you do after a big meal."

Nelson cocked a half smile. "Ha-ha. He's got you there partner."

Orlando almost smiled too. Knowing what lay in store at their next stop made him hum inside. It started to feel like old times riding in the car with Nelson and that's what Orlando was afraid of.

When the car pulled in behind Duke's plumbing van at the rear of the shop, Brother Breedlove appeared to be more interested in the Bentley parked long ways and taking up two parking spots than he was eager to go into the building with old washing machines leaning against it.

"I hope you won't be long Pastor Clay. I'll remain here and make some calls while you're in… there."

"I don't think so Brother. This here is MEGA church business," Orlando told him, with a tinge of self-righteousness thrown in. "You want the top spot, you have to get your hands dirty. Leave the phone and come on."

Orlando and Nelson were both out of the car and heading to the back door before Breedlove had a chance to decline the offer.

Orlando opened the heavy steel door with Nelson on his hip, just like they'd done too many times to count. When Nelson instinctively went to draw his gun, Orlando waved him off. "Uh-uh. This is a family business." He looked past Nelson to find the visiting minister tip toeing up behind them. "We're not breaking in the place. Still, it's probably better if you don't touch anything. Fingerprints have a bad way of showing up in court evidence," Orlando warned.

The men walked in the door of what used to be a busy convenience store before drugs hit the city hard. The store suffered too many losses to remain open when a lot of the warehousing and manufacturing business shifted further south. The lighting was poor. The floor was dirty and tacky beneath their feet. Orlando pretended not to notice but Nelson knew right away what made that gritty sticky feeling as they walked deeper in the store room.

"What is on this floor?" asked Brother Breedlove. "It's filthy."

"Mind how you talk about the property of my two most loyal church members. They don't come in often but they tithe religiously. I see to that."

"Something in here lost a lot of blood," Nelson said, with his right hand on his firearm.

Brother Breedlove sided up Nelson and reached for his arm. "Hey man! Stay behind me," Nelson said, "and not that close behind me neither."

"I think they're in here," Orlando said, as he pulled opened the silver door of the insulated room that was designed to be a beer and beverage cooler. As the foul stench hit them, each of the men winced. Brother Breedlove held a handkerchief over his nose.

"I hope ain't nobody dead in there, Orlando," Nelson threatened. "Or else I got to call it in."

"Perhaps *you* need to go wait in the car," Orlando fired back. "Maybe letting you tag along with me wasn't such a good idea after all."

Orlando was also hoping they didn't find a corpse. He didn't want Nelson to be faced with a decision that might get Duke and Grunt sent to prison for life. Then, Orlando would have been faced with the dilemma of killing his former partner as a result.

118

"I'm still here ain't I?" Nelson hissed. "I'm getting a little tired of you snapping at me too."

"Y'all gonna come over here and help out or stand there arguing like a couple of females," Duke reprimanded them.

Orlando flipped on another light and looked around the room. There were trails of blood leading from the center of the room to the back door, three dried urine stains and the smell of human feces in the air.

Duke rolled a 100 gallon drum from the corner of the room to the side of a hooded man who was still tied to the folding chair in the center of the room. Duke ran an industrial-sized hose into the large drum, from the facet, then sneered at the hostage slumped down in the seat, dressed in jeans, tennis shoes, and a thick light-colored jacket. He was motionless.

While the drum was filling, Grunt hooked up the jumper cables to a diesel truck battery on the floor then touched the ends together causing bright orange sparks that popped and crackled.

"Y'all came just in time for the fireworks."

Mosley slinked out of the other corner, holding a gallon-size water pitcher. "Welcome to the dungeon," he said, in a business-as-usual tone. Sorry about the smell. Maid's day off." He dipped the pitcher down into the drum then pulled it out filled with water. "Bring him to."

Grunt kicked the man's foot. He didn't move.

"LaDuke, tell me y'all didn't go too far before getting the information we need," Orlando asked sharply.

"Don't put that on me," he said, in his own defense. "If he ain't breathin', then it was a minor miscalculation as to his pain toleration."

Orlando looked him over, curiously. He noted the dark stains on his pants, jacket and hood. "When was the last time you fed him?"

"Huh? Didn't nobody say to feed him," Duke answered, scratching his head.

"Oh my Lord. Is he dead?" whispered Brother Breedlove, placing his hand over his mouth, in utter disbelief.

"I said to wake him up," Mosley growled, while socking the man in the stomach. The captive coughed, sputtered, and gasped for air. Mosley held his head back then poured water from the pitcher over the sack where his mouth and nose were underneath.

"Hold him down Grunt!"

Nelson moved in to stop Grunt but Orlando jumped into his way.

"You are merely an observer here. Stay back or get tied down until we're finished."

Listening to the man gargling loudly and squirming to keep water out of his lungs, inspired Nelson to do something after what he'd witnessed. "You think I can stand here, watching y'all water-board a U.S. citizen, and let it go?"

"This is a U.S. terrorist," Orlando shouted. "I put him on the watch list my damned self after he fought his way into my church on a Sunday morning then scared my congregation with the ravings of a lunatic."

Breedlove gasped. "That's why he's being tortured like this?"

"Yeah! So the next time he is deterred from coming back ministers before his clip is empty."

When the water was all out of the pitcher, Mosley looked at Orlando who was obviously in charge.

"Hit him again?"

"No. Take that hood off and let's have a look."

Grunt pulled the wet sack off of the man's head. His eyes were swollen half shut, lip busted and nose broken. Stale blood had marked the front of his jacket. Sweat and human waste saturated the bottom half of his clothing. It was completely demoralizing, just the way Orlando ordered.

Duke told Grunt to move onto the next phase. "Go ahead Grunt. I'm getting hungry. You hungry?"

"I could eat," he said, nonchalantly, as he ripped the front of the hostage's jacket opened. "We could get those street burritos from the food truck you really like." Grunt pulled on yellow rubber gloves then hooked one of the battery cables to the captive's nipple. "This might be your last time to come clean, *Christopher*. I haven't figured the right voltage yet."

"Won't matter if he won't talk," Duke said, determined to end this interrogation. "Light his ass up."

"No! No! Please don't do that again," the church intruder begged, as Grunt connected the positive cable onto the man's zipper. "Nooooo! Please don't!" he screamed, as the battery current flowed through the cables, sending a powerful jolt to his chest andcrotch simultaneously.

They all watched as his body seized and floundered until Nelson yelled to stop it. "You're killing him! Turn it off now." Nelson pulled a gun on Grunt, who reluctantly disconnected the wires."

"Ahhhh! Uhhhhgh! I can't breathe," the hostage whimpered, with foam coming out of his mouth.

"What do you know, I'm getting better at this," Grunt said, to toot his own horn.

Brother Breedlove was throwing up his lunch on his shoes. "I can't do this," he gasped.

Duke nodded his agreement then looked at Orlando, who had drawn Mosley's gun on Nelson, pointing it at his head.

"I told you, this has nothing to do with you Nelson so don't make this about you," Orlando told him. "You point that thing at my people again and there won't be nothing else to say between us."

"Please let me go," the tortured man cried. "Please, I'm begging you."

Orlando stared a hole into the captive but kept a gun trained on Nelson. "Shut him up before I put a bullet in him myself," Orlando said, sharply.

Duke smiled. He took one step toward the fellow, ready to reconnect him to that diesel truck battery.

"We won't spark him again fellas but you'd better holster that gun and keep it there," Orlando said to Nelson, with little regard of human life at that moment.

Just as the seriousness of the situation was clear to Breedlove, he doubled over holding his stomach. "I think I'm going to be sick."

Duke shook his head disapprovingly. "What, again? Who's gonna clean that up?"

"I don't know what's gotten into you," Nelson complained to Orlando, while choosing his words carefully. "You're treating me like a stranger because I wasn't there when your life fell apart. I need you to be sure you're not going to shoot me over that, instead of this."

Duke grabbed a shot gun then cocked it. "Hey, I thought y'all was friends."

Nelson's words cut Orlando deep. The pastor was ready to blow Nelson's brains onto the floor because of the pain he endured alone, after being deserted by his former partner and the department he had worked so hard for.

Suddenly, Orlando lowered Mosley's weapon.

Nelson sighed hard, put his pistol away and then cleared his throat. "I'm sorry and I don't know what else to say about that."

"Heyyy! Hey, don't apologize to him," the prisoner clamored. "Help me. Help. Me." When Nelson walked over to him, the man began to nod his head feverishly. "Yes, thank you man. Thank you."

"See. Y'all going about this all wrong," Nelson said defiantly. "Grunt, you got any other ideas before we end this?"

"I'm surprised he hasn't died yet," Grunt answered.

"Duke, any more tricks up your sleeves?" Orlando queried.

"Nope. He won't talk or he's got nothin' to say."

"I. Ain't. No. Rat," the captive barked. "Snitches get stitches."

"And holdouts get rolled out," Nelson countered, then wrapped a rope around the man's neck. "If he won't talk, we're done here. String him up!"

"Help! Heeeelp!" the frightened man yelled. "Don't let this white man hang me."

"You'll wish I strung you up once that acid singes off every square inch of your skin. Duke, get that other barrel. The one with acid."

Duke was confused until he realized what Nelson was trying to do, then he carefully dragged another barrel beside the one filled with water.

"Good, now drop this tough guy in the acid alive. He'll scream out any secrets he's holding on to."

"Whoooa! Hell naw. I'll talk. Ain't nobody dumping me in acid? I'll snitch on my own momma first. I'll tell you everything I know," the hostage ranted.

Nelson laughed aloud then took the rope off of his neck. "Hot damned. "It's a miracle!"

"Amen," Brother Breedlove agreed. "Wonders never cease."

"It was St. Nick," the captive said, angrily. "He's the devil that made me do it. Uh-huh, he said to run up into the auditorium and embarrass you, throw so much shade that those good church folk turned on you. Nick said if I got caught to keep my mouth shut *or else*." He leered nervously at the barrel he believed to be filled with acid. "It can't get more *or else* than that."

"So we got to let him go now?" Grunt asked, with a look of sorrow.

"Get him some new clothes and enough money to leave town for good," Orlando said, handing Duke a plastic bank card with $5,000 stamped on it. "Here, give him this once he's changed into something decent then *put him on a bus*."

"Give him a bath!" Breedlove said, to offer his two cents. "They do not want him on the bus smelling like that."

Duke took the bankcard and pushed out a thought that came to mind. "What if he doesn't run? He could tell the police what we done to him."

"Oh, he has to run now. Can't show up at Nick's or they'll know he ratted them out and kill him on the spot." Orlando said that, just in case their captive was stupid enough to return to home base.

"Besides, after all he's been through, I highly doubt he'll tell a soul."

"I could clip him for good luck," Duke suggested.

"Do you want your pinky fingers cut off?" Orlando asked the captive, nicely. "No? Then make sure nothing that happened here ever comes out of your mouth. I have people all over who would love to collect a bounty on your head."

"Can I go now?" Brother Breedlove asked. His hand on his forehead as if he were about to swoon.

"Nelson, please take him out to the car," Orlando suggested.

As they left the room, Orlando patted his foster family member on the shoulder. "Well done Nephew. Grunt, you too. Be certain this gentleman gets away clean and without another thing happening to him."

"I'm hungry too," the man said abruptly.

"Alright, and feed him," said Orlando, much to the prisoner's delight. Find out where St. Nickolas is holding up."

"Oh, he ain't hiding," the captive quipped. "Nick n'em over at the Craw Daddy Breakfast Bar. He's there all the time if he's not at the Windsor Hotel or at that big house he bought last month."

"Then there it is," Orlando said, turning towards the exit. "You know what to do if *snitchy* here reneges on our deal."

"Then I get to clip him and dip him," Duke said fondly.

"Let the church say Amen," Grunt answered, with a bright smile.

Duke was a good soldier who always followed orders, even when he collected rent from the Orlando's tenants. Once, when a renter couldn't pay on time, Duke kicked the door off the hinges and threatened to put his family out in the cold, butt naked. Duke offered them a choice to get their pinky finger sliced off or agree to an uncontested eviction. He never had a problem getting tenants to clear out or dealing with any fussy legal battle which could take up to 180 days before going to court. Orlando told him to fall back on those threats as illegal evictions are frowned on by the state and punishable by law. Still, Duke managed almost twenty rent homes at times for his Uncle without incident, although he'd rather clip a few of the tenants when the rent was past due instead.

As soon as Orlando stepped outside, he was confronted with three men arguing in the back lot. Mosley was trying to get Brother Breedlove to go with Nelson so he could take Orlando where ever he needed to go next. Nelson, had the same idea, only he wanted to pawn the minister off on Mosley so he could hang with his old partner.

"I'm only suggesting that Brother Breedlove might be more comfortable in that fine luxury automobile than stuffed in the car with me and Orlando," Nelson said, heatedly.

"Yep, there's plenty of room in this Bentley for Pastor Clay and this one here," Mosley said, pointing dismissively at Brother Breedlove.

Orlando stepped between the men, both posturing for his attention. "Hold it guys. Hold on. Brother Breedlove, you are free to take my car back to your hotel if you like or ride with me in the Cadillac back to the church so you can go run and blab to Sister Burlington for all I care. Which is it?"

"Hell no! I am not going to the hotel or to meet with the selection committee. I have seen enough to let me know that I don't want to be a part of this crazy church or this silly scandalous situations y'all got going on in this God forsaken city. Take me directly to the airport my good man," he ranted, while awaiting Mosley to open the back door of the Bentley for him to get inside.

"You heard him Mosley," Nelson teased. "He wants to be chauffeured to the airport so he can ride a fast plane away from here."

Orlando reached out his hand toward Breedlove, who looked at it like a pile of dog poop was sitting in the middle of it.

"I'd rather not Pastor Clay," he answered, then sat in the back seat comfortably. "I'll send for my things, thank you. To the airport please."

Nelson reached into the Cadillac and picked up Breedlove's cell phone off the back seat. "Here you go. Your *publicist* is probably getting concerned that *she* hadn't heard from you in a while." Breedlove took the phone and closed the door, refusing to look at them for another second.

"Bye," Nelson said, as the Bentley pulled way. "I wonder what the selection committee would say if they knew about his publicist."

"Nowadays, probably not a damn thing," Orlando answered, correctly.

9

WOULD I LIE TO YOU

Neither of the men said a word on the way to Orlando's home. The past few hours were filled with quick-draw gun play and staring down the opposition much like the old west. In life or death situations, trust came at a premium. A single mistake, one misguided association or misjudgment in where a man's loyalty lay, could have spelled doom. Orlando learned that the hard way. Nelson was having a devil of a time atoning for his.

Sitting in Orlando's den sipping twelve year old scotch, Nelson looked around the large room. He noticed the latest electronic equipment, an 80 inch wide screen TV, built-in cabinets and suede fabric over distressed wood furniture.

"So, do mega church preachers need a special license to go water boarding their disgruntled visitors or is that just a black thang?"

"If they walk, talk, and quack like a terrorist something has to be done," Orlando answered, while looking over a glass of ginger ale. "Whether foreign or home grown, I'll do whatever is required to keep my community safe from terrorizers."

"Were you going to shoot the fella back at that filthy room?" Nelson asked.

"If I thought he might cause future harm to my congregation, in a heartbeat."

"You don't think it's illegal to use military interrogation tactics on civilians inside the United States?"

Orlando decided on his words before using them. "Now you sound like a lawman. Are you setting me up for a confession on what happened today?"

"No, I was just saying…"

"Because I would gladly sit in the defendant's chair and try my chances with a jury box full of white people than a church house full of dead members after a mass shooting that I could have prevented." Orlando took a gulp of soda then sat the glass on a coffee table. "I would rob a man of his civil rights in order to save lives." While he believed in civil liberties, averting a terrible incident ranked higher on his list of importance.

"Well, since you put it like that. Can't say that I blame you." Nelson looked at crystal vases and expensive trinkets on the granite cabinet top. "You're a dedicated man, Orlando. Steeped in principle. That's always been easy to see."

"And since you knew that about me, why was it so easy to sit back and watch the FBI sic their lawyers on me to save their high-profile drug case?"

Nelson stared into space for a moment, as if traveling back in time. "Who said it was easy?"

"Oh it had to be, right? I mean, you never came to visit me or sent mail and even when Shonda and the kids died, not a single card or anything."

"Orlando listen. I'm not even supposed to tell you this but I had to stay away," Nelson said, with all sincerity. "The OIG, FBI, and the Department of Treasury had this joint task force working to nab a big fish. It meant taking a half billion dollars of cocaine off the streets."

"What did that have to do with me?"

"Everything. As soon as you stumbled onto that meth lab in Rustin."

"Tommy Eckert's business?"

"Yeah, you pinched the nephew of a San Pablo drug kingpin. Seems the U.S. Government was right in the middle of a collaboration that took years to build. They had old Tommy boy setting up his aging uncle to take a big fall. Was even gonna let that dopey kid keep a tiny piece of the family business to see if he'd lure other heavy hitters in."

"And I walked in on three government agencies with their pants down?" Orlando asked, already knowing the answer.

"Oh yeah, they had all agreed on a buck-naked circle jerk. You walked in on it when you busted Tommy Eckert's backyard science project. Hell, he couldn't spring the final trap and screw over his dear Uncle Brewster then."

Orlando wrinkled his brow. He was pressed to remember the parts of his life he spent four years trying to forget. "I'm still listening," he said, with a quickening heartbeat.

"That's where St. Nick comes in," Nelson said, quickly.

Orlando leaned back to take in Nelson's implication.

"What? How?"

"Turns out you were a causality of the failed war on drugs."

Nelson poured two more fingers of scotch then he sipped a bit before continuing. "You and me had already taken down Nick on wire and credit card fraud. He resented you because you found the deeds to his commercial properties and that swanky plantation home outside of New Orleans, all purchased by a shell corporation he founded with drug money."

"Yeah, that's the bust that earned me a gold shield and promotion. You deserved one too Nelson."

"You had seniority between us. It was your name in all the paperwork so your name landed on a burn list."

Orlando couldn't believe there was once a contract out to ruin him. "Who in the government was out to get me?"

"The FBI, Treasury, and Office of Inspector General."

"That's bullshit!" he grunted. "No way my own department would promote me then turn around and throw me the wolves. No way!"

"How else do you think the FBI built a case on you overnight and wrecked your career while our bosses sat idly by and let those *feebs* do it?"

"They didn't lift a finger to help me," Orlando said, remembering sadly.

"They were in on it Orlando!" Nelson shouted. "Wheeew, I've been waiting a lot of years to say that."

Orlando laid back on the sofa and let it sink in. "Now that I think about it, there had to be a conspiracy. I thought it was odd that no one at the department returned Shonda's calls when she went to them for help. They even refused to offer legal advice or suggest competent counsel."

"I didn't have any answers then but I went to your house, looked in on Shonda and the kids a few times until I was ordered to stand down."

"I didn't know Nelson. Thanks."

"It tore me apart watching that happen to you. I refused another partner the whole while you were locked up. I couldn't bear riding along with someone else with word on the street saying you were dirty."

"Shonda went to her grave thinking that I was," Orlando said, in retrospect. "Probably a good thing that Wallace and Lacy weren't old enough to believe their father was a crook." He felt like the scab was being pulled off a wound he thought had healed.

"You probably don't want to hear this either but the whole thing popped off on account of a chance meeting between St. Nick and Tommy Eckert during the time they were awaiting trial in Louisiana." Nelson leaned forward with his elbows on his thighs. "Nick told Tommy how he could beat the wrap you put on him. Tommy said if someone could make it happen, he'd make sure it was worth their while. From what I understand, your favorite *Christmas character* bit on it and somehow arranged drugs, money, and guns to be hidden under floorboards in your garage."

"How did they get my finger prints on the suitcases filled with cocaine and cash?"

"You were being followed for weeks until you wondered into a luggage shop at the mall and picked out a lovely matching set for you and the family."

"Yeah, I remember that. Four piece. Samsonite. The sales lady kept trying to get me to buy this ugly brown hard shell set.

She made me look it over pretty good before I convinced her it wasn't my style."

"You want to know what the money and drugs were hidden in?" Nelson asked.

"Ugly brown hard shell luggage?" Orlando answered, while shaking his head.

"Bingo, partner. You didn't want it but Tommy's boys sure did love it for setting you up."

"I knew I was done in by someone with connections but I never could figure out how they got my prints all over those bags."

"I can't prove any of it but you deserved to know."

"Wouldn't change anything. They dropped the case all of a sudden but not before they smeared my name all over the papers and evening news, for eighteen months. When I walked out of the prisoner's release station, I had nothing to come home to. My family was killed in a hit and run. Aunt Theresa died soon after. All I had was a ton of rage and a bounce back plan."

Nelson glanced at the biggest TV he'd ever seen in anyone's home. "Looks to me you found a way to make that plan work in your favor."

"Hell yeah, I did."

"Well, I need to get going," Nelson said finally. "I know what I've told you doesn't get everything fixed between us but I hope it helps."

"I do appreciate it partner. Explains a lot," Orlando conceded. "Is that why you came and found me today?"

"Believe it or not, I'm in town on business. Working out some tips. You know how it is." Nelson didn't want to give away the real reason he was in town. "Hey, I've been hearing about a slew of violent deaths in this part of town lately, your part of town. I'll keep my ears open if I hear anything that can help."

Nelson didn't let on that St. Nickolas Boudreaux had moved his illegal enterprises to Dallas from New Orleans shortly after St. Nick was released from prison. He also neglected to report that St. Nick refused to turn in his drug supplier or stolen credit card connection. He proudly served the full five-year stretch in a federal penitentiary with a smile on his face. Once Orlando's credibility as a governmental fraud dawg was destroyed, Tommy Eckert beat the meth distribution wrap and kept his promise. When St. Nick hit the streets, he had money coming out of his ears. With too much competition over drug turf back home, he decided to adapt to the changing landscape. St. Nick also learned how to cover his illegal pill mills for bored housewives and soccer moms in North Dallas with legit businesses in the neighborhood. St. Nickolas had devised a bounce back plan too. One that included Orlando.

The next day, Mosley sat across from Orlando at Denny's Restaurant. It was the one place where he dreamed about eating while stashed away in prison. At least once a week, he visited the same location off of Interstate 35 and ate three fluffy pancakes, crispy bacon and skillet fried potatoes. Mosley wasn't the biggest fan of eating breakfast during odd times of the day but Orlando was the boss.

"You know they got a lunch and a dinner menu too," Mosley said, to no immediate response.

"Just thought you'd put it out there like that?" Orlando asked, eventually.

After flipping the picture coded menu book over several times, Mosley waved the waitress over. "Ma'am, I would like to order for the both of us."

The food server was white, middle-aged with short graying hair, and very fit for a woman in her mid-fifties.

"Hey guys, you finally decide on something to eat?" She began to write on her note pad before Mosley opened his mouth. "Okay, so that's a three-stack of pancakes, four crispy bacon and firm hash browns."

Orlando glanced up from the menu to read her name tag. "Thank you Cindy but how did you know I would order the usual? I could have changed my mind."

"Honey, that order isn't your usual, it's your only," Cindy said, smiling over her brown, oval sharped reading classes. "'Sides, most men don't change their minds about a darn thing, ever. They eat what they're used to, get goofy over the same type of women they did as young boys and rarely deviate from either." Orlando smiled. Cindy noticed Mosley had picked up his menu again. "What you want, Sugar?"

"Gimme what he got, ma'am. Substitute sausage links for the bacon."

"Got you down fellas. Holler if you need a refresher on the coffee." With that she was off to visit an Asian family, who'd just been seated two tables over.

"*Gimme what he got*," Orlando teased. "You turned down lunch and dinner to eat breakfast?"

"That lady made it sound so good. Like she was gonna get back in that kitchen and cook it herself."

Orlando laughed hard. "Oh man, I really needed that."

"Where'd she go? Probably to whip up the pancake batter."

"Hey deacon, I meant to say thank you for yesterday. Nelson popped up and jumped in where you normally fit. You rolled with it though."

"Wasn't anything. You'd have done the same for me."

"That's real talk. I appreciate it." Orlando glanced down at his cell phone when it buzzed. "Did you ever get Brother Breedlove to the airport alright?"

"Yeah man, that cat cried three times on the way there. He was sniffling and whispering to some woman on the phone, a pub'cist I think. Said for her to meet him at the terminal with a sedative so he could ride the plane in peace and rest his last good nerve."

Orlando hadn't heard his friend yap so much in years. "Breedlove really had an impact on you huh?"

"A bad one." Mosley wiped his mouth with the back of his hand. "I almost had to pull the car over, he showed out so bad."

"Pull over and do what, deacon?"

"Put that bratty minister over my knee and whoop his tail."

"Ha-ha-ha! Come on now. It couldn't have been that bad."

"The hell…"

"Okay, okay. I won't put that on you again."

"You could try, pastor. I wouldn't recommend it though," Mosley said, assuredly.

During their meal, Orlando caught Mosley up on the discussion that he and Nelson had about St. Nickolas' wire fraud bust and his own incarceration. He didn't share every detail but explained how most of it made sense.

"If I wanted to set someone up, I would have gone about it the same way. If you remove every avenue to deny the charges, the court of public opinion will find you guilty," Orlando said, as if he was playing his court case back in his mind. "If they can make your family doubt your innocence, you'll break for sure."

"I didn't get to know your wife Orlando before the good Lord took her," Mosley said, fiddling with a bite size piece of potato. "Can't see the momma of your kids losing faith in you. No, I can't."

"It was the toughest time. I thought I'd die in prison," he said, thinking back. "Maybe get shanked in the shower or hang myself with a bed sheet. Didn't much matter. The FBI put together a case so tight, I didn't see no way out."

"God did though. He was your way out of no way."

Orlando was so proud to have a God fearing man like Mosley on his team, he felt undeserving. "Look, if anything was ever to happen to me. I want you to take everything I own and see that it all gets used for good. Get out of Dallas, take your family and run. Don't stop until you're ready to get out of this kind of life. Let it all go and walk away, Mosley."

"Why you saying all of this?" Mosley asked. "You sick?"

"Nah, nothing like that. Things might get kinda testy around me. St. Nick blamed me when he went down. He did a nickel bid. I put that time on him. It might come down to me taking what's left of his life if he's still in his feelings about it."

"We're in this together, pastor. That cat comes for you, he'll have to deal with me too."

The men bumped their fists together as a sign of solidarity then settled up for their meals. Shortly after Orlando received a text.

He realized he was short on time so he sent Mosley to pick up rent collections from Duke then make a bank deposit.

When Orlando suggested he would catch a ride later, Mosley figured he had some more catching up to do with Nelson but didn't want to talk about it. He was floored when Sister Carolyn Drew stepped out of a white BMW 7 Series, threw a black designer bag over her shoulder then headed inside of Denny's like a woman who knew what she wanted and how to get it.

The moment Carolyn walked in and stopped at the hostess stand, Orlando knew he had underestimated her. Clad in a black fitted sweater and light blue denim jeans that taper off directly at the top of black four-inch ankle boots, she was casual chic and prettier than all of the times Orlando had seen her before. Dressed in comfortable clothing that softened up her stiff persona and perfectly managed behavior, Orlando stood to greet her with a Christian hug but she kept her distance just in case there was more to it than brotherly love.

"Wow. Just wow," he said, softly, with a smile in his eyes. "Thanks for coming Carolyn. Please sit."

"So, this is your secret hide away?" she said, looking the place over. "I would have pegged you for a Bentley in the valet of the Grande Lux kind of man. "Excuse me, *pastor*," she said, when the waitress floated near their table. "Hey Cindy, glad you're working today."

"Hey Girlfriend. I thought that was you," the waitress replied. Her hand was on Carolyn's shoulder but her eyes on Orlando. "So how do you know my favorite customer?"

"Who, him?"

"You could do worse," Cindy said, doting over the couple.

"Thought I was your favorite customer," Carolyn pouted, behind a beautiful smile.

"You're my prettiest. *He* leaves huge tips. I pay my car note with those tips."

Carolyn turned to Orlando, with a look of surprise. "Really?"

Cindy wrinkled her nose and scoffed jokingly. "Nah."

Orlando laughed out loud. "Ahh, that was cold."

"I'll start your lunch if you're ready," Cindy said, while pouring ice water for Carolyn.

"That would be great. I'm starving," Carolyn answered.

"Okay, that's eggs scrambled hard, a three stack of pancakes and crispy bacon."

"That's me," Carolyn answered her. "I love their fluffy pancakes Pastor Clay. What are you having?"

"Nothing, actually. I ordered the same exact thing with Deacon Mosley. I'm surprised you didn't pass him in the parking lot."

"That would have been awkward," she answered, more reserved then. "I agreed to meet for just coffee and discuss your impending tax audit but I am not comfortable at all with people seeing us like this."

"Carolyn, its Denny's not the Do Drop Inn." Orlando had to push back an impish grin when the actual thought of them tipping off to a secret love nest came to mind. "Huh, I'm sorry what did you say?"

She looked at his thin lips, swooping into a smile, then she smiled back. "See, this is why I probably shouldn't be here."

"What I do?" he asked, innocently.

"Blessing everyone with that boyish charm is a trap," Carolyn said, with a side-eye expression. "I see the way sisters at MEGA look at you. It's downright sinful."

"Don't know about them but I like the way you look at me, or try not to," Orlando replied.

"And how's that?" she asked.

"Like we could be friends. Maybe go out for a drink or just coffee."

"And then what?"

"That's it," he responded, fighting off a subtle smile that would not be denied.

"Uh-uh. Strictly business. I can't with you, Pastor Orlando Clay. You don't even know me outside of the church building," Carolyn joked.

"You're thirty-seven. Atlanta roots. Economics B.A. from Clark. MBA from Spellman and a very capable chief financial officer."

"You've done your homework. LinkedIn or Facebook?" she joked.

"Does it matter?"

"That's it? My college bio is all you got on me?"

"Oh you want my unabridged analysis?" he said, smiling handsomely at her.

"Yes, hit me with what you see in me," she said, laughing at herself for talking fresh with the pastor.

"You're beautiful. More striking than pretty in my opinion but some men go for the drop dead gorgeous type. Obviously you know how to laugh at yourself. You don't take things too seriously or come across as prudish.

"Really?"

"But I can tell, you get your kicks once you decide to let your hair down."

Carolyn was impressed but wanted to keep Orlando guessing. "You can tell all of that by looking at me?" she said, secretly thinking how much he'd gotten correct.

"Nope, but I have watched you run finance meetings, counsel young girls, teen mothers and women who's sons were arrested doing things they were old enough to know better."

"I have seen you do all of that as well and more but thank you, pastor."

"I love the way you navigate. Would it be so bad if we hit it off? I mean, after your time of mourning has passed," he assumed.

"Again I say, and then what?" Carolyn repeated herself, to make a point. "Men, these days don't care to know what a lady needs. Most of y'all don't even try to figure out what we want half the time."

Orlando smiled again. "I haven't thought it out that far down the line but wouldn't it be a shame if what you needed, what you wanted, was right in front of you?"

"Oh Pastor Clay, *whatever do you mean*?" she said, in her deepest southern belle voice.

"Sister Carolyn Drew, I am merely suggesting that whatever you might be looking for, you could be looking at."

"Okay, y'all knock it off before somebody in here calls her ex-husband for a do over and a ton of new headaches that I don't need," Cindy said, as she lowered two plates onto the table between them. "You need salsa, Carolyn? Let me get you some cold water too."

Cindy dashed away, leaving them to settle their heated anxiety alone.

"That went well," Carolyn said, like a guilty lover who had just been found out.

"I refuse to put you in this position. I'll have Jessika send you my forms, receipts, and returns for the past three years."

"Can I ask you one question before we get down to this strictly tax business?" she asked, with a serious tone.

"Sure, I have no secrets. Well, not many," Orlando said, to keep the mood as light as possible.

"You and that lady detective, what's her name?"

"Vera Miles."

"You and Vera Miles were really close once. I remember her stopping by the church a lot. What happened between y'all?"

"She's a good woman. Smart, giving, and a talented cop. I loved her enough. It could have worked, I guessed," Orlando said, without admitting who was at fault for the breakup. "We couldn't figure out a way to get along."

There was a look of admiration in his eyes for Vera but not one single hint of regret. "I see how that could become a deal breaker. It does take more than love to stay in love. Excuse me for a second," Carolyn said, closing her eyes to pray over the food. "Amen."

"Indeed. Amen."

10

IF I WAS YOUR GIRLFRIEND

"Are we on a date now?" Carolyn asked, when Orlando invited her into Posh Nails salon. "I am not trying to be seen with you in public, Pastor Clay."

"Denny's wasn't public?"

"That was breakfast."

"Point taken," he said, smiling at her. Orlando enjoyed the thought of them getting to know each other better. "I appreciate the ride over here. I thought Deacon Mosley would have been back by now," Orlando lied.

He knew good and well his friend's list of errands was designed to keep Mosley away long enough to require getting a ride from Carolyn.

"Look, Sister Carolyn, this is a nail shop. No one in here will know us."

"Then please stop calling me Sister Carolyn like we're playing church games."

"Cool, and just to make you feel better about the situation, you could come in five minutes after me and get those cuticles of your looked at. Maybe get your feet scrubbed."

She smiled big, with her mouth purposely closed. "Okay, I actually like that idea. I could be a voyeur to see what it's like to be the sexy minister that all the girls are crazy about."

"You think I'm sexy?" he asked.

"A little bit. If I squint real hard and turn my head sideways."

"Ba-hah-hah! You're a riot and I'm late for a standing appointment," he said, wanting to hug her goodbye. "If you choose not to come in, I'll understand. Besides, Deacon Mosley really likes this place more than Sister Mosley would appreciate. By the way, thanks for the ride."

"Yeah," she answered, watching him through the glass door with a heavily tinted screen on the inside.

Orlando came in with a handsome smile. "Hello Ladies, how's it going today?"

Several women in the shop looked up from magazines and cell phones to acknowledge him, waved hello and returned his smile with plenty of their own."

"Who is that?" a woman asked, from the last spa chair in the right. "He looks like new money."

"Oh snap, that's my big sister's old love jones," Boojie answered, from the next spa chair. "Posha! Get out here," she said, before Orlando came into earshot. Boojie started texting on her phone while her feet were dancing anxiously in the water.

"Come on girl, read your screen."

Orlando looked over the magazine selection, which stood on a black wooden wall wrack. He selected an ESPN issue then waited until the hostess put away a stack of white towels to greet him.

"Oh, I'm sorry Mister, didn't see you standing over there," the young woman said, with a gold tooth gleaming as she smiled. "We can get you in but it might be a minute. There's a one o'clock appointment that's gonna have two of the girls busy."

"I have an appointment already. It shouldn't be a problem."

The hostess seemed concerned. "Then what's yo name?"

"Orlando," he said, while reading his name on the appointment book upside down.

"Yes, we have you down for one o'clock. What you like to drink?" She gestured towards a tall, narrow, stainless steel cooler that sat behind the reception desk. "We out of Crown though," she said, before allowing the customer a chance to consider selections.

Orlando pretended to be interested in the miniature bottles of premium alcohol which were displayed through the glass refrigerator door.

"Good thing I didn't want Crown, huh?"

"Yeah because we out of that. Got that Grey Goose though. Got that Absolute. That Jack and we got that Henney too." She seemed so proud of their liquor offerings that Orlando couldn't find it in himself to refuse.

"I'll try some of that Grey Goose with a splash of Sprite if you don't mind."

"No, I don't mind. That's why I'm here, to make your salon experience more remember... remember-erable," she stammered, as if reciting lines from a school play.

"Ohhh, memorable. Thank you. That's very nice."

"Uh huh, you welcome," she said, while handing him a mixed drink. Orlando, reached in his pocket then handed the girl a twenty dollar bill.

"Oh, you don't have to pay. It's free for customers here at Posh Nails."

"I know," he answered, feeling sorry for the young lady. "That's to say thank you for making my Posh experience more *rememorable*."

"You welcome. Melissa will see you now, Mr. Orlando."

"Thanks, wait you haven't told me your name."

"Nobody ever axed me that up here at the front desk. It's Teresa but people call me Reesie."

"Thank you, Reesie." Orlando took a seat in the spa chair that Reesie ushered him to, the last one on the left. As she bounced away with youthful vigor, he realized the advantages that Jessika had by being in his home for the past three years. Jessika had also used awkward grammar when Orlando met her and she was just as unaware of the world around as Reesie. He was thankful that Jessika flourished in her education due to strict rules, good study habits, and demands that books be read and discussed on a regular basis. Orlando wondered if Reesie could have been more polished if someone had taken the time to invest in her and made demands that benefited her future. Then, just as quickly as that thought appeared, it was chased away with bothersome clicking of long acrylic nails on a cell phone screen.

"Hey," Boojie Queen said, sitting directly across from Orlando.

"Hello," he answered casually, while stuffing both socks into his leather loafers. Something about her drew his attention as he noticed the woman wearing tight pink sweat pants and a silver athletic bra. Her breasts were spilling out of it but he gathered that's exactly how she liked it. "Bonita Holywater, is that you?"

"You know it is Orlando," she responded, just this side of flirty.

"But I don't go by my government name no more. I'm Boojie Queen, right about now."

"Well, Boojie Queen, it's good seeing you again. You grew up very nicely."

"Thank you very much," she cooed, blushing at her sister's former lover as if he were her own. "You always were so nice to me. Man, I had a thunder crush on you." She looked him over thoroughly with a naughty thought behind it. "Wish you had stuck around longer."

Orlando ignored Boojie's last comment when the lady sitting next to her was ear hustling and seriously wanting to know if he had any interest in seeing firsthand how much the young woman had grown.

"Well, all good things must come to an end. It's good to see you though. Tell Posha I said hello."

An Asian woman wearing jeans and a black smock told Orlando to put his feet into the water. "Put both in please. Let soak," she said, then dashed off to see about another customer.

Boojie and her sidekick laughed as they shared a private secret. "Why'ont you tell her yourself, Orlando. She's in the back office, wrapping up a business meeting."

"Mmmmm hmmm," the girlfriend moaned. "She'll be happy to see you. Know I am."

"Right, right," Boojie cosigned. "Yuma, go get Posha for me," she said, wanting to be left alone with Orlando. "She's not answering her phone."

"My polish isn't dry yet."

"Maybe it'll dry on the way, now go," Boogie insisted, playfully.

"Baby, you like this color on me?" Carolyn asked, as she approached Orlando from the other side. "I think it's time for a change." She looked at him with admiring eyes then smiled knowingly at the other two women.

"Hey y'all."

"Hey girl."

"What's 'sup?"

"Uhhh, yes. Sure, that's a beautiful color," he answered cautiously, with five pairs of eyes watching his every move. He didn't see two people leering through the blinds of the manager's office.

"I can't leave you alone for a minute, Baby, without you making new friends," Sister Carolyn said, placing her hand on his shoulder.

"You don't have to mark your territory," Boojie said, as she checked out the way Carolyn's pants fit nicely on her behind. "We're all friends here. I know Orlando from the old days."

Orlando felt obligated to introduce the ladies as tension continued to rise between them.

"Carolyn, this is Bonita. I meant, Boojie Queen. Boojie, meet a friend of mine, Carolyn."

"This my ride or die home-girl, Yuma," Boojie said, as she smiled at her friend lovingly.

Yuma pointed at Carolyn's outfit. "I like how you put that together. Casual yet chic," Yuma complemented.

"Good taste, Orlando," Boojie commented, with her eyes sizing up the competition. "I'm really digging those boots."

"Thank you ladies. I'll go so y'all can get back to talking about old times." Carolyn spun away slowly, sweeping her hand across Orlando's cheek.

They observed her walk away for apparently the same reason.

"I think my polish is good and dry now. You still want me to go get Posha?" Yuma asked, in a semi-shady way.

"Nah, we good. She'll be out as soon as her and Nick strike a deal."

Orlando closed his eyes for a moment. He couldn't imagine a scenario where St. Nick and Carolyn would be in the same place, at the same time. If he had any plans of keeping his new association with Carolyn miles away from his nemesis, that no longer seemed possible.

"Mosley, where are you?" Orlando whispered, into his cell phone.

"Over off Red Bird Lane. I'm dropping off a deposit at the bank like you told me to."

"Okay, stay put. I'm at the world's busiest nail shop where all hell is about to break loose."

"Want me to hurry over there?" Mosley asked.

"You're more than fifteen minutes away. I'll call you later."

"You sure, Brother Pastor?"

"Yeah. I'm good." Orlando ended the call then looked at the other end of the shop where Carolyn was nose deep in a Cosmo magazine. He wanted to tell her to go but it would have presented more questions than he was prepared to answer at the moment. There was nothing to do but play it out whenever St. Nick exited the manager's office with Posha.

Orlando tried to remain calm when the door in a shallow hallway finally opened minutes later. He texted Mosley as voices spilled out of the small office.

Call Sister Carolyn Drew. Get her to go and look at her tires. Nail in the rear. Immediately! 214 555-4510.

Orlando pressed send with his fingers crossed, hoping Mosley read the message and was able to respond in time.

"That's why you should keep it to yourself," Posha answered, jokingly. "Remember that you're the silent partner of Posh Nails. You need to remain *silent!*"

St. Nick laughed with his mouth open, like he was thinking of a clever comeback until he stepped out of the hallway and discovered Orlando's shin deep in bubbling water. "Ain't this about nothing! Man, what you doing up in here?"

Boojie and Yuma looked on as Orlando blew off St. Nick's boisterous insult as he observed Carolyn heading out of the door with a cellphone pressed against her ear.

"Posha, you should watch who you let in the gate. Some visitors get settled in and start to think they're running the place," Orlando fired back.

"Good afternoon, pastor. It's always good to see you here at Posh Nails. I'd like to think I can always count on your support even though St. Nickolas is partial owner now," Posha informed Orlando.

"Show some respect or you might have to deal with Tony Tubbs," St. Nick said, as if he were introducing a force of nature. Suddenly a man walked into view from the hallway. He wore a tight long sleeve shirt, dark slacks and a pistol tucked into the back of his waistband. His menacing smirk was rock solid until he recognized Orlando from the barbershop.

"You hiring muscle now?" Orlando asked St. Nick, but he was looking dead at the bodyguard.

The man's tough guy persona faded when the minister stared

him down until breaking him. "It ain't going down like it did the other day, playa," the enforcer replied, after he'd blinked first.

"Not unless it has to," Orlando said, dismissively. He looked at the front door casually as Carolyn returned. "Tell Slim Woody I said to hit me up," Orlando mused.

"Tell him your damn self. I don't work for that pimp anymore."

"We both know why, don't we?" Orlando said, as if he'd just tattled on the coward who ran out of Bishop's barbershop like his shoes were on fire.

"Looks like y'all already bumped heads before. Good, no love lost then," St. Nick said, with a curious look at his guard. "Me and Tee Tubbs got some corners to turn. Tip my girls good, now, you hear?" He turned and headed towards the front door. "Boojie. I'll see you tonight. Be on time for once when I send the car service."

"You know me, fashionably late makes all the tricks wait," she answered St. Nick, while looking right through him. Orlando's face was all she wanted to see. St. Nick missed it but Posha and Yuma clocked it immediately.

"Alright then Posha," was St. Nick's final goodbye before he left the shop with his muscle following closely behind him. Both of the men took time to notice Carolyn, who had watched the men's interaction closely from her vantage point. "Yeah, I like the nail business already Tee Tubbs. Lots of pretty things to look at."

"Yeah, I saw that too," he answered, when they exited the building.

Orlando glanced at Carolyn while the nail tech dried his feet with a bath towel. He couldn't tell how much she'd overheard, if anything, but he had to find out and administer damage control.

"Pastor Orlando?" Boojie said, to get his attention. There was a twinkle in her eyes that made him uncomfortable with Posha looking on. "You and St. Nick got beef? Interesting."

"Not really," he said, while putting on his socks. "Bunch of old news mostly."

"Was it over some female?"

"You know it had to be," he answered quickly. Orlando wanted to keep the conversation moving and far away from the real reason for the troubled waters between him and her new boyfriend.

"I knew a woman was involved. Who came out on top?" Boojie asked, with her mouthwatering.

"We both lost out on that one."

"Then why y'all still at each other like heart-broke homies?" Yuma questioned.

"It should have been squashed a long time ago," he answered finally, for every interested party.

As Orlando stood up to leave. Posha shooed the other ladies away. She didn't like the way that conversation was going or the fact that Boojie was already thinking of ways to get closer to Orlando. Yuma had no business poking her nose in from the sidelines.

"Maybe this is a good time for y'all to get on home and prepare for your sets tonight." They caught the drift and quickly collected their things.

"Nice meeting you, Sir," Yuma said, with a long leer before she decided to go. Her thirsty expression revealed that she wanted to know more about him until Boojie nudged her to move it along.

"See you around the church, *pastor*," Boojie joked, as she leaned in closer to Yuma.

"I can't wait to join his church. Fine ass man like that, I'll bet its standing room only up in that piece," Yuma stated giddily.

"I always wanted a church hat," Boojie said, fondly. "Now I got me a reason to shop for one."

Orlando paused until the women were paying their bill at the front of the shop. "I have to run Posha. Seems that St. Nick is biting off chunks of your businesses and carving out a groove with *Boojie Queen* at the same time."

"She's a child and he's only getting the pieces I break off for him." Posha had no idea of the kind of man she was dealing with. Orlando didn't have the time to tell her how hard it would be to root St. Nick out of her life once his hooks were in deep enough. She'd have to learn that the hard way.

"Is that your new boo?" Posha asked quickly, as Carolyn stared their way more than once. "She's cute."

"So are you."

"Yet, I'm not the one you're leaving with," the shop owner answered, correctly. "Don't be a stranger Orlando. Next time drop by alone maybe."

"Good bye, Posha."

Orlando paid at the front. Carolyn stood closely by his side, once again, unsure why she felt compelled to protect unchartered terrain that did not belong to her. He said goodbye to Reesie then walked out with Carolyn on his arm.

"That was different," Orlando said, as soon as they entered the parking lot.

"What, women coming out of the woodworks to flirt with you? No sir, that's the same thing I see at MEGA."

"If you say so, Carolyn. I went in for a pedicure but felt like I'd signed up for a cavity search instead."

"That's what you get," she chided. "Shouldn't be so darn charming to random women."

"I knew two of them," he answered in his own defense.

"Really? How many of them have you already been with?"

"What? You're serious?"

"That means one, maybe two," she answered.

"Two of those women are sisters. The one I did have a relationship with has been over me a long, long, long-long time ago."

Carolyn opened her car door then smiled at Orlando.

"Can't have been too long ago. Neither of those ladies have been grown but a hot minute."

"Yeah, they catch on quick around here though," he jested.

"Ha! And you're the one to teach them, huh?"

"Someone has too."

They sat in the car exchanging glances until a thought rolled off Carolyn's tongue.

"You'd better be glad I needed some laughs today. You'd be walking home."

"Don't do that. Please don't put me out on the street," he pleaded, impishly. "I just had my feet done."

11

HOTTER THAN HELL

No one noticed as an old brown Toyota Corolla abruptly pulled into the parking lot and slammed on the brakes. When an angry man jumped out of the car and hurled loud insults into it, a woman's shrill voice hollered back. What appeared to be a lover's quarrel suddenly turned violent when the man began punching the woman repeatedly. Onlookers in the strip center craned their necks as loud screams emanated from the car but the windows were dark and tinted so no one could see inside. The angry man darted away from the car then hopped into a green truck waiting a few yards away. The truck burned rubber from the lot towards Westmoreland Road as smoke began to rise from the Corolla.

Jessika exited a custom jewelry shop just as people milled around watching the smoke grow thicker and darker. Several people who exited clothing stores along the strip dialed 9-1-1 as smoke poured out of the partial open car windows.

"Heyyy, there are people in that car!" an old man yelled, then pointed feverishly.

Several onlookers became alarmed but no one moved closer to check out the old man's claims.

Jessika stepped off the cement walkway into the parking lot when she heard the man's proclamation about people being inside of the burning vehicle. She threw her shopping bag onto the ground and sprinted across the parking lot. As she approached the car, a man grabbed her off her feet and pulled her back.

"Don't let her get too close!" someone shouted. "Everybody stay back!"

"That old dude said some people are inside," another person said, while filming the event with her cell phone. "I don't hear anybody though."

Suddenly, a child's loud cries could be heard above the murmuring audience.

"Put me down!" Jessika pleaded. "Somebody's got to help!"

Numbers was walking up and down the street as usual when he saw smoke billowing into the air. He arrived just in time to drag Jessika further away from the burning car and then hand her to another man to hold her back.

Bishop walked to the front of the shop when he heard a commotion outside. He peered out of the window to see the car on fire. He couldn't believe people were standing around to watch it burn. "Get that fire extinguisher out of the back," he demanded. "I'll take this one now."

By the time he pulled a fire extinguisher off the wall and hurried out of the barbershop, shop, the flames were higher and tons of heat was coming off the car. Jessika shouted for people to do something but it was too dangerous to get any closer.

Numbers paced back and forth rubbing his head with both hands. It was a terrifying scene. "Those people gonna die," he muttered. "Somebody help!"

When it was clear that no one would, he pulled off his long sleeve shirt and wrapped it around his hand. He moved in slowly then charged at the front passenger door. The hot door handle burned his palm when he tried to open it so he punched the window hard until it shattered. People stood idly by while he removed the remaining glass with his other hand.

When Bishop arrived, he moved in closer and began spraying the flames with his fire extinguisher. His protégé Byron was too afraid to get that close. Mosley had driven up and seen the car burning but wasn't interested in getting involved until he saw Jessika trying to help. He snatched the red fire extinguisher from Byron then approached the fire from the other side. What his eyes found almost dropped him to his knees. He continued to battle the flames while hollering anxiously for help.

"Hey, there's some children in here!" Mosley shouted. "Somebody help get these kids out!"

Numbers pulled the woman out of the front seat. He carried her to the covered walkway. Bishop sprayed the hem of the woman's dress that was still smoldering. Before anyone could see to the woman, Numbers raced back into the smoke filled car again.

"That fool's gonna burn up," someone heckled. "The car might even blow."

Dozens of people looked on with their cell phones recording the horrible scene as a few shop owners pitched in to spray the fiery car. After several moments passed, Jessika became worried for Numbers as well as the children in the backseat.

"Help Numbers!" Jessika pleaded. "Somebody has to get him out of there."

Mosley tried to get closer but the heat was building. He noticed exhaust smoke was coming out of the tailpipe. "Get away, this car is still running!"

People moved further back as the sound of ambulances and fire trucks roared in the air.

Jessika prayed that Numbers would make it out before something worse happened. "Please God," she said. "Please wave your hand over this fire and calm it down, Lord. You have some angels inside of that car and they need your protection, Father. Please God, bring them out alive. In Jesus holy name I ask it all. Amen."

The man holding Jessika tightly, felt ashamed that he hadn't done more to help. In his quiet humiliation, he whispered, "In Jesus name. Amen."

The crowd cheered to the heavens as Numbers stumbled away from that burning inferno, covered in black soot and grime, with two little girls kicking and screaming in his arms. Once Numbers made it to the walkway, he handed the girls off to the women who were seeing to the adult victim's injuries. Then, he collapsed in the parking lot.

Jessika raced to his side, placing clothing from her shopping bags beneath this head. She doted over him despite the pungent smell of burnt flesh filling her nostrils. She tried to cover Number's charred hands but they hurt too badly to be touched, so she rocked him back and forth while he writhed in pain on the ground. Jessika held onto him tightly , whispering words of encouragement and appreciation until several firemen and emergency medical techs forced her to let him go.

When Carolyn pulled into the busy strip center's parking lot, she looked at the ambulances curiously. She notices firemen watering down burnt rubble on the ground. Orlando watched as firemen stacked a wide white water hose back onto the side of the long red truck.

"I hope everyone is okay," she said, just above a whisper. "There's always something going on over here."

"Yeah, and not always good," Orlando answered, as a slight brush-back regarding her comment. "This isn't anything but bad. See how that car is completely charred down to the frame? They don't burn like that unless an accelerant is used."

"You're saying someone set that car on fire?"

"In broad day light too." Orlando unfastened his seatbelt when he saw Mosley holding someone close to him. "Thanks for the ride Sister Carolyn. Something is wrong." He hopped out of the car then disappeared into the crowd of people still lingering around.

"They said the lady ain't gon' make it," an old woman repeated, what she'd heard, with a hand laid over her heart. "What kind of person would do that to some kids though?"

Orlando zigzagged past bystanders until he reached the broad walkway in front of the shops, where Mosley was standing. His heart shuttered when he heard Jessika's distraught voice. Fear washed over him as his eyes found her face and hands battered with dark ash.

"Why did this happen, Deacon Mosley?" she wailed, her eyes filled with tears.

Orlando reached for her arm cautiously. "Jessika, are you hurt, baby? Were you in that car?"

"Wh-whut?" she replied, surprised to see him. When her eyes discovered grave concern on his face, she shook her head.

"No, no, sir. It all happened so fast. Everything was on fire, Uncle." Jessika fell into Orlando's arm like a young child when she broke down emotionally again. "They were all burning alive."

Orlando looked to Mosley, who was biting his bottom lip to hold in the sorrow he felt.

"Deacon? Tell me, something."

"They say a man was arguing with a woman. Said he jumped on her pretty good then he ran to a green truck and tore out of here like the devil was after him."

"The fire? Who set it?"

"Had to be the dude who took off. From what I hear, wasn't nobody else close enough."

"There's cameras installed all up and down this walkway. I saw to that myself. I'll get Vera on it and see what she can come up with."

Jessika wiped her tears away with a tissue that someone handed her. When her eyes were clear, she smiled.

"Thank you, Sister Carolyn. What are you doing here?"

"I was uh… just in the area," she answered, then glanced at Orlando.

Mosley caught on fast and wondered how well their meeting went that Sister Carolyn was having to lie about it in front of Jessika. Then, he realized Orlando would rather hear the worst of the news from him since he was there to witness it firsthand.

"That woman, she had half of her body burned, smoke was coming out of her mouth and her stomach swelled while they tried to resuscitate her."

"I heard she's in pretty bad shape," Orlando said, looking on, as the second ambulance doors closed.

"There were some little children inside of the car, pastor," Mosley informed him, as if those words cut him deeply. "Two girls."

Orlando's arms fell by his side. "Are they both...?"

"Oh my God," Carolyn gasped, fretfully.

"They're still breathing for now but swallowed a lot of smoke too," he said, nodding his head slightly to suggest their fate appeared grim.

Orlando turned to look at the car again as a tow truck elevated it onto the back of a flatbed. He'd heard of honor killings among some middle-eastern cultures but didn't want to jump to any conclusions. "A woman and her daughters most likely," he surmised, with a thought that came to him out of nowhere, like a finding money in his pocket.

"Who got that woman and kids out?"

"Numbers," Jessika said, her eyes widening with pride.

"Numbers!" Orlando said, as horror pushed him back an entire foot. "Where is he Mosley? Where'd they take him?" he demanded.

"In that ambulance about to leave now."

Orlando sprinted through the parking and reached the white emergency vehicle as the paramedic closed one of the doors. "Wait a minute! Hey wait. Wait. I need to see this man."

"You any relation? He doesn't have any identification on him."

"Yeah, yeah. I'm his guardian," Orlando told him.

"He's in a lot of pain and talking out of his head."

"But he's alive though?"

"For now but we have to get him to the hospital."

"Okay just one second, please. Please," Orlando begged until the medic obliged him. "Thank you, sir, thank you."

Orlando climbed into the back of the truck and took a knee next to the gurney where Number laid with both hands wrapped up to the elbow.

"Man, look at you. A real live hero," the pastor gushed with praise. Orlando saw first and second degree burns on the left side of the Number's face, smeared with antiseptic gel. "You're an amazing man, Numbers. Amazing!"

"I saw the chances falling from the sky and they flashed in front of my eyes, Mr. Clay."

"Chances?"

"Chances, probabilities, that those four angels were all gonna die," he winced, sorely. "If I didn't do something they'd be in Heaven by now."

"Four," Orlando said, questioning what he had heard about the victims in the car.

"Three to one, we all make it. Two to one everybody watches them die," Numbers muttered. "I had to do it. Heaven sent me some gooood odds."

The paramedic looked on, concerned about his patient's mental state. "I told you, mister, he's not making any sense. This man needs better attention than I can give him in the back of this bus," the paramedic said, insistently.

"Okay. Okay." Orlando climbed out of the back and they secured the gurney. He looked at the clear I.V. bag that dangled from a metal hook. "Where are you taking him?"

"Parkland Burn Unit," the EMT answered.

"Methodist is closer," Orlando argued.

"Parkland's the county hospital so unless he's got damn good insurance..."

"Get him to Methodist. I got this," Orlando said, irritably. "That man is a hero."

"What's his name?"

"Daniel Ashland. They call him Numbers."

"Got it."

"I'll be right behind you," Orlando said, with a mountain of concern.

"This victim is going to be in surgery for hours, sir. No need to rush."

Orlando nodded that he understood then closed the door. He slapped the side of the vehicle to let the driver know the cargo was ready for transport. Orlando remembered the last time he'd done that. It was seven years ago when he took a victim's death bed confessions and it didn't seem likely he would make it to the hospital alive.

Mosley walked beside Orlando as the ambulance pulled away. "His hands are burnt pretty badly. I still can't believe Numbers jumped into a car that was on fire, not once but twice, when all of the other men were too damned scared."

"He said that heaven sent him some chances, some probabilities, about making it out alive and everybody watching the angels die."

"Maybe the Holy Spirit spoke to him in the best way to reach him," Mosley said, "with numbers."

"God always knows what He's doing, no doubt, but there's something else I didn't understand. I think numbers had a Shadrach, Meshach and Abednego moment."

"The three Hebrew boys who the King tossed into the fiery furnace?" Mosley asked, as he recalled the famous bible story.

"Yeah. Remember they put three boys in the furnace and even the King himself saw a fourth person in there with them?"

Mosley folded his arms and tilted his head back like he was contemplating the possibility of that happening today. "Did Numbers say he saw somebody else burning in that car?"

Orlando shook his head. "He said there was a 50-50 chance that four angels were going to be killed if he didn't react."

Mosley turned and looked at Jessika, who was explaining to Carolyn how things happened. "Jessika. She's the fourth angel."

"But she said she never got into the car."

"Because Number ran up and snatched her away from it, pastor." Mosley's mouth was dryer than drugstore cotton. "I'd just come out of the bank when it happened. I know I couldn't have done it, saved those people. Numbers stopped your niece from jumping into that car herself."

Orlando stood there motionless, nearly speechless, and more thankful than he had ever been. He was visibly shaken but tried to hide his face, turning it toward the ground. "My God," were the only words Orlando could muster.

"Thank God. And Numbers too."

At the hospital, Jessika slept in the visitor's lounge for hours. She was tucked beneath a blanket that Carolyn convinced the charge nurse to scrounge around for her. Orlando watched as the local news station ran a series of stories about the woman and girls who were pulled from the vehicle as it burned. They had the scene covered from several angles as a number of people filmed the whole horrid scene with cell phones.

Carolyn sat close to him on a comfortable love seat. She shook her head every time they ran another segment from a different angle.

"Look at all of those people standing around," she said. "It could have been a horrific ending."

"Every time I see Jessika running toward that car and Numbers grabbing her, I feel like a man who let his daughter down. Then immediately, I'm filled with joy that God sent a protector. A super hero from the hood," Orlando said, accompanied by a soft chuckle.

"We need to find a way to bless him. Honor him."

Jessika's eyes fluttered then opened. She heard Orlando's words and took them to heart before pulling the covers tighter then drifting back to sleep.

Carolyn looked at Orlando as if she was seeing him for the first time, looking past his strong jawline and deep set eyes that mesmerized her. She was seeing him for what he truly was, a caring and compassionate father figure to a girl he'd taken in and a congregation he was taking care of as best he could.

When he noticed that her glances had evolved into an adoring stare, Orlando smiled at her. "Thank you for coming down here. Thank you for consoling Jessika while I checked on Numbers in the ambulance," he said, with utmost sincerity. "So much has happened today and I don't want it to end without showing some proper gratitude."

"You're welcome Brother Pastor," she said playfully, while throwing a look at Jessika.

"Oh, it's like that? That's how we're going to do this?" Orlando asked.

"I'm sorry but I don't know you. Not like that anyway," Carolyn replied.

"How do you mean, *like that*?"

"I don't know where you're from, how you knew right off that someone set that car on fire. I heard that you were some sort of an agent before, then found yourself in a lot of trouble with the law."

"Seems to me, you know a lot more than you give yourself credit for," he said jokingly.

"What happened? If you don't mind my asking."

"Its old news but not anything you couldn't read about online, if you were so inclined to look it up. Knowing you, that'll be soon enough."

She leaned her head on his shoulder. "I'd rather hear your side of it."

"I didn't know you thought enough of me to care about my side of the story."

"Before today I didn't," she answered, honestly.

"I grew up in a little town in central Texas called Marlin. It's mostly pasture and poor people. Good people." His eyes floated upward like he was thinking back on the gentler times and dirt roads of his youth. "My mother was a teenager. My papa ran off to join the Army shortly after I was born. It didn't take long for him to discover that he was too scared to be a father but not for the military. By the way, did I mention he was a chicken shit?"

"Pastor Clay, your language."

"Well, you wanted to know me. I'm a cussin' Christian. So, now you know."

Carolyn gave a disapproving look. "Who said you had to be proud of that?"

"I'll work on it," he promised, with his fingers crossed.

"I was good at sports in high school. Even better with books. Went to the Lamar University. I did the high jump and pole vault. Mostly carried the long pole around to show it off to the ladies."

"Oomph, you are so disgusting," she said, rather amused.

"Oh, I forget to mention that. I like to cuss and disgust."

"Back to the story please, only without the innuendo."

"You want the clean virgin then?" he teased.

"Did you say *virgin*?"

"Just wanted to see if you were paying attention. Now I know that you are, I'll make it a clean *version*."

"Thank you."

"College days don't last forever but the memories do. There was this one time that me and some fellas were on our way to the Kappa Beach Party in Galveston when our car broke down. It was Vee Scott, JJ, Clayton, Craig, Keith and Andre the Cajun chemist we partied with. Oh man, if I told you all seven of us went and…" Orlando said, until he realized that some school shenanigans should not be told, ever. "Never mind all that but yeah, I was a college graduate before I knew it and had no idea what to do about it. I delivered furniture because I liked being outside. Even spent six months as a chicken catcher at this East Texas poultry plant."

"Ha-ha-ha!" she laughed heartily. "Chicken catcher? There is no such thing."

"Yeah there is too. Least there use to be. Guy by the name of D.C. Mitchell was so fast, he could wrangle ten chickens in thirty seconds. Never seen anything like it," Orlando said, still somewhat amazed. "How else do you think they get those hens to the slaughter? They don't walk up to the death pen and say, *I'm ready to be plucked and packaged now*."

"I would think not but what's the deal with a degree and a chicken catching job?"

"I was young and bored. Hadn't figured out what I wanted to be yet?"

Carolyn crossed her legs and leaned a bit closer. "How did you decide?"

"I saw a Want Ad in the paper. *Wanted: Honest Young Men for Government Jobs.* Well, I was at least two out of the three so I applied. Didn't make the cut the first time but I dangled my chicken catching credential again and they bit."

"The FBI hired a chicken catcher?"

"Hell no, not the forbidden *feebs*. I signed on with the OIG," he scoffed, until she pinched his arm like a big sister. "Ouch, you hurt me."

"That mouth is going to get you into some trouble," she snapped, then rolled her eyes playfully. "And what's the OIG?"

"Office of the Inspector General. They're over fraud against the government. Mostly white collar thieves who think they can get over then get away with it. Many of them don't make it. That's why there are new federal prisons going up every day." Orlando smiled big and grand when he remembered one of his first cases. "I wasn't off the desk but a month when I caught a bumble-dick assignment."

When he felt Carolyn moving in for another pinch, Orlando moved away in the nick of time.

"Hey, that's what everyone called a simple bust because you'd have to be a bumble *penis* to screw it up."

"Then tell me about this bumble dick assignment they gave you."

"I remember like it was yesterday. I went out alone to this farm, after a hurricane had swept through the east coast like a hand of

God. I'd never even been on an airplane before but there I was trying to burst some sorry soul for fraud when her life was falling apart in every way imaginable. On the outskirts of Jacksonville, an elderly woman who needed a new roof was living in a horse trailer out behind the house."

"You're serious?" Carolyn questioned.

"Yes ma'am. Hurricanes are mean sons of... well, you get my point. This one demon of a storm left a poor woman roofless and knee deep in water. She and her husband got a Small Business Loan, which against common belief does apply to homes that are damaged due to natural disasters."

"Thanks for clearing that up," she said, to make him smile.

"You're welcome, so listen, the husband dies as soon as the woman gets the check for seven thousand. She forges his name on it and deposits the dang old thing in the bank."

"Ha-ha-ha! The what?"

"Now you got my country boy spilling out. I tend to slip a bit when I get excited."

"I can see that," she said, totally feeling his vibe.

"So I'm sent out there to take a random look at the progress of the roof repairs only to find that this woman was spending her low interest government loan to bury her dead husband."

"You're lying?"

"Not this time. She really went and did it. Now, I drive up and introduce myself to her in the backyard like some kind of big shot government law man and this little bitty woman said I could come on down to the cemetery and enjoy the big send off or I could stand around scratching my ass until she returned to be arrested."

"Okay, wait. Wait a minute," Carolyn huffed, between laughing. "She was in the wrong but told you where to get off?"

"To my face and I was wearing a badge. She didn't think much of it though."

"What did you do? Arrest her?"

"I went to the funeral to see how Uncle Sam's money was being spent and I mean it was a spectacular send off. She hired a horse and glass-covered carriage, white-gloved pallbearers, and the whole nine yards. She even released some doves and had a fireworks show."

Carolyn found it hard to believe. "She did not."

"Okay, I threw that in but it was a fine send off. I wouldn't mind going into the great hereafter in spectacular fashion like that."

"Did you send that poor, old woman to prison Orlando?"

"She was short of funds when it time came to do the repairs on the house. So I got her to promise to use her husband's veteran benefits to fix the roof. She agreed and gave me her word. I falsified documents on the plane ride back."

"You put your career on the line?"

"What kind of man sends an elderly woman to prison for doing what her heart told her to?"

"Wow. Just wow."

"Sometimes people are dead wrong and still deserve just a little grace."

Carolyn let the next question do a couple of laps around in her head before she spat it out. "How did you land in one of those federal prisons?"

"I can't tell you the particulars but I was a good agent. Earned a gold shield by then. I was told not to trust the FBI but I buddied up with a federal agent against my better judgment. My partner was on vacation and I was supposed to be minding a desk but this big drug bust fell into my lap. A notorious pusher named Tommy Eckert was cooking backyard meth with the SBA money he was supposed to be replacing his water-damaged first floor with." Orlando eased out a sigh then leaned back against the love seat. "I don't know for sure how it turned on me, Tommy's case got kicked and I got the boot."

She leaned away from him to collect herself. "Are you a felon, Orlando?"

"The FBI must have gotten what they wanted out of me because they dropped the case. I was just as shocked the day they let me go as I was the night they kicked in my door and cuffed me to the back seat of a black Crown Victoria."

"Yes," she responded, behind a deathly serious expression.

"Come again?"

"Yes, I will be your accountant and see why the IRS is looking into you."

"Oh, yeah. That's what I am talking about. Thank you," he said, while Jessika stretched and yawned next to them. "Yes, Sistah Carolyn, I appreciate that."

"Y'all can cut the *Sistah* Carolyn and *Pastah* Clay routine," said Jessika, with a knowing shrug. "I haven't been asleep the whole time."

"You are too slick," he said joking, while wondering how much of his truth she had heard. Just as another news story about the heroic car rescue came on the television, a black female surgeon waked into the waiting room.

She was dressed in green scrubs and built like a fitness model. Orlando pretended not to notice her small waist and muscular thighs.

"Are you the family of Daniel Ashland?"

Orlando stood up first. "Yes Doctor. How is he doing?"

"I'm Dr. Quinn, the surgeon for your Daniel and I'm happy to report the best possible outcome."

"He'll be alright then?" Jessika asked, with hope in her eyes.

"It's a miracle the smoke didn't affect his bronchial lining. Daniel must be living right or have some fierce prayer warriors on his team."

"What about his hands," Carolyn asked, looking at footage on the television of him being attended to by the paramedics.

"He will have to undergo a few more surgeries and skin grafts but he will keep most of his fingers," Dr. Quinn told them. "You can come back tomorrow and look in on him if you like. He'll be sedated for the pain. Mr. Ashland has a rough go ahead of him."

"He doesn't have to be awake to know we care about him," said Jessika. "Numbers saved my life and hopefully the others too."

"I heard the grandmother and girls were taken to Parkland," the doctor informed them. "The grandmother didn't make it."

"Grandmother?" Orlando questioned. All of the early reports listed the woman as the children's mother.

"The little girls experienced burns on over thirty percent of their bodies," Dr. Quinn explained. "It'll be touch and go for a while."

"Thank you Doctor Quinn," Carolyn said, as the physician headed off in the other direction.

Jessika watched the news story on repeat and grew more upset each time the reporter referred to the car-fire hero as *Numbers*.

"We've got to do something," she hissed. "He was the only person brave enough to help. All of those people were standing around and nobody lifted a finger. I was one of them and I'm so ashamed of that. I stood there too and did nothing. Tonight I'm changing that. Right now, no one knows who Daniel Ashland is. Tomorrow, everyone will know his name and what he did."

12

SEX, LIES AND CHOIR HALLS

The following day, Orlando was called to the church by the leadership who were none too happy about a blabbering report from Brother Breedlove. He turned down a second interview but not before he praised the hard work that Pastor Orlando Clay and Deacon Mosley had to do on the congregation's behalf. Breedlove added that he would never be up to such a task as to pastoring a church body that God had obviously forsaken.

"What did you say to Minister Howard T. Breedlove?" Sister Betty Burlington spat, from the other side of her desk. With her meaty finger pointing at Orlando's face, she awaited his answer. Two elders sat next to one another on the old leather sofa as Orlando stood in the middle of the room, like a child being reprimanded by the school principals. Brothers Langston and Simons were rusty relics who had long outlived their usefulness. If they ever had a backbone between them, Sister Burlington crushed it and carried it around in her purse.

"That poor man was terrified when we spoke with him this morning. He said that he would never, under any circumstances, ever set foot in this church house again," she informed him.

"He really said that? Never, ever?" Orlando asked, with a smile hidden directly beneath his lips. "Deacon Mosley and I showed Brother Breedlove around the neighborhood and took him to the airport after that. Just like he asked. Maybe he has bad nerves."

"Don't you get cute with me Interim Pastor. Something happened that he was either too afraid or ashamed to talk about." She waited for an admission but none came forth. "Perhaps you can start by telling us who the white man was that open-carried during your little field trip."

"My old partner Nelson was in town so he came with us," Orlando answered, with a brewing attitude. "Is that what this was about? Brother Breedlove doesn't like white people?" he asked, knowing that wasn't what spooked the visiting minister.

"I don't believe so," Sister Burlington answered, somewhat sorry for bringing up Nelson. She was out of sorts and had no idea which direction to go in. "You have nothing else to say about it?"

"Not really. No," he answered quickly.

"Well, that puts me at a rare disadvantage because we have another minister visiting later in the week. He would like to meet you and sit in on a message this Sunday."

Orlando shifted his weight as his brow wrinkled behind a mountain of questions. "Let me get this straight Sister Burlington, I'm supposed to show another minister around town then do a dog and pony show? Hell, am I auditioning or is he?" Orlando said, glaring at the old men who kept quiet.

"I would remind you to watch your mouth Brother Clay! You are in the house of the Lord."

"Actually, I'm in your office but I will apologize for my language. Although, not for showing my true feelings about the sheer ridiculousness of your requests. I went along with it when Breedlove came because I was curious what kind of man you thought could replace me. Now, I find myself becoming less curious every day."

"Are you telling us that you no longer care who leads this congregation into the next chapter or how it's lead?" Sister Burlington assumed that line of questioning would paint Orlando into a corner. If he said yes, she would have blasted him for turning his back on the congregation. If his was answer no, he would have been compelled to continue playing the role of Mr. Hospitality to men who wanted his job.

Orlando felt like Jesus when given questions by the Sadducees that were meant to trap him, so the pastor did what Jesus would do, he fashioned his answer in form of a question to show how defective their supposition was.

"Why would you be looking for a leader who is capable of growing the congregation by twenty-one percent in fourteen months and then double the weekly attendance to worship when I have already completed the task? Why would you be so eager to pay a pastor to watch over our people, the homeless in our community, while protecting many of them from drugs and spousal abuse without asking for a dime in return?" he added. "Just another question if you'll indulge me. Why would you seek a man who connects with the children of this body and inspires them to become more than they can imagine, all while donating his salary back to help those same children with college scholarships?"

Suddenly Brother Langston leaned forward with his elbow resting on his thigh. "Those are very good questions."

"You and I know why!" Sister Burlington said curtly, to hammer the old man back into his place. "Brother Clay, you run with pimps, prostitutes, loose women and immoral men."

"So did Jesus," Orlando said, in his own defense.

"You've been seen eating with drug dealers, thieves, and violent enforcers."

"So was Jesus. He was often seen around men of low stature and character in his day."

"People are whispering about you Orlando. They're saying you regularly take up with non-Christians who don't even believe in one true God."

"So did Jesus," he responded, matter-of-factly.

"I hope you aren't putting yourself on the same level with the Savior?" Sister Burlington asked, all dignified and self-righteous.

"I most certainly am not. While I make no misgivings about who I am and what I do, I ask that you search your hearts as to what it is that you truly seek for this position of pastor at the Methodist Episcopal Greater Apostolic church. Because the obvious can at times be so glaring, it is often over looked. It's a common occurrence for people who do not know what they are looking for to fall into a ditch, over something they did not recognize they already possessed."

"Brother Clay!" she yelled, as he turned and walked away. "Orlando Clay, you get back here! I'm not finished with you!"

Orlando was good and finished playing Sister Burlington's games. He loved what he did. How he went about executing his role was successful. Members who had been delinquent and considered other congregations were returning in droves. More impressively, they were bringing their children to worship as well. High school aged membership doubled and for the first time,

M.E.G.A. had a teen choir that won city-wide awards and rocked the house every fourth Sunday. Orlando was proud of that but was often reminded that worldly problems came in along with people who sought refuge from the world. It was predictable yet unavoidable.

As soon as Orlando rounded the corner from the hallway, it opened into a large office suit. He saw two teenage girls sitting on one side of the room with their heads down and an angry woman standing between them, wearing a wounded expression. On the other side, two young men in letterman jackets sat motionless, both avoiding eye contact with everyone else in the room.

"What's with all this," he asked, but no one spoke up. Carolyn stood in the doorway to the pastor's office, shaking her head as if to warn Orlando not to investigate the situation further until she clued him in first.

Once inside of the office with the door closed, Carolyn pressed play on the DVD player on the credenza to the right of his desk.

"Just watch what's been going on in the choir hall, after song rehearsals," she said, with the video running on the monitor.

Two girls walked inside of the large room and sat down on the first row of risers. Seconds later, two boys came in. Within seconds, the girls unzipped the boy's pants then took out their penises. Orlando looked at Carolyn in disbelief as the young ladies, who sat right outside of the office, began to preform fellatio on the older boys. Carolyn had to hold her mouth closed as the girl's displayed skills she would have guessed were beyond their knowledge.

"On my Lord," Orlando sighed. "These children are growing up way too fast. Pause the tape, Sister Carolyn."

"I'll turn it off," she said, in response.

"No ma'am, please pause it and leave it up on the screen," he argued. "How did you get involved in this anyway?"

"You don't have a secretary, remember?"

"Haven't needed one before now," he answered. "We have deacons and deaconesses and staff for most everything that comes up."

"Not for this, Brother Pastor."

"You're right. Who else knows about this?"

"The leadership and security."

"Let me make a quick call then send in those boys," he said, picking up the office phone from his desk. "Where are the boys' moms and dads?"

"Single mothers but both on their way. Had to take off work."

"That the girl's mother out there?" he asked, noticing how the young ladies looked enough alike to be sisters.

"Is their father in the picture?"

"No. He divorced Sister Spencer and his girls, right along with her. Hasn't been around for a number of years now."

"And this is what happens when men don't play a part in raising their daughters."

"What about the boys?" she said, as if he'd forgotten about their part in the shenanigans.

"Oh, they're about to catch hell. Wait sixty seconds then send them in whether their mothers are here yet or not."

Carolyn nodded assuredly even though her puzzled expression suggested she didn't know what was about to go down or if she would have been on board with it. "Yes, pastor," she answered, on her way out of the door to fetch the young men.

"Hey Sederrick," this is Pastor Clay. "Yeah brother, I know this is a pickle we're in and it could very easily tear our congregation apart. I'm about to handle it but I need something from you on that end. I know the leadership has heard about this circumstances and you were right to share it with them but from now own, come to me first. Now, listen to me and I don't really care how you feel about what I'm asking. It needs to be done right. Torch any copies of the DVD you've set aside for parents or whomever. If any of this gets out there, it could ruin the church and the children who got caught doing grown up things. I believe they deserve to see the error of their ways and be redirected in the paths of righteousness." Orlando listened while the line was silent. "If you're thinking about disobeying my orders, imagine if it were your daughters on their knees when this video goes viral. Won't ever be a chance for them to outlive this moment in time. Everyone they'll ever work with on the job will have access to this footage. Sooner or later, even their children will too."

When Orlando heard what he'd been waiting on, he thanked the director of security then placed the office phone back on the receiver.

Carolyn had been listening on the other end of the phone line, at the receptionist desk, like she'd done when her husband was discussing serious issues with female members and his secretary was out. After Orlando convinced the security director to erase proof of the sexual conduct between minors, she hang up then ordered the boys to go inside of the pastor's office. Reluctantly, they opened the door and walked in with their tails tucked between their legs.

"Close the door and sit down," Orlando instructed them.

As soon as they were alone, Orlando pulled a gun out of his drawer and placed it on the desk. Both boys recoiled when they saw the shiny steel.

"Sit your narrow asses down until I tell you different," he grunted. "It's not loaded, yet."

"Pastor, pastor, Pastor Clay, we're sorry," one of them apologized heartily.

"Yeah, we real sorry for disrespecting the church building, Mr. Pastor," the other wailed, nervously.

Orlando placed a box of 45 caliber rounds on the desk then shook out a handful as the boys watched him load bullets into the circular chamber.

"Now look at the TV screen over there. Look at it real hard," he ordered.

The boys turned to find images of themselves on the screen with their penises in the girl's mouths. One of them begun to water at the eyes. It didn't matter if he was overwhelmed with remorse or consumed with fear but he had a right to be scared. The other boy, who seemed a bit tougher, simply turned his face away from the screen.

"Damn," he whispered.

"Yep, that's what I thought too when I saw it," Orlando told them. "What are your names and ages so I'll have it right if this goes sideways and gets into the public eye."

"I'm Derrick Eddins, sixteen years old," the bigger one said slowly, as if his words cost him a thousand dollars each.

"My name is Marcus Glen. I'm fifteen, sir. Could you please turn that off?"

"Not yet. Your mother's need to see what you've been up to."

"Oh God please no!" Derrick begged. "She'll kill me."

"What do you think is going to happen when the girl's father gets a look at how you defiled his children?"

Marcus leapt to his feet and considered bolting for the door, until he heard Orlando's revolver handle click.

"You're going to shoot me?" he asked, with a hint of defiance.

"I could pop you both and get away with it or would you rather the girl's father, Mr. Spencer, catch up to you on your way from school one day? Him and some of his homeboys could do to you what you've done to his daughters, maybe pump a few holes in your head then leave your bodies somewhere for buzzards and possums to pick at."

"This is so messed up," Derrick whined.

"So, you thought it was a good idea to get your knobs polished in this building?"

"It's wasn't our idea," Marcus said, after falling back into the chair.

"It wasn't our fault," Derrick co-signed.

"Let me explain something to you fellows," Orlando said, in a professorial tone. "The police don't care who started it."

"Police?" Derrick clamored. "You gonna call the police?"

"You are young black men who had sex with teen aged girls. The law doesn't see that you're the girl's classmates but rather overdeveloped sexual predators. Ones, who deserve to be imprisoned with grown men who would love to tear you two boys apart in their cells at night." Both of the boys were sobbing and wiping their faces then.

"This is what I propose we do about it. You will agree to any and all of the punishment I deem necessary to avoid police and prison."

"Anything pastor," they pleaded.

"We'll do anything you say, mister."

"Your bodies are a temple of God. Did you know that? Those girl's bodies are also temples of God. You went and put your peckers inside of God temples and dirtied them up pretty good. So, there should be some cleansing going on, I do believe. First, you will be punished before you leave this office. Secondly, you will pick up trash around the building. You will also help the cleaning crews sweep up and mop the building after Sunday worship, of which you will attend for seven straight weeks without fail. Miss one week and your punishment will start all over. Do you understand me?"

"Yes sir."

"Yes, I do."

Orlando took off his a long black leather belt. He separated the boys on opposite sides of his desk then took turns whipping their behinds until his arms were worn out. The boys started out swallowing their pain until it came storming out in unyielding yelps and howls.

Breathless and tired of seeing young men make mistakes they had to live with for the rest of their lives, Orlando composed himself and allowed time for the boys to wipe tears and snot from their faces.

"Do we need to have another discussion about this?" he asked the boys, as they limped around the room wincing and rubbing their butts.

"No sir. Never!"

"Ain't nobody ever whipped me like that. No, no, no. I heard you the first time, pastor."

"Is anyone going to hear about what happened in this office?" Orlando asked them.

"Uhhh-uhhh."

"Whew! Not from me."

"Good. Then go on home and I'll see y'all bright and early Sunday morning."

When they opened the door, limping and repentant, they were met with wide eyes and sorrow from even the girl's mother. Carolyn stood up from the secretary's desk and gawked at Orlando as he fastened his belt around his waist. She'd heard what went on inside of the reckoning room and wondered what was in store for the girls who were now mortified and drowning in their own tears.

Marcus' mother Erika stood in the mouth of the office suite when her son shuffled by. She arrived too late and asked what was going on. Her son pulled on her arm like a small child who had been acting up at school and wanted to go home before she got the whole story from his teacher.

"Come on, momma. Pastor Clay set us straight. I'm good now. Come on momma, please let's go." She looked at Carolyn, whose expression displayed sincere regret for everyone involved.

"Call me later Sister Glen," Carolyn said. "This will all be taken care of."

"I sure will Carolyn. And somebody had better tell me everything."

"Thanks Erika. I will," Carolyn promised.

She watched her Zumba partner leave with her son, who had

received the whipping of his life and probably not a minute too soon. Carolyn didn't necessarily agree with Orlando's tactics but knew something had to be done to curtail the boy's mischievous sexual behavior.

Now that time had come to deal with the girls, Carolyn was concerned how the Interim Pastor would handle a room exploding with estrogen once the girl's mother laid eyes on the video of her daughters servicing high school jocks in the deserted choir hall.

"Come on in ladies," said Orlando, from his perch on the edge of the desk. He glanced at the image on the TV monitor, a freeze frame of the girls square in the middle of a sex act and seemingly enjoying it. "Please have a seat."

Carolyn stood beside Orlando as he looked the girls over like a concerned parent.

"I've seen you girls in the church before but we haven't formally met. I'm Pastor Clay, what are your names and ages."

"Pastor, I don't know exactly what we're here for," the mother said, hoping whatever the reason was, passed quickly. "I figure it has something to do with those boys who just left."

"I'll get to that shortly Sister Spencer. I need to get some information first. Girls, how about it?" he continued, with a questioning look.

"I'm Lucinda," the oldest one said, with her head down. "I'm fifteen."

Just above a whisper, her sister answered eventually. "I'm Charlotte Spencer. Fourteen."

"Do you girls know why you and your mom were called in today?" he asked, with an eye on Carolyn.

Orlando wondered what she told them to get the quick meeting. When she looked away, he knew the girls had some idea but the mother was practically in the dark.

"I was at work when the call came in. Sister Carolyn said to get the girls and get down here. I was mad that I'm losing time at the job but after hearing how rough you handled those boys, I knew it was something serious enough to miss work for."

"I think I can help explain matters," Carolyn said, as she moved strategically in between Sister Spencer and her daughters. "Gwen, there is no easy way to say this so I'll just show you." Carolyn pressed the green button on the DVD player. "The girls already know what happened last Friday night after teen choir rehearsal," she said, to bring their mother up to speed.

Sister Spencer's eyes narrowed as she studied the monitor.

"What in God's name is going on here?" she groaned, in a low strained tone. "Were my girls watching that trash in choir practice? I'll have a talking to them because I'm raising them better than that."

When Gwen recognized her children's faces on the screen, her voice began to rise as she surrendered to her shocking discovery.

"Ohhhhh Myyyy Goddddd! That's not right!"

She tried to run for the door but Carolyn stopped her. "Gwen, we're going to address this here. In a controlled environment."

Before Carolyn realized it, Sister Spencer had spun around and swung her purse at Lucinda. "You got my baby sucking on some nasty little boy's thang up in this church house."

Sister Spencer was fraught with emotions. She felt as though she'd witnessed her daughter's innocence vanish right before her eyes.

Her head swam as the room began to spin. Washing out their mouths with soap was her initial response which was quickly followed by killing the boys who participated but she fought to keep her composure instead.

"I'm sorry momma!" Charlotte screamed, with her hands up high in a defensive manner.

Lucinda didn't move an inch when her mother threw windmill punches at her face. Orlando stepped in when the second blow landed on the teenager's eye.

"Sister Spencer try to calm down," Orlando suggested, firmly.

"Hell no, I won't either. These fast tail girls want to act like grown women in private then they got to deal with me like grown women in public."

Sister Spencer wanted to shame them publicly but only after a sound thrashing. She pushed past Orlando to slap the taste out of Lucinda's mouth then she tried to choke the life out of Charlotte.

"Putting your hands on them might lead to bigger problems," Carolyn argued, while pulling Gwen off the younger girl.

"They need their asses whooped like those dirty little boys who talked them into doing this," Sister Spencer howled, while pointing at the TV screen. "I can't wait to show this tape to their daddy."

"You can't show him this momma," Charlotte whimpered, hysterically. "He'll never come back if you do."

"He's not coming back anyway, stupid!" Lucinda shouted, with her hands balled into angry fists. "He divorced us and got himself another family."

"Stop it!" Charlotte screamed. "You don't know everything. daddy is coming back. He still loves us."

"Then why did he leave?" Lucinda snapped, angrily. "Momma, why did you let him leave?"

Suddenly Sister Gwen Spencer's knees buckled.

When she hit the floor with a solid thud, her head bounced off the carpet. Orlando ran to help her.

"Carolyn call 9-1-1. I think she hit her head pretty good."

"I'm so sorry, momma," Charlotte cried. "I didn't mean to hurt you."

"Momma get up," Lucinda pleaded. "Please get up, momma."

Carolyn raced to the other side of the pastor's desk then grabbed the telephone receiver. "Is your mother diabetic?" Carolyn asked the girls.

"Yes. She takes insulin," Lucinda answered.

"Yes, she is diabetic," Carolyn repeated, into the phone. "Okay, I will. Please send someone in a hurry. She hit her head pretty good. Thank you."

Orlando kneeled down to comfort Sister Spencer, who was breathing but unconscious.

Sister Betty Burlington busted into the room when she caught wind of what was going on in the pastor's office. "How long has this been going on Sister Carolyn? There's no use in asking Pastor Clay because he's on the fence about sticking around here in the first place."

"Nothing you should concern yourself with Sister Burlington," was Carolyn's response. "I believe we have it covered."

Sister Burlington caught an eyeful of the video, which was still rolling. "Good Lord Almighty! What's has gotten into people these days? Shut that thing off and call these girl's father to handle this."

Immediately, everyone in the room argued against that move. "No ma'am. We're good," Orlando said, then promptly turned off the TV monitor.

"Our father won't forgive us if he sees what we've done," Charlotte cried. "He won't come back home then."

"We really messed up and now our momma is hurt," Lucinda said, sorrowfully. "Please don't call him and make this worse than it already is."

It was apparent the girls were seeking the love and affection their father wasn't providing so they acted out in a way they thought would provide it. They were desperately seeking validation from a man but it rarely worked out as intended when girls set out to fill that void. The steep rise in sex trafficking was largely due to young girls chasing validation and affirmation of worth.

When Sister Burlington slowed down long enough to survey the entire situation, she clearly understood what was going on already. She stormed back to her office then called 9-1-1 so many times that emergency dispatch sent three ambulances and a firetruck to the church.

Almost an hour later, Carolyn agreed to take the girls home while their mother was rushed to the hospital. Orlando was on his way out of the door when Jessika met him, totally unaware of what had transpired less than an hour ago.

"Uncle, check this out. I set up a Go Fund Me account for Numbers, I mean Daniel Ashland's doctor bills. See, watch." Jessika pressed play on her Samsung Galaxy phone then smiled proudly as the video footage she produced rolled along.

Jessika stood in front of the burned out car in the police impound.

"A tragedy occurred in Dallas when someone set this car on fire, with a woman and two little girls inside of it. Someone wanted them dead. Almost everyone stood around and watched as it happened in broad daylight."

Several seconds of viral footage flashed of the scene in real time, all of it captured from cell phones that people held still to get a good video stream instead of helping those trapped inside to get out.

"Then someone risked his life and limbs to save them when no one else was brave enough or cared enough to help."

More footage of Numbers dashing to the rescue. He darted in and out of the car, each time salvaging another life in the process.

"By now, millions across the world have seen the videos. Millions have been shaken by the heroic courage of one man but very few know his name. Daniel "Numbers" Ashland is a Dallas native who lives in a group home when he's not on the street. Daniel isn't mentally ill, he just sees the world a little differently than most of us. And, thank God he does."

In the video, Jessika begins to tear up but she refuses to wipe them away. "Daniel saved my life too that day and I am grateful. Now, I get to show my thanks for his unbelievable bravery. Numbers lost most of the skin on his hands. He will probably lose some fingers and has already undergone very expensive surgeries on his arms and face. I've been saving for college but this is more important to me. I am starting a campaign for his doctor bills and after care with a donation of nine thousand and seventy-two dollars. That's every penny I own in the world. Please help me say thanks for my life, the lives of others and for being living proof that people still exist who put others before themselves. Please help me repay Daniel 'Numbers' Ashland, a real American hero."

When the video stopped, Orlando was speechless. "Where did you get this idea? I hope it works like you want it to."

"No hope needed. I've been praying, Uncle."

He was surprised but Jessika prayed many times when she was homeless, abused and mistreated even though nothing usually happened to fix her situation.

"You prayed? I thought you'd given up on talking to the Lord, Jess."

"I was desperate when I saw that car burning and heard people screaming for help inside. I wanted someone to save them and when no one did, I prayed for God to do it. I realized when a homeless man pulled off a miracle, that prayers do works. Maybe not on my account but I'm praying for good and decent people to help Daniel now."

Orlando's heart swelled with pride. "I don't know what to say. This is something else. This is beautiful. And where'd you get almost ten thousand dollars to donate?"

"You give me money all the time and reimburse me for the things I spend money on," she answered. "When you're busy, you give me money to get out of your face."

"I do not," he said, wondering if he actually did.

"When you go out of town, you leave me money. When my grades are really good you throw money at me to celebrate."

"Is that bad parenting?"

"I don't think so," she said, laughing aloud, then she became more serious. "You don't have to give me a dime and I would still know how much you love me. You're a business man with money. You're a giver, that's what givers do so why fight it. Guess this funding campaign for Numbers means I'm a giver too, huh?"

Orlando pulled Jessika closer and looked her in the eyes.

"No one knows what I'm about to tell you so I'm betting on you to keep it between us." She nodded her head quickly. "Numbers helped to save my life too once. When the federal charges were dropped and I was released from prison, I went straight to this restaurant to get some breakfast."

"Let me guess, Denny's?"

"Of course but check it out. Numbers was hanging around outside counting blue cars. He didn't want money and didn't seem to need anything. I asked if he'd mind me hanging out with him for a while. He said as long as he didn't lose count. So I stood by him for over an hour. I saw the simplicity of his mind and the complexity at the same time. He didn't have a care in the world except to know how many blue cars passed by that morning. He's read somewhere that blue was once very popular but it was being replaced by various shades of silver. Numbers didn't want to believe it because blue was his favorite color." Orlando smiled to himself while remembering back on that day. "Well, after we ate, he asked how long I'd been behind bars when I hadn't even told him about it. He said it was a Thursday afternoon when I was arrested because he'd read it in the *Morning News*. It was in a throw away paper he'd found at a bus stop, so he didn't have the full story. Yet, he remembered me."

"Is Daniel special?" she asked.

"He's a genius, hiding in plain sight. We've been business partners for years after he gave me a stock tip that made me a lot of money."

"So, he isn't poor or homeless?" she asked, with wide eyes.

"Not hardly. I don't know if he clearly understands his financial situation half the time," Orlando answered. "I bought him a group home where he'd always have a safe place to lay his head, good food to eat, and people to look out for him."

"So, the funding campaign I set up for Daniel is useless? He doesn't need the money."

"But people need a reason to believe that honor and selflessness still exists. You did a good thing Jessika and I know God is pleased."

"I shouldn't take it down then?" she asked, unsure of the campaign's purpose.

"Don't block people's blessing Jessika. Let's leave it up so people can thank him like you did. Who knows, maybe some of them who view your video need to give more than my buddy Numbers needs to receive. That's not always a bad thing."

Jessika understood immediately that he was including himself in that number who had giving spirits. He often felt compelled to help others financially when he could. "It's settled. I'll leave the campaign up for a week and see how it goes."

"I think that's fair and I'll match it up to twenty-five thousand, if we can reach that amount."

"What if the fund grows to fifty?"

"In a week? It'll never happen but yeah I guess so," he said, slightly concerned that it could. "I'll match that too."

Jessika smiled to herself then to Orlando. "You know, sometimes people have to be convinced that their donations will amount to something."

"What do you mean?"

"How do you feel about me going public with your agreement to match contributions up to fifty thousand dollars?"

"Are you trying to break me?" he joked. "Whew, uhhh, alright. I'm in if you think it'll make an impact."

"Uncle, you're the best. Lemme get that up right now."

"You're welcome, I think."

"Yes, yes, yes. Thank you so much. I've got to go. This could be big," Jessika chattered, as she hurried toward the computer lab to add new information about Orlando's money matching commitment. "This could be big Uncle Orlando."

Her head was racing and his was in the clouds. Orlando felt good about his and Jessika's relationship, especially after witnessing how a lack of male role models could affect a young woman's perspective and self-esteem.

Carolyn and Sister Burlington had watched the pastor and his niece's interaction from the older woman's office doorway. They couldn't hear the discussion but they were clear the interaction was powerfully uplifting to Jessika as she bounced away joyfully. They had no idea that it meant just as much to Orlando.

13

AFTER THE FIRE

Mosley was noticeably quiet as he navigated the spotless Bentley sedan south on Interstate 67. He'd lost a ton of sleep and wasn't much for words all the way to Methodist Hospital. He didn't know how to process the feelings plaguing him. Watching Numbers risk his life when others refused to give it a thought, made him feel less of a man than he was a few days before. It had Mosley out of sorts and wondering how Orlando felt about him.

"It's a shame about Numbers," he said, softly.

"Yeah. I'm trying to be optimistic he'll still have that same spirit of giving, fearlessness, and blind faith that separates a lot of men."

"You ever see anything like that?" Mosley asked, his eyes frozen straight ahead. "I mean, a man jumping into a burning car to save people from being cooked alive?"

"I haven't even *heard* of anything like that," Orlando answered, knowing what the deacon was getting at. He understood how life or death emergencies effected men, especially if someone didn't have what it took to accept the challenge and take it head on. A moment like that could ruin a man. Orlando didn't want that to happen to his friend.

"I've been in my share of gun fights. It is *not* like what you see in movies," he joked, "where the brave Marshall stares down a bad man in the middle of the street, draws him down and then fires hot lead into him without batting an eye. Nah, it's nothing like that. When bullets start flying and whizzing by your head, everybody and I do mean everybody ducks for cover."

When Mosley didn't respond, Orlando let him marinate on what happened the day before and what he said about facing life or death situations. There were also a million things on Orlando's mind so he didn't push. "When we get to the hospital, I got dibs on Number's jello if he ain't got into it."

Mosley was still smiling about the jello joke when they stepped off the elevator on the third floor. "It's this way," he told Orlando, when they came to a roundabout nurses station that split off into four hallways.

"You have ESP or something?"

"No sir, I was here earlier," Mosley admitted. "Came about three in the morning and couldn't seem to leave," he said, staring through the doorway at Numbers lying in bed. Orlando walked into the room but Mosley held back and leaned against the door frame.

"Looks like somebody beat us both to the dessert."

Orlando looked at the serving tray. The metal plate cover hadn't been removed nor the other items on the platter touched. "I see," he said, while squinting at the grape jello container that was empty and laying on its side. Numbers appeared to be asleep with both hands wrapped heavily in white gauze and covered in sterile bandages.

"Numbers certainly couldn't have pulled that off."

"Pulled off what?" Nelson asked, while juking past

Mosley at the door. "I wonder if I could order another dessert, maybe chocolate pudding or something?"

"I can't believe you ate a sick man's sweets." Orlando said, with a disappointing tone.

Nelson smiled at him. "You must've had dibs? Haha, I beat you to it."

Mosley lumbered into room and took a seat by the bed. He could barely look at Numbers.

"What is he doing here?" Mosley asked somberly.

"Besides stealing jello? I have no idea." Orlando replied.

"I'll get that cute nurse of his to bring you boys some dessert too. It ain't that serious," Nelson said. "Look, I haven't been hungry much lately with all of the bodies stacking up."

Mosley frowned. "It's not about the food, stupid hick."

"He knows that," Orlando replied, before Nelson and Mosley got into a room clearing disagreement at Number's expense. "What are you talking about, Nelson?"

"In the last twenty four hours, there's been three homicides within a five block radius."

"So, bangers and bad boys get testy every now and then," Orlando reasoned. "Drives the murder rate through the roof."

"Not this time. Something wicked is going on. Mostly girls, bodies cut up and burned. Down south of San Anton', they had this problem last year, except for the cutting. Coyotes who didn't get paid their transport fees, torched the merchandise."

"Coyotes?" Mosley said, with his mind trying to recall something he'd heard the night before.

"Yeah, Mexican smugglers who get paid to sneak people across or under the border," Orlando answered him.

"Mean rattlesnakes is what they really are. Human traffickers don't care how young or old their cargo is as long as they get paid the freight fee."

Mosley turned to look at Nelson. "What happens if the fee don't get paid?"

Nelson threw a questioning glance back at him. "You know something deacon?"

"Just that when Numbers talked in his sleep early this morning, he screamed out a time or two. *Coyotes*! *Coyotes*! Like that."

"He's on the street most of the time, could have heard it any-where," Nelson said, dismissively.

"But I didn't," Numbers answered.

Orlando walked closer to the bed. "Hey Numbers, if we're too loud, we'll go."

"I didn't hear it on no streets," he answered defiantly. "That women… in the fire told it to me. She said it like that was his name."

Mosley placed his hand on the bed and leaned in. "You don't have to talk about that now. Go head on and rest."

"*Coyote*. That's the one who did it to those girls," Numbers said, then drifted out of consciousness.

Nelson thought about Number's declaration. "Poor fellow, he's not talking out of his head at all. I'll bet the woman knew she was going to die and wanted to tell somebody why she was being killed."

Orlando suggest they take the conversation out of the room so Numbers could get some decent sleep. While they were standing in the hall, he put on his investigator hat. "Since when did Mexican traffickers start delivering this far north, Nelson?"

"They'll transport as far as Oklahoma if the price is right.

The fees go up with the risk. The farther north they have to deliver, the higher the risk for them making it back home too."

"Hmmm, let's get a bite to eat. I need to make some calls," Orlando said, as his eyes narrowed in on someone walking down the hallway towards them.

"Well I'll be," Nelson hummed, "the pretty detective is stalking you partner."

"I thought you'd be here sooner or later," Vera said, as a hello to Orlando. She nodded salutations to the other men. "I came by earlier to interview Daniel Ashland but he was out cold and so was the deacon."

"I must've dozed off," Mosley said, shamefully.

"Grief is heavy," she answered, quickly. "It tends to wear people down and that's why I need to get some info from our hero as soon as possible. We already lost the woman late last night and one of the little girls is hanging on by a thread. Too much of her skin gone."

"Maybe you ought to talk to Deacon Mosley about that. He's got some ideas that might help your case," Orlando advised.

"Really?" Vera questioned.

"I'm going to visit one of my female members who was brought in a bit ago."

"We going to lay some hands on her?" Nelson smarted, with a childish grin.

"You're staying here with these two and out of my way, while I do some serious ministering to one of my wounded sheep," Orlando said. "I'll call you when I'm done. We need to talk."

Mosley stopped him before he left. "Hey, back at the church, there was some girls and boys waiting to see you. What was all that about?"

"Believe me, you don't want to know."

Orlando walked away from them, each of them important to him at various periods of his life. Each of their eyes followed him down the hallway. He had a heavy heart when he headed towards the stairs to visit Sister Gwen Spencer. He didn't know what to expect. At least Number's injuries were visible and Orlando could see the damages. With the mother of two girls who acted out in lewd sexual behavior, he couldn't have known how badly torn she was on the inside, simply by looking at her.

As he pushed through the doors from the stairwell onto the second floor, Orlando peeked at his cellphone. He had received a text message from Carolyn. Sister Spencer was flat on her back with tubes in her arms when the nurse opened her door to exit.

"I'm Pastor Clay," he said, politely. The young white nurse smiled and waited as if he had more to say. "May I go in and visit with Sister Spencer?"

"She's awake but I don't know if the patient is up to seeing anyone," the nurse with freckles and a brown hair bun replied, as she read over her chart.

"I'm willing to chance it but could you tell me how bad off she is."

"She took a rough spill and bumped her head pretty good. Ms. Spencer is going home tonight. She can leave after her I.V. is empty and the doctor releases her."

"Good. No head injuries?"

"None that we could see," the nurse said, with a roll of her eyes. "She's not too happy about her daughters though. They must've have done something pretty dangerous."

"Yes, I would agree. Must've been dangerous alright." Orlando stuck his head in the door then walked on in.

"Sister Spencer. Gwen, you up?"

The covers stirred then the woman turned her body toward him.

"Hey, Pastor Clay."

Her voice was much smaller than it was earlier. Also absent was her thunderous reprimands and snarky threats from that woman who dropped to the floor at the church building. The woman lying in the hospital bed was altogether different.

Orlando walked over and shook her hand softly. "It's good to see you're alert. The way your body went limp, I thought you'd broken something."

"Only my heart, pastor," she said, barely above a whisper. "Where are my girls?"

"Sister Carolyn Drew is watching them at your place. I'll give you her number if you'd like." Orlando didn't know what to say but he did not want to delve into what her children had done.

"You think my girls are sexually active?"

"I think that maybe, well, at least once," he answered, honestly.

"Yeah, I guess you could say that for sure. You think some man has been molesting them?" she asked, while staring at the silent TV.

"I don't know but we can find out. However, if you haven't noticed any changes in behavior or attitude until now, I'll bet they're acting out because there's no male authority figure to validate them."

Sister Spencer laid there for a long time without moving. She pondered what the minister said then wiped a fallen tear from her eye. "I've tried to do the best I could to raise them by myself, be momma and daddy so they wouldn't want for anything or anybody."

"I know you don't feel like it now but your daughters love you."

"You're right, I don't believe that. They've always been daddy's girls and since Richardson left us, it just seems like a big hole has been ripped through what was left."

"They respect you too, Gwen. You need to remember that"

Her voice grew shaky. "How can you say that after what they did, in the church?"

"They made mistakes and none of their behavior is excusable. On the other hand, they are both still children. They're still growing morally. Their brains are still developing and God knows their hormones are having a block party inside of their young bodies."

Sister Spencer laughed a bit then pushed out a giant sigh. "All of this makes me want to holler! And cuss!" she yelled. "Especially that. I want to cuss out the girls, those nasty boys that were in the choir hall too. And, most of all, I wish I could cuss out their daddy to his face for not being around the past three years."

"I could call Brother Spencer right now," Orlando teased. "I think I still got his number in my phone."

"Bah-hah-hah! You are one funny man. I thank God for you, Pastor Clay," she said, lovingly. "And not only for handling things today, like a father would have, since there hasn't been one in the mix. I am thankful for the way you raised Jessika, and how you look after the students who win those MEGA church scholarships. Some people say you're scandalous but not me."

"Some people, huh?"

"Okay so a lot of people," she laughed, "but I don't care. You're a good man and a fabulous preacher."

"That's very kind of you to say. I didn't hear all of that. Say it again," he joked.

"Ha-ha-ha-ha! Whew, you crack me up." Suddenly Gwen's eyes watered as streams poured from both eyes. "They say I can leave here with this headache. What are they gonna give me for my heartache?"

"Can I pray for you?" he asked, reaching for her hand again. "Father God, we come before you with bowed heads but unbreakable spirits. We come to petition you for relief and encouragement. You knew before we did what sorts of things our young people were getting into at the church. We ask for your love and temperament when addressing the children, going forward. Please place the right words in our mouths as we come seeking the perfect utterances to remedy and redirect the roads our young women and young men are traveling down, Father. Let us look deep within ourselves every step of the way as we repair what is broken and lacking in them, Dear Lord. Please be our light in darkness, our compass in the wilderness, and our shelter in the storm. In your Son, Jesus' name we ask it all. Amen."

"Amen, Pastor Clay. Thank you for stopping by. Whew, I think you prayed my hate away. Don't even feel like cussing nobody out anymore either."

"Praise God for that."

"When I get released, I'll go home and hug my daughters real tight."

"They'll appreciate that Gwen."

"You think I can catch an Uber from here?"

"You will do no such thing," he scolded her. "Deacon Mosley is right upstairs visiting a friend of ours. He'll be honored to take you home in my car."

Gwen threw a saucy look at Orlando. "In that beautiful Bentley everybody's been talking about? Oomph, what did they do with my shoes?"

"Ha-ha-ha! Okay, now you're the one cutting up Sister Spencer."

"I know you need to go. Thank you and God bless you."

When Orlando left the room, Gwen Spencer was in good spirits. Contemplating what she would say to Lucinda and Charlotte played softly in the back of her mind. But, taking a long ride in the two-hundred and twenty-five thousand car would have made her worries and woes a tad bit more tolerable, at least for the moment.

Orlando found Mosley and Nelson eating peanuts next to an out-dated vending machine.

"Considering her current situation, that's the least I could do," Orlando said, when Mosley tried to get out of it.

Nelson listened in but it was church business so he butted out.

"I'll take your orders and your word for it, Pastor Clay," he agreed, "but something devilish must be going on for all of this secret society jive."

"It's necessary Mosley or I would've filled you in on it already. But on this, I just can't do."

"Understood. I'll wait for Sister Spencer to get her release papers then get her home alright."

"Thanks, and deacon, take the scenic route. Put her in the back seat and put on some soothing music."

When it appeared that Nelson might crack wise about Mosley's chauffeuring assignment, Orlando shut it down quick, fast, and in a hurry. "If you even think about making a joke about Mosley being a taxi driver, I will break my foot so far off in your behind."

"Hey man, don't get so touchy," Nelson said, as he backed out of Orlando's range. "Deacon is doing the Lord's work. Ain't no way I'm cracking on that. You think I want to be cursed and have a root growing out of my pecker?"

"What? No," Orlando said. "That's not how any of this works."

Mosley put his hand over his mouth to stifle a laugh that wanted to erupt. "Nelson, who you been talking to?"

"If God wanted to punish you, he'd just strike you down where you stand," Orlando informed him.

Nelson pushed his hands down inside the pockets of his suit pants. "That'd be better than the root if you ask me."

Mosley walked away laughing. "What is wrong with that dude, I just don't know."

After Orlando followed his former partner out to the parking garage, he looked at Nelson like a disapproving older brother. "Really? You'd rather be struck dead, by the hand of God, than to have something growing out of your Johnson?"

"Well yeah. Might as well be dead if that happened."

"For an educated man, you sound dumber than a box of rocks right now."

"What can I say? I love my pecker," Nelson answered, as Orlando walked away shaking his head. "Hey partner, don't be that way. Okay, I'm sorry." Nelson laughed when Orlando turned just enough to toss him a glaring expression.

"Get in the car. I'm driving."

14

MY WICKED WAYS

Orlando drove out of the hospital parking garage then looped the building twice before Nelson noticed they were going in circles. "Hey, we already passed this way. You lost?"

"Just making sure we leave this place alone," Orlando answered, taking peeks at the rear view mirror. He wasn't positive but he couldn't shake the feeling that someone was watching their moves. "Maybe it's nothing or maybe it's everything."

"I told you I wasn't traveling in a pack, *Orlando*."

"Actually, you haven't told me much of anything. You've been here more than a week, popped up and vanished like a ghost and not once have you been forthcoming about why."

Nelson stared out of the window a while then chewed at his bottom lip. "I did come here to look into someone then thought you might know a thing or two about those bodies turning up everywhere. You know a lot of people who might whisper some information in your ear that would never think about saying a damned thing to me."

"I have no idea and I don't like the idea of you dancing around the truth," Orlando said, taking a left onto Polk Street. "Who is this someone you're looking into?"

There was a long pause before Nelson responded.

"I'm supposed to keep an eye on St. Nick and... dig up any intel on you if it happens to fall into my lap."

"Haaaa-hah, the truth will set you free," Orlando howled thankfully, then he slammed on the breaks in the middle of the street.

"Get out!"

"What! Hell no, I won't," Nelson wailed, as cars zoomed past with horns blaring. "Man, you're gonna get us hit. I can't file an insurance claim if you get us hit on purpose."

Nelson kept looking through the back window.

"Come on man, please. This is not cool."

Suddenly the car pulled back into traffic. Orlando whistled as if nothing happened.

"Whew! What is the matter with you?"

"You're looking into that fat rascal Nickolas? I get that but you should have told me you had eyes on him. Not telling me that *I'm* a target of an investigation is inexcusable."

"Because you're not a target. Although, some people are asking how you're living so large without taking money from the church."

"I don't rape the church of finances because that's not who I am. I would never take from people who need money more than I do. Plus, I learned a long time ago that nobody can tell you where to get off, if they haven't put you on their payroll."

Nelson wondered if he'd done the right thing. Before they reached the next destination, he knew he had.

"So what do we do now?"

"We make an important stop. You leave. I stay. We part ways."

Orlando stared straight ahead at the road. He was concerned that saying too much might have put Nelson in a bind with his bosses.

"Just so you know, I've been on to you. I knew you were snooping after me, Nelson. You pushed too hard at first. You always do."

"I do not," Nelson said, as he contemplated his investigation tactics. "Do I?"

"What you want is written all over your face. Always was."

"Why haven't you told me this before? I thought we were partners."

"When we *were* partners, I told it to you all the time. *Nelson don't show all your cards*, I said. *Nelson be smooth on the introductions so you don't spook the people we might need to double back and talk to on the low.*"

He rubbed his nose then made a pouty frown with his lips.

"Sheeeesh, you did say that," Nelson remembered.

"Yep," Orlando agreed. "More than once."

"Can't believe I still give myself away after all this time?"

"Every man has a tell. A little inkling, a wink, a pause or flinch that conveys he's about to lie or do something to you that you're not gonna like."

"Sure am glad I came out with the truth then," Nelson sighed. "What a load off."

"Should have told me sooner, before I figured it out on my own," Orlando said, disappointedly.

"You trust me now though, right?" Nelson asked, like a small child wanting to be believed.

"We're here, get out."

Orlando pulled in behind Duke's white van in the rear of the plumbing shop. He climbed out of the Cadillac and waited until Nelson got out then he handed over the keys.

"You know something? Man, I am waaay past tired of you talking to me like I got a tail and I am sick of coming to this stinky place."

"This is it," Orlando replied, matter-of-factly. "You can come in or drive away and stay the hell away from me altogether. Your choice. Either way, I hope you find something to hang on St. Nick before I have to kill him." Orlando pulled on the heavy back door and entered the building. After he took a few steps inside, he heard Nelson's footsteps pacing closer behind him.

"Hold on," Nelson said. "I'm here, may as well see what Doom and Gloom are up to."

"Duke and Grunt," Orlando corrected him.

"Whatever."

Orlando gave a quarter smile that quickly vanished as soon as he stepped into the walk-in cooler that was currently used as air conditioning for the entire room. Orlando stopped when he saw a light brown man slouched down on a chair with is pants pulled down around his ankles. His hair was shaggy and unruly, beard overgrown and wild. His hands were tied behind him and his mouth was gagged with a red shop rag.

"Hey Duke. Hiya doing Grunt?" Orlando said, calmly.

Duke placed two thirty-pound dumb bells down on a wooden work table then wiped his face with another of those dirty red shop towels. "Hey Unca'," he answered, as he caught his breath.

"Preacher Man," said Grunt, with his eyes locked onto the motionless man sweating bullets in the folding chair.

"He dead?" Nelson said, like he was aggravated by the entire scene.

"Nah, just scared to death," Grunt responded, still stalking his prey with a cold haunting gaze. "Who's asking?"

Orlando looked at Duke cautiously then answered. "I brought him here before."

"Unca', I know that and I didn't question it but a white man who keeps coming around my place has got to be a known quantity at some point. In case something comes back on me when it shouldn't, I need to know where to aim my retaliation."

"This is my old partner, Nelson," Orlando said, in a 'please relax' fashion that his nephew totally disregarded. Duke took two steps in Nelson's direction before Orlando put himself in the way.

"You brought him here twice, Unca'? That's the rat bastard who left you rotting in a federal prison when the FBI flipped on you?"

The man in the chair opened his eyes, looked at Nelson like he was a devil, then he shook his head disapprovingly.

"Calm down now LaDuke. Let those bygones go," Orlando told him.

Nelson smiled, nice and easy. "Don't let this smooth suit fool you, LaDuke."

"Don't nobody call me that but family. You ain't blood and unless you want some blood spilt, you need to shut the hell up."

Nelson was getting visibly frustrated. "I've had about all I can stand of this posturing like we're on some ghetto sand lot."

"You's a bitch for leaving my Unca' in jail on some trumped up charges."

"That's enough nephew," Orlando said, with a raised hand that put an end to it.

Nelson didn't say a word. He couldn't refute Duke's assertions. He turned red with anger then turned to storm out. "This is some horse crap! And y'all know it."

Nelson had enough of being degraded and scoffed at so he left. Besides, he knew they were correct and there was nothing he could do to change what happened years ago. Nothing at all.

Duke stared Nelson down as he walked toward the exit. "Don't come back Huckleberry Finn, unless you want to tussle!"

"Fellas, who is that you got in the hot seat?" Orlando asked, nicely. He was concerned they had been freelancing and settling scores in the shop that he was partial owner of. A closer look revealed the man had a tire chain around his waist. The other end of it was attached to a lawnmower.

"This Harvard Grady," Grunt said, with a metal tape measurer in his hand. "Guess who ever named him had some high hopes."

Duke was still upset about Nelson but he tried to pull it together.

"Brother Grady here, is the woman beater you had us to go and talk to."

"So, how'd it go?"

"This joker told us to stay out of his business and he can whoop on his woman anytime because she's his wife. Said he got papers on her to prove it."

Orlando bristled at those harsh words and old-fashioned rhetoric. "LaDuke, did he really say that? Oomph. Take off that gag from around his mouth."

"You think marrying a woman makes it okay for you to punch her in the face, huh? Bounce her off the walls? Twist her arms and stomp on her?"

Duke did as he was instructed then shrugged at his captive.

Harvard Grady sat uncomfortably for a while until Duke pressed the issue. "Don't you hear the pastor talking to you?" Duke asked, then kicked the chair out from under Harvard.

Sitting on the cold floor, Harvard brooded a while then finally pushed out an answer. "My daddy kept my mom's in check that way. It worked for them."

"It worked for who, Brother Grady?" Orlando asked. "I'm sure you saw how it did not work out well for your mother. How many black eyes did she have to endure? How many bruises? How many times did she have to hide her wounds from friends and family before he killed her?" Duke and Grunt looked on with a level of disdain that worried Orlando. "Now tell me how exactly how that worked out for them?" he asked insistently.

When Harvard didn't answer. Orlando backed out of the way.

"I don't know your wife, Sister Grady, but I like her way better than you," Duke said, as he sharpened gardening tools and long carving knives. "I think the Mrs. deserves to feel free and unafraid in her own house." The man's eyes started watering and it didn't sit right with Duke. "What you crying for? You're the big bad terrorist at your house. Oh, you didn't know you were a terrorist? A good man never beats on a woman. You gotta learn how to talk it out or walk it off. Punk ass coward!"

"Hey, it's about to go down like this," Grunt said, evenly and without malice. "I'm going to snip your scrotum at the bottom, right here at your taint, with those pruning shears he's sharpening. Why they call it the taint beats me. I guess it 'taint really the buttocks and it 'taint the ball sack neither."

"Please don't do that y'all," Brother Grady whined. "I won't hit my wife no more."

"You haven't learned your lesson. We can all see that you're just as black-hearted as when you raise your hand against her," Grunt surmised, correctly. "After the initial snip, I'm going to cut your nuts lose and unravel them thusly, thereby stretching them out that way over yonder. Maybe you'll be more docile and agreeable around the house then. The last fella who wouldn't stop terrorizing his woman is now carrying lip gloss in his knockoff designer clutch, but that ain't on me."

Duke gave Orlando a questioning look, as if to ask if they could keep going down the same path. Orlando wasn't convinced how far they were willing to go but he didn't want to be presiding over Sister Grady's funeral either. "Go ahead. Just make it quick."

"Please don't let them do this to me, Pastor Clay!" Harvard pleaded. "Please make them let me go."

Orlando shook his head. "I'd rather watch them torture you to death than watch you murder your wife. Sister Grady sings in the choir, she'd a good woman. She might not be a perfect wife but she didn't sign up to be abused." Orlando sent a text then said his goodbyes. "Later y'all. Remember to make it quick then do what we talked about." Orlando washed his hands of it. He walked away without so much as smudge on his conscience.

"Come on brothas," Harvard whimpered. "I know it was wrong to beat my wife but I lost my job and I can't deal with her disobeying me."

"This fool thinks he can raise a grown woman," Duke said, with a hearty laugh. "We about to snatch that stupidness right out. Twenty-two inches of testicles is the record but you got a lot of nuts talking crazy to my Unca' so you might break it. Gets real bloody but I like to have the measurement precise." Duke pulled out a red, stained, measuring tape then marked off two feet directly in front of Harvard's crotch. The man tried to scoot away on his behind until chain snagged him.

"Oooouch!" he bellowed.

Duke clapped excitedly. "Yeah, I think we can get three feet out of this one."

Harvard Grady's eyes rolled back in his head. He gasped for breath two times then fainted. Grunt laughed and stomped his Timberland boots on the floor.

"Awe man! You said he was a punk, Duke! He passed out cold on the floor."

Duke placed the knives and shears down on the table then walked over to get a closer look. "Damned if he didn't punk smooth out. You owe me a hundred dollars. Never met a woman beater yet, who ain't a coward."

Grunt doled out five twenties and then handed the bills to Duke with a frown. "I'll tell you something else he ain't."

"What's that?"

"Breathing."

Duke sneered at him. "Untie those ropes on his hands so the coroner can't tell he was still tied up if this rough-and-tough cream puff kicks the bucket. Unca' Lando said to make sure he's good and shook then put him on a bus like the last dude."

"Guess his ticker must've gave out. Let's hook up this cat to the diesel truck battery and see if we can bring him back."

"Breathing or not, he's getting out of town on a bus," Duke said, in a serious tone. "It's either him or us."

Orlando had managed to push those sordid details of punishment and pain out of his mind by the time he paid the taxi driver who let him off at HE Spa, a chic massage parlor that catered to high-end male clientele and adventurous women who wanted something out of the ordinary. All of the amenities were strictly confidential and guaranteed to satisfy.

The pastor was greeted in the office suite, a modified rub-and-tug hideaway. The registration desk was made of mahogany wood and covered with a light granite counter top. Expensive leather chairs sat in the reception area with beveled glass tables. Built-in racks, filled with an assortment of sports and real estate magazines, gave the establishment a look of legitimacy and class. Since the owners had to be vigilant against robberies and jealous spouses, there was an off duty police officer who protected the clients and the worker's assets. He kept his eyes peeled at the TV monitors in the manager's office.

Soon after Orlando signed in under the name of Grand Poohbah and took a seat, Jessika texted him that the Go Fund Me campaign to help Numbers was going surprisingly well. He responded with a few words: *That's good to hear. So proud of you. Let's talk about it later today.* His mind was stuck on getting the royal treatment from two of the prettiest massage therapists in the business.

Just as he responded to Jessika's text, Asia and Amani paraded down the hall toward him from their VIP room called The Owner's Box.

Orlando stood to greet them, with every inch of him eager to see the dynamic duo. Asia, the oldest twin by six minutes, stood five-eight in light-brown six-inched red bottoms and a peach colored sarong. She planted a soft kiss on his right cheek then handed him a glass of merlot.

"Welcome to Happy Ending Spa," she said, with the politeness of a foreign diplomat. "It's very good to see you again Grand Poohbah. We've been waiting for your arrival."

The hostess didn't know Orlando's name or ever referred to him as anything other than the one he signed in with. They kept records but there could not be any illegal implication without names or credit card receipts. The HE Spa had a way of handling things delicately. Confidentially and caution were included in the packaging.

"Thank you Asia. I've had such a difficult week and a few kinks that need some attending to."

Amani, the younger identical twin, was dressed like her sister but opted for a short yellow coverall. She handed Orlando a small black pouch to inspect then rubbed her hand up and down the front of his bulging slacks. "Whoaaa, daddy, as long as this is one of those kinks, I have a few ideas how to get the knots out," she whispered.

Orlando leaned closer to breathe in her scent. Hints of vanilla and expensive, he thought. "Very sensual Amani. Very, very, nice selection in deed."

"Shall we then?" Asia said, while taking him by the wrist and leading him down the hall with Amani following closely behind. On cue, the off duty police officer exited the manager's office then headed towards the front door to stand guard.

"Heyyy, am I too late y'all?" Mosley asked, as he slithered inside the building with a hopeful smile.

"You're right on time deacon," Orlando answered.

"Lock the door."

Mosley twisted the deadbolt lock then flipped the red neon *OPEN* sign off. He nodded hello to the officer then shook his hand with a hundred dollar tip.

"Enjoy yourself, sir," the middle aged Sargent said, maintaining strict professionalism.

"Mmmm hmmm," Mosley responded. "That's what I come for." He followed the others in the last door on the right.

The Owner's Box was the largest room. It was decorated to resemble a pro sports team owner's suite. The walls were adorned with original oil paintings of athletic scenes being played out on expensive canvasses. A buffet tray was fully stocked with finger foods and assorted liquors and mixers. The tray was positioned in front of smaller area built like a country-club locker room with two individual stalls, both equipped with plush white spa robes, towels, mouthwash and spray on deodorant.

Mosley was undressed and out of his clothing in a jiffy. He slipped on the robe hanging in his stall then tip toed into the steam room. He felt like a millionaire when he turned the steam up, turned the music on and then disrobed.

When he sat on the teak wood bench and placed a bath towel over his lap, he sipped from a cognac snifter. A petite Columbian woman entered the steamy room wearing white nylon shorts and a matching halter top. She sprayed incense into the air and poured water over the lava rocks until the sauna was nearly filled with thick vapor and the smell of spearmint.

The room attendant whispered something in Spanish into Mosley's ear until he giggled like an enchanted monkey, fawning over his companion's alluring dialect. Even though he could only make out half of what she said, he was totally mesmerized by the entire monologue. Things went on like that until she opened a jar of warming oil and removed the towel he had used to cover his throbbing manhood. Mosley's embarrassed expression caused the masseuse to blush as well. They exchanged glances and fingertip touches as she fulfilled his order to the letter. He enjoyed a solid hour of hot oil rubbing and tugging from head to toe and everything in between. His exclusive membership at the HE Spa was a birthday gift from Orlando and beneficial in more ways than he could count.

For the past sixty minutes, Orlando hung out in the jacuzzi with the twins discussing business tips and island trips mostly. Amani rolled two fat blunts from the small black pouch she presented to Orlando earlier. He huffed and they puffed, passing marijuana joints and chilled cocktails between them. The twins laughed out loud each time Orlando tried to hold in a steep hit of the chronic herb but choked and coughed miserably. It was clear that weed toking was not his thing but Asia knew what he could handle without any trouble whatsoever.

"Lie down on your stomach, Poohbah," she moaned.

"Oh, we're doing that now?" he asked, with his eyes half-closed and glassed over.

"Mmm hmmm, right now," she answered, while loosening the top on a jar of warming oils. "I'll start up here." Asia wrapped her long black hair in a bun then poked a thin bobby pin through to hold it still.

Orlando did as he was told and stretched out, face down on the tall oversized massage table which had a cutout at the head for his nose and mouth to fit nestled down in it comfortably. Then, Amani pulled the folded towel from underneath his mid-section, which revealed a sizable hole in the table. Orlando laughed when he realized it was designed to accommodate lowering his privates into the middle of it.

"This is super freaky ladies. I approve y'all. Oh yeah, I definitely approve." He closed his eyes and laid out comfortably as instructed. Orlando was thoroughly enjoying his special time with the twins at HE Spa. He spent another hour getting his kinks worked out by Asia above the table and the rest of him pleasured below it by Amani's very skillful methods. It was a refuge Orlando didn't take for granted. Everything that happened at HE Spa stayed at HE Spa, even between the best of friends.

As Orlando awakened on the table after a peaceful nap, Amani wiped away every ounce of evidence with a warm towel.

"So, Grand Poohbah," she said, holding him in her hands and admiring it. "How are you feeling now that you're had a chance to visit our new Owner's Box VIP room?"

"Rather satisfied Amani, thank you," he said, in a free and easy tone. "Yes, I'm feeling undefeated if I do say so myself."

"Same time next month, then?"

"Yeah. Put me down in the book. Same time." He handed her a thousand dollar gift card then thought better of it. "Here take this, just in case the deacon wants to come back on his own." Orlando passed the gorgeous masseuse a card with $2,500 stamped on the front.

"I got you covered Poohbah, and the deacon too. Don't be a stranger."

He said goodbye then tried to gather his faculties once she left the room. Orlando shrugged his shoulders then rolled his neck around. "Wow. Feeling this good has got to be illegal."

After Orlando showered and changed back into his clothes, he looked for Mosley until he found him asleep in the front seat of the Bentley. Orlando got in and closed the door.

"Hey deacon, let's go."

"Oh, sorry. Must've dozed off waiting on your *meeting* to end."

"Did you get Sister Spencer home to her daughters alright?" Orlando asked.

"Yes Sir. She said to tell you thanks for the ride home and your nice words at the hospital."

"Good. Good." Orlando looked at Mosley and wondered if he felt guilty about getting attended to in a place like HE Spa.

"Is there anything that happened during your *meeting* you want to talk about?"

"Sister Carolyn Drew said to call her. She was at Sis' Spenser's when I pulled up."

"Is that it?"

"Everything that's gonna get talked about, yeah."

"Good. Good."

15

RASCALS AND REDEMPTION

The following morning, Orlando made a few calls to get a jump on his day. He reached out to Carolyn but she hadn't returned his text. It had been so long since he fussed with his own taxes, he didn't know where to begin. Carolyn agreed to help him with the impending IRS Audit and he believed she was more than qualified. Nelson's revelation that he was in town to see if he could gather information on the source of Orlando's wealth made him anxious to get his business affairs in order. He sat in his home office, flipping through boxes of receipts while growing flustered.

"*Entertainment*," he said, when a thought came to mind to write off his membership to HE Spa. "I wonder if there's a section for *adult* entertainment." Orlando looked over the papers awhile then he began to sort out pages of auto repair bills, house maintenance, commercial insurance premiums, and bank statements for a number of his rental properties.

When someone rang the doorbell, Orlando shouted for his junior accountant.

"Jessika! That's who needs to be sorting these out."

The doorbell summoned him again.

"JESSIKA," he yelled. "PLEASE GET THE DOOR."

Orlando went to the front door and peeked out through the curtains. He recognized the car in front of his house but didn't expect his tailor.

"Pierre, did I miss an appointment?" he asked, after opening the door.

"No sir," the thin clothing designer said, behind thick sunshades. "I was in the neighborhood so I decided to bring these by."

He handed a long white garment bag to Orlando then turned to leave. "If that will be all. Thanks for your business."

"Hey, hold up Pierre. Come back here for a minute," Orlando demanded. He laid the suits on the sofa arm then met his tailor on the walkway. "What's going on?"

"Yes, Minister Clay?" the young man said, standing as still as possible, although he did flinch when Orlando reached toward his face to remove the dark glasses. Pierre was embarrassed, his right eye was black and swollen shut.

"Pierre, was this personal or business?" Orlando asked, in a way that suggested he wouldn't stand be being lied to.

"It's nothing really. And I don't think it would solve anything so...," he answered quietly. "I'm sorry but I can't service you anymore. I had to, uh, take on an exclusive customer who doesn't want me designing suits for anyone but him, and especially not for you."

"You don't have to be afraid of anyone, especially on my account. Just tell me who the person is and I will have a talk with him."

"Pardon me but you don't know the kind of man he is. He offered me ten thousand dollars and when I refused," Pierre said, before his gaze fell towards the ground in shame. "I shouldn't even be here. I have to go."

Orlando looked at the damage done to an innocent man's eye.

"Did St. Nick do that to your face?"

"I can't say. Thank you for understanding, sir."

"I'm sorry you got mixed up in this. I really am," Orlando told him, with an honest measure of remorse. "This has nothing to do with you."

Pierre's black eye said differently, even though he tried to see Orlando's point. "Okay, then," he said finally, then turned slowly and headed back down the walkway.

Before the tailor made it to his car, Orlando knew it was St. Nick who was sending an indirect message to get Orlando's attention. Orlando didn't have to know why St. Nickolas Boudreaux came to Dallas of all places to set up shop or why he had determined to be a thorny prick in his side. However, Orlando needed to know how embedded his adversary was in the community before reacting with his own brand of annoyance.

Orlando hung up the suits Pierre delivered in his massive walk-in closet. The semi-formal clothes were arranged by color and rows of expensive shoes were organized by their practical use. All of the leather loafers and ankle boots were aligned on the first row, lace-ups and slip-ons were next, then casual canvas shoes and leather house slippers on the top row.

While busying himself in the garage, Orlando remembered why Jessika didn't answer his calls around the house. She agreed to be interviewed by a local news station regarding her funding campaign for Numbers. He shot into the house to turn on the TV when the front door opened. Jessika and Carolyn walked in with lively conversation about bright lights, cameras and show producers, who all thought his niece was a natural. Orlando was caught off guard and woefully unprepared.

"Heyyy Uncle. Did you see the interview?" Jessika asked, in a sing-song manner. She was still bubbling over from her moment in the spotlight. "It was so much fun."

"Oh, uh. I was about to," he said, then closed his mouth when Carolyn gave him a look that told him to keep quiet and go with it.

"Sister Carolyn drove me to the station where everyone was so amazing and treated me like a celebrity," Jessika continued. "They did my makeup, pinned up my hair and even told me what questions they were going to ask so I wouldn't look stupid."

"She did such a good job, Pastor Clay," Carolyn chimed in, quickly. "I do believe a star is born."

Jessika blushed and leaned into Carolyn like a gushing younger sister. "Ahhh, thanks Sister Carolyn. Thanks for driving me and telling me to relax."

Orlando figured it was only a matter of time before he was questioned with what he thought of her performance, so he held his breath. "I am very proud of you and your chaperone for representing Numbers' cause. What is the total now?"

"I'm so glad you asked," Jessika said, with her cell phone in hand.

Orlando walked across the room to see the campaign app at work. "Hold on, let's see how things are... coming... along," she said, while dabbing and sliding her fingertip over several places on her phone screen until she had logged into the app.

"Yes, here it is. Oh wait, something is happening Uncle."

Orlando leaned over her to see the screen better. The numbers were changing like a running stock report. Once the numbers remained static long enough to lock on the totals, his smile began to fade.

"What were the totals before the show? It'll be interesting to see how successful your interview was."

"Around sixty-thousand dollars," Jessika answered plainly, as if she were talking about pennies.

"Now it's climbing passed a hundred and seventy thousand."

Carolyn stepped beside Jessika to look on as well. She was standing so close to Orlando that she felt him breathing.

"Uhh, whew! Look at it go Jessika," she said. They were intrigued at the outpour of support for a man that few would have tossed pocket change at before his heroic rescue.

Orlando noticed how close he was standing to Carolyn when Jessika received a text that broke their spell.

"Who's Latonya On TV?" he asked, after reading the name attached to the text message.

"Duh, LaTonya Stillman from Channel 4," Jessika answered, turning on the television. "She's the reporter who interviewed me this morning and said to tune in right now." She walked closer to the big screen Smart TV and found the channel.

Orlando smelled Carolyn's sweet perfume when she walked over and stood next to him. He tried to pretend it didn't affect him.

"How'd you miss the interview?" Carolyn whispered. "Don't know if I can keep covering for you." She smiled then walked away to join the star of the hour.

Orlando hung back, admiring Carolyn's physique from behind. Her green off-the-shoulder sweater looked especially classic against her even, apricot-colored skin. She seemed quite at ease playing the doting talent manager who genuinely cared about her client's success. Orlando enjoyed the attention Carolyn devoted to Jessika, even though it was only for a brief time, it meant a lot to him. Suddenly, his thoughts were shattered when he was jolted back to reality by Jessika's conversation.

"OMG! Ohhh Emmm Gee!" Jessika screamed over and over again. "This is bananas. What am I going to do?"

"About what?" Orlando asked.

Carolyn shook her head at him while Jessika texted the news reporter back. "Weren't you listening? The fund total just hit a quarter million."

"Dollars?" Orlando asked, with a ton of surprise in his voice.

"When you match the first one-hundred thousand, Uncle Orlando, it will reach almost four hundred thousand," Jessika tabulated, in her head. "This is big. This is really big." She continued to send texts while watching the totals climb on television. "Thank you LaTonya," she mouthed, while texting her gratitude.

"You're matching donations of one-hundred thousand dollars?" Carolyn asked the pastor. "Well, thank you *Uncle Orlando*," she said, affectionately.

Jessika glanced up from her cell phone screen to throw him a smile. "Yes, and thank you too Uncle Orlando. This is so great. Thank you LaTonya, Uncle, and God. Oh my God." Jessika went upstairs with her eyes trained on her phone until she entered her room and turned on the laptop.

She began sending out personal thank-yous online and text messages to organizations who helped to publicize her efforts.

Downstairs, Orlando took a calculated step away from Carolyn.

"Thanks for covering my lack of support for the interview. I got side-tracked and completely forgot."

"You were supportive in spirit," she teased, with a sly wink. "And wonderfully compassionate with your wallet." Carolyn looked in Orlando's office then pointed towards the stacks of invoices and receipts on his desk. "Will I be able to find where the one-hundred thousand donation is coming from if I dig deeply enough in that office?"

"Why don't I deliver the boxes to your office at the church then..."

"...that's a conflict Pastor Clay," she interrupted. "I cannot work on your personal accounting at the church. Why don't you have them shipped to my home," she suggested cordially, "with the two previous year's tax returns then I will reconcile them. In my experience as a CPA, when there is nothing to hide, there is nothing to worry about." Carolyn looked closely to see if Orlando revealed any tale-tale signs that he might have been financially involved in illegal activities.

"It's the IRS Carolyn," he answered, plainly. "There's always something to worry about."

On the other side of town, Duke sat behind the wheel in his plumbing van staring at the active Greyhound bus station downtown. Grunt, who wanted no part of the "ditch and body dump" thought leaving a dead body on a private bus was a horrible plan. So he busied himself by reading the sports section cover to cover instead.

In the thirty minutes they surveilled the depot from a parking lot directly across the street, Duke shooed away several crack and refer dealers and one desperate dope head trying to score. Duke also saw two buses pull in, unload the passengers and their luggage from an underneath cargo compartment.

"Look at that one, Gee. It's empty," Duke said, as he titled his head forward to patrol the loading bay for security.

Grunt peered over the newspaper then shook his head. "There might still be people on the bus who didn't need to stretch their legs. Anyway, it's too many people who could see us with that dead dude either before we drop him off or when we try to get away."

Duke looked at his watch. "It's already after four o'clock. He'll start stinking if we don't come up with something."

"Let's set him on fire somewhere. Everybody else is doing it," Grunt answered, dismissively. "Lazy way to handle business but it makes a big mess of the evidence."

"Yes, it's very unprofessional," Duke agreed. "But I know a real business-like way of getting the same result." He turned the key in the ignition to start up the van then said goodbye to a very bad plan.

After driving to South Dallas, Duke pulled into the unloading dock in the back of South Side Mortuary. Grunt folded the Real Estate section of newspaper over his knee to survey the new location. "Yeah, this could work."

Once inside, they hoisted a large black body bag onto a stainless steel examination table. It made a loud thud.

"Chi-Town, my man with a plan," Duke exhaled, excitedly. "What's good homie?"

The nervous embalmer tried to quiet him. "Shush! What you think this is, an amusement park?" Chi-Town Brown was the Assistant Manager who facilitated over fifty embalming services a week.

He hated the job but it paid well and he thoroughly enjoyed washing the female corpses before the embalming process began.

Chi-Town rubbed his bald head then brushed his manicured beard before leaning his stubby frame against the wooden counter.

"What's *that*?" he asked, suspiciously, as he stared at the long dark bag on his table.

"Don't you mean, *who* is that?" Duke asked.

"I'm assuming there's a deceased individual over there and I don't much care *who* it is. I'd like to know *what* I am supposed to do about it."

"Man, we want you to torch this dude that we croaked by accident," Duke told him, as calmly as if he was asking to have a car washed. "Just go ahead and cremate him then we'll be out of your hair, I mean your scalp," Duke stated, once he realized Chi-Town didn't have any hair.

"Hell no, I won't. No way!" the assistant manager refused. "I left Chicago to get away from this sort of stuff. Take it somewhere else."

"Sorry Chi-Town, but this dude is hella heavy," Duke said. "We should have gutted him, before we left the plumbing shop to let all of the blood drain out first."

"It would have made packing him around town a lot easier," said Grunt, while smacking on a green apple.

Duke leaned his head to the side then pursed his lips disapprovingly. "You must've forgot that little thing we took care of for you, Chi."

"Nah, he ain't forgot," said Grunt, with a mouth full of apple. "Yeah, you was having a problem with the boss of your fine ass neighbor. He told her to give up the drawers or get gone."

"When you went up to her job, trying to regulate, old dude told you to step off or get broke off, didn't he!" Duke argued.

"Yeah, he was bigger than I thought," Chi-Town admitted. "He must've worked out and everything."

"So work this out for us," Duke said, insistently.

"Yeah," Grunt co-signed.

"Okay, that was real cool when y'all ran up on my girlfriend's manager and got all Country BUCK!" Chi-Town became sentimental about the professional manner Duke and Grunt threatened a workplace bully. "I appreciate y'all handling that like some original gangsters."

"So, we good on this here request?" Grunt asked, gesturing at the body bag.

As Chi-Town went over to open the long bag, it moved a little.

Grunt's eyes narrowed.

Duke took a step back.

"Don't worry about that," said the mortician, "sometimes the body has one or two last good twitches in it. By the way, my girl thinks I personally straightened out the situation with the jerk at her office so I get to do… whatever I want to… as a reward for my bravery."

When the bag started moving again and flopping erratically on the table, Chi-Town screamed and hid behind Duke.

"Uhhhhhggggg! Man, what y'all put in there?"

Duke threw up his fists and prepared to scuffle.

Grunt whipped out a large hunting knife and assumed a battle position. "This is some bull! I ain't going out like that."

"Texas Voodoo Zombies!" Grunt hollered, as he advanced towards the floundering bag that flopped up and down like a fish out of water.

He had second thoughts when an arm suddenly pushed its way through the top of it.

"You got to cut off the head to kill them thangs." Grunt raised his knife overhead but Duke stopped him after Brother Grady reached both arms out and unzipped the body bag. The other men watched perilously as the wife-beater popped his head out of the bag like a jack-in-the-box. His matted hair and nappy beard were dripping with sweat as he gasped for breath.

Harvard Grady peered around the embalming room excitedly, as his chest heaved in and out violently, thirsting for oxygen. "Where... in hell... am I?" he huffed between breaths, in a rough voice.

"Nah, you're not in hell yet," Grunt said, irritably.

"It's a funeral home," Duke replied, still in shock. "The embalming suite to be more accurate."

"Whewww! Thought I was dead."

Grunt shrugged it off. "I thought you was a zombie."

"It's a miracle," Duke surmised, as he crossed his chest with his right hand. "Go forth and sin no more."

"But I'm not Catholic," Grady answered.

"And I ain't the Pope so get your woman-beating ass out of here before I dead you myself."

Harvard jumped out of the bag like a trained ninja. He landed on the floor wearing soiled drawers and white tube socks.

"No cause for that. I'm a changed man with a second chance. I'm changing my ways," he announced.

"Change your skid-marked drawers too while you're at it," Grunt heckled, as Grady bolted out of the door.

"Well, that didn't work out like I thought," said Duke. "Not even close."

Chi-Town looked on in amazement. "That's the first time one ever got away."

Duke agreed it must've have been rare to lose a body once it was delivered in a bag. "You still owe us one then?" Duke asked, as an afterthought.

"Yeah-yeah. Y'all got the hookup on the next one. Just make sure he's good and dead first."

Duke was relieved to hear that he could stash a corpse at the South Side Mortuary if it came to that. However, he was not eager to tell Orlando that Harvard Grady, his wayward church member, was still in town and very much alive. Since he didn't see any cause to hurry up and inform his uncle, Duke figured he would bring it up after morning service on the following day. "It can't hurt to wait a day, right?" he asked Grunt, who was the only person that cared less than he did.

When Sunday morning rolled in right on schedule, Methodist Episcopal Greater Apostolic Church seemed to be ready and waiting. Colors of spring were everywhere. Little girls, adorned in vivid orange-crème, sunny yellow and pink dresses by the dozens, showcased their mother's taste as well as their pride. Some of the men burst into the auditorium like rays of sun with bright pastel suits and neckties in various hues, as vibrant as a sixty-four count box of Crayons. There was something special about the signs of spring, especially after a harsher than typical winter.

It was the last Sunday of the month, which meant the teen choir was due to deliver some soul-stirring selections for the congregation. Orlando was warned that news had gotten out about the choir hall incident. He didn't know how to address it but he was dead set against it ruining those children's performance.

The church leadership sat on the front row, just to the right of center where most of the wealthiest members were seated, as a rule. Although Orlando didn't like the thought of doctors, lawyers, business owners and politicians getting preferential treatment. Since seating arrangements were as baked into the church's culture as its hallelujahs and amens, Orlando kept his complaints to himself. He'd learned to pick his battles and kept his powder dry for fights he could win.

At ten o'clock on the nose, Harold Bennet rose to his feet directly in front of the teen choir that was wearing white robes with white satin trim. He stood at attention like a drill sergeant proudly looking over his well-trained recruits. Thirty-three seats were taken by young adults who were sitting perfectly straight with their backs erect and hands placed on their knees. When the choir director stomped his left foot one time, the entire heard of singers stood on one accord.

Orlando watched from sideline as the director raised his hands and pointed upward. Immediately and without fail, every choir member threw their heads back and gazed toward the ceiling. The audience was attentive and waiting to see what happened next. Softly the boys in the choir began to hum in a syncopated beat.

"Mmmm, mmm-mmm-mmm-mmm. Mmm-mmm mmm-mmm. Mmm-mmm-mmm-mmmmm-mmmm." Then they started swaying to the left and right in striking precision, not one of them in a hurry or out of step.

Suddenly, the elderly pianist got up and walked off stage. Lucinda, the oldest girl caught up in the choir room controversy, sat down on the bench and banged a single white key that meshed heavenly with the choir members hums. They kept humming and swaying, all while looking up. When some of the older members in the audience realized what song Lucinda was playing, they stood up too.

Out of nowhere, a strong high pitched voice spilled out of the speakers like an angel's breath on the winds of God.

"Some… times in our lives, we all have pain. We all have sorroooow. But, if we are wise, we know that there's always tomorrooow," Charlotte, the younger sister sung.

She was on fire, filled with the spirit, unabashed and more importantly unashamed. She was standing proudly before many of the same people who were saying vile things about her. Charlotte was fearlessly giving it to them good, unapologetically, and with both lungs.

"SANG THAT SONG, BABY GIRL!" a woman shouted, from the balcony.

"Lean on Jesus! He won't let you down," Gwen Spencer said, to encourage her daughter.

The chorus lowered their heads towards the audience and sang boldly, "Lean on me, when you're not strong. And I'll be your friend. I'll help you caaaarry on. For, it won't be long, til I'm gonna need somebody to leeeeean on."

234

As the young members lifted their voices in song, more people stood up and clapped on beat or sang along with Charlotte. She promised herself to go out on stage and deliver the message that Sister Carolyn Drew made her believe in, that everybody needs somebody to lean on from time to time.

Before this Sunday, Gwen Spencer, the girls' mother, began receiving calls asking whether the rumors about her daughter's sexual behavior were true. Carolyn warned her that might happen so she was prepared, telling them that if their children never made a mistake they were embarrassed about, then she would be happy to share every sordid detail. Not one of those busy bodies had the nerve to cast the first stone. As her children's amplified sounds of joy and forgiveness rose in the auditorium, church members knew it wouldn't have been in their best interest to keep that bit of gossip going.

By the end of the song, almost every girl in the choir was wiping away tears and so were a many of their mothers. There must have been more than enough untold stories and family secrets to go around the congregation that day. No accusers could be found among them.

When Orlando took the stage, his smile was wide. His face glowed with a magnificent hope that people could change and even learn to mind their own business every now and then. He approached the podium at center stage with his hands held high.

"Hallelujah church! Can I get an Amen?" he roared.

"Amen, pastor!" someone answered.

"Yes lawd. Amen," another responded.

"Glory," Sister Spencer said, sitting next to Carolyn.

Orlando was hyped and overzealous. Each time he tried to steady himself, his feet were moving again. He walked along the stage, in front of the choir then slapped high fives to the singers as the drummer and organist played along. He paused long enough to give Lucinda and Charlotte hugs, while they sat in their rightful places. It was a joyful jam session until the pastor circled back around and stopped at the podium again.

He tried to reign himself in but seeing those sisters who faced their fears and confronted a multitude of people, who had unkind things to say about them beforehand, kept him revved up. Watching the girls step out of the shadows and rock the house was incredible.

"Can I get a grand amen for the teen choir this morning?" he said, shaking his head and surging with vitality. After his 'Amen Corner' came through with a chorus of support, Orlando opened his bible. "If you brought your swords, hold them up and say, I do." He laughed out loud when he noticed something strange in the audience's reaction. "Now how come only the sisters and married brothers said *I do*? Single fellas were like, *Uhh-uh man, I ain't ready to say that in no way and no where.*"

The audience howled and erupted with laughs and merriment. Even Deacon Mosley's wife cracked up because she knew he was right.

"He's so silly," Carolyn said, to Sister Spencer. "This week has been hard for him too."

"I could tell when he came to the hospital," she agreed. "He's a good man, Carolyn."

Carolyn Drew cut her eyes at Sister Spencer like, *I know what you're trying to do Gwen.*

"Uhh-huh," was all Sister Spencer had to say. Carolyn understood exactly what the girls' mother was getting at. Regardless of what people were saying behind Orlando's back, he was still kind and caring to them, even when they didn't deserve it.

As the audience began to calm down, Orlando gave a serious expression then jumped right in to his lesson.

"Okay then, I came to preach the word and y'all came to get the word. You might not believe everything I tell you but you need to keep up with this sermon and best believe everything that I show you." He wiped his forehead with a folded kerchief with a blue paisley design. "Do you believe that God talks to you? The reason I ask because some people do and others do not. Even still, some believers do and others do not. Well, let's not fight about it. Let's see what the word has to say then we'll both be alright about it. Turn with me to Second Timothy, chapter three and verse sixteen. All scripture is what?"

"God breathed," the congregation replied in unison.

"That's right, God breathed, and is useful for our teaching, rebuking, correcting and training in righteousness," he read aloud. "I know what some of y'all are thinking because I thought it too, a long time ago. You're saying to yourselves, of course the Word of God is His voice but that's not really what I'm talking about." There were lots of heads nodded and agreeing so Orlando knew he had a captive audience who wanted to learn.

"What else you have to say about it, Preacher?" an older man said, from behind a thick pair of bifocals.

"I'm glad you asked," Orlando answered. "Meet me in the good book at John, chapter ten and verse twenty-four. Now this was happening at the last Winter of Jesus' life. How do I know that? Verse twenty-two says it was winter and I know that the Jews were tracking Him, trying to trap Him and were even lying on Him. Jesus was a marked man and even though he was healing the blind and casting demons out of people, some people still wanted Him dead. Y'all still with me?"

"Yes sir," Mosley answered, with his nose in the bible. "Get on with it."

"Look at verse number twenty-four. It reads, the Jews gathered around him saying, 'how long will you keep us in suspense. If you are the Christ, tell us plainly.' " Orlando looked up from his bible and smiled cunningly. "See, I told you they were after Him and He knew it. My question to you is, if you know this winter we just had was your last, would you do anything differently? Everything differently? Some of y'all sisters need to wear your clothes differently," he joked. "At least in the church house, but I digress."

Several people shouted their agreement but a multitude tightly-skirted sisters refrained from supporting that notion altogether.

"Back to the Bible I go. Verse twenty-five, Jesus answered, 'I did tell you but you did not believe me. The miracles I perform in my Father's name speak for me. But, you do not believe because you are not my sheep. My sheep listen to my voice. I know them and they follow me.' " Orlando walked in front of the podium to get everyone's attention. "So, first of all, we know that Jesus speaks for God, amen?"

"Yes, He does," Mosley answered.

"You get an amen on that preacher," said Brother Simon, after he woke up from a cat nap.

"Good, that's at least two of y'all still hanging on," the pastor remarked, cleverly. "Some of you all have to be thinking that Jesus isn't here. Who talks to us now? Good, back to the book we go. Let's head on over there to Hebrews three and seven. It reads... 'So, as the Holy Spirit said, today if your hear His voice, do not harden your hearts as in the rebellion, on the day of testing in the wilderness, where your fathers tested me, tried me, and saw my works for forty years.'" Orlando stroked his chin and eyed the audience suspiciously. "Was it the Holy Spirit that had those Hebrews roaming the wilderness after freeing them from Egyptian bondage? No, it was God but he sent the Holy Spirit to speak on his behalf."

"I'm half way there but I need a little push, Brother Clay," Sister Betty Burlington shouted, from her perch.

"Oh, I like a challenge. Let's go all the way back then and settle this right here and right now. I will prove that the Holy Spirit is God's Spirit. And in saying that, the Holy Spirit would have had to be here as soon as God was here. I see some of y'all shaking your heads and still need some convincing. Good, look at Genesis one, verse two. That's right, y'all just told me the Holy Spirit had to be in the beginning if it was speaking for God. So look, listen, and watch. Verse two of chapter one, a few words after *In The Beginning*... 'Now the world was formless and empty, darkness was over the surface of the deep and the Spirit of God was hovering over the waters.' Who was hovering over the waters?"

"The Holy Spirit!" shouted Charlotte, from the choir stand.

"I bet y'all heard that," Orlando said happily. "Then after God made the light and the land and the vegetables and fruit, then he separated night from day and he saw that it was good. Then in verse sixteen he created two great lights, meaning the Sun and Moon. In verses twenty and twenty-one he got around to making birds and creatures of the sea and now we get all the way home in verse twenty-six."

Orlando dusted his shoulders off and tugged at his French cuffs before he wrapped his sermon up with a beautiful spring-time bow. "Verse twenty-six of Genesis, Chapter One reads, then God said, let Us… let who?"

"Us!" the congregation answered.

"That's right. God said. Let Us make man in Our image," Orlando said. "Not if, but since, God said let Us make man in our image, God was not talking to himself and God was not alone. In all of the verses before this point, who have we read about being with God, hovering above the water?"

"The Holy Spirit," sighed Sister Betty Burlington, from the front row. "Okay, you got me good, pastor," she admitted loudly.

"Go head on preacher," Mosley said, prideful and loud. "Go head on then."

Orlando signaled to the organ player to crank it up and start out low. "So listen church family. God's actual words would probably pierce our eardrum because they're so pure, powerful and mighty so he gave us a comforter that talks *to us* when we need to hear his voice and direction. The comforter also speaks *for us* when we pray to God because we are not worthy enough to go directly to the King of Kings. The Holy Spirit is our advocate and one heck of a diplomat. He can get prayers through that have no business flying out of our mouths."

The choir began to hum a few bars of *Take Me to The King* as some of the deacons stood up to pass the collection baskets.

Orlando paced slowly on the front of the stage, collecting his thoughts, while bringing the message home like a trained actor nailing a monologue to close the show.

"Church, the next time you say, *something* told me this or that or *something* told me to call and see about you, that's the Holy Spirit reminding us to be there for each other, to lean on one another like the Holy Spirit has been *for* us from the beginning of time. Amen."

"I GOT TO DO IT!" a man hollered, from the back of the room.

Mosley stood up from his position in the second row, just to the left-center of the stage. He took a protective position on the stage in front of Orlando, who was thinking, *not this foolishness again.* Although this time was much different.

"I want to be baptized, pastor! Don't let them take me out. I WANT TO BE SAVED," the stranger hollered, as Duke and Grunt grabbed him. "Tell 'em to let me go, pastor. HOLY SPIRIT, HEEEELP!"

This disruptor had a medium brown complexion, wore a fitted tan-colored suit, and was clean shaven with a closely cropped hair style. Other than the loud outbursts, he looked normal.

People in the audience were moving out of the way, as he raved on like a lunatic. Orlando watched the scene play out from the stage while Duke and Grunt marched in step with their hands firmly around the stranger's arms to restrain him.

"Let him go, brothers," Orlando said, before he recognized who the disrupter was. "Bring this man up here."

Duke and Grunt reluctantly ushered the man up the stairs leading to the stage.

Once he was free to say his peace, he made the most of it. "Brother Preacher. I'm sorry for what I done," the tormented man said. "Sorry for the pain I caused, for the times I raised my hands to my wife, Sister Grady."

The sight of the man standing before Orlando caused him to recoil when the man's identity hit the pastor like a ton of bricks. He leaned away to study the disruptor better. Harvard Grady had shaved off his nappy beard and also hacked off all of the matted mess of an afro. He looked a great deal more presentable than the angry wife-beater that was chained to the lawnmower in Duke's plumbing shop.

"So you want to testify, Brother Grady?" Orlando asked, then glared curiously at Duke for letting this man escape. "Go ahead brother, the stage is yours."

Grady grabbed a microphone from Orlando then walked to the edge of stage to address the congregation in his own way.

"Baby, I'm sorry but first I want to say hi to my momma and Auntie Jane. Oh, and a shout out to the people from my block. What's up Cisco, Donny Jr., Pookie... Ray-Ray. They're my boys and they know me. They know I get mad sometimes but that's no reason to hit a woman," Brother Grady relented, with tears streaming down his face. "I was sure it was the right way to do things in a marriage but I was wrong. Yesterday, I died y'all. DIDN'T I DUKE?" Grady asked, while staring naughtily at the plumber who had terrorized him.

When Duke made an attempt to climb the stage from the right side, Brother Grady gripped the microphone tighter. To be safe, he dipped onto the other side of Orlando then continued his testimony in the spotlight. Mosley quietly entered onto the stage from a side door. He sneaked out onto the platform slowly then prowled behind

242

Grady while he was busy saying more than he should have.

"And I was dead but I rose like Jesus and I'm gonna do better with my second chance. God heard my humble cry y'all. I'm sorry and I am a better man because of the mean things some people did to me," he said, before Mosley slapped the microphone out of his hand.

As Mosley grabbed Grady around the shoulders and wrestled him off the stage, the audience cheered. Some of them were renewed by a repentant man's apology but all of them were thoroughly entertained by his bold antics.

Orlando picked up the microphone then held it up to his mouth.

"Amen!" Orlando shouted. "Get that man into some water and dunk him good too," the pastor instructed, quickly. "The Bible says in Mark, chapter sixteen and verse sixteen that 'Whoever believes and is baptized will be saved but whoever does not believe will be condemned.' " He looked over the crowd as Mosley lead Harvard away to the baptismal pool. "I know some of y'all don't believe in baptism or second chances but I got book, chapter, and verse. Acts second chapter, verses thirty-eight through forty-one says Peter replied, 'Repent and be baptized, every one of you, in the name of Jesus Christ for the forgiveness of your sins. And then you will receive the gift of the Holy Spirit.' " Orlando closed the bible then wiped his brow. "Don't hate me if y'all don't agree. Take that up with the Lord. Now, let the church sing."

As some of the church members stood around gawking at yet another spectacle at M.E.G.A., others sung praises to God. The tithes and offerings baskets were passed and the choir harmonized sweetly. Orlando's eyes found Carolyn's glimmering back at him in a sea of beautiful colors and convicted Christians. The pastor didn't have any idea how Brother Grady made it back to church with a kinder, gentler spirit and he didn't really want to know. Something had transformed a black-hearted husband. Orlando hoped whatever happened to him could have been replicated on other men who struck their wives. That was a sickness he never learned to understand.

16

MOJO MONDAYS

The last Monday of the month was special to many of the local pastors, who made it a point to have fun and fellowship, let their hair down, and spend time with their side chicks. Because it was problematic to participate in romantic flings in the public eye, ministers often found other avenues to take out their *other women* on dates and make them feel appreciated.

Pool halls, veteran lodges and even barbershops provided a secret solution for powerful married men of the cross to take girl-friends and consort with less desirables, without being seen by members of their congregations. Bishop's was high on the list of most mega-church ministers and visiting clergy who wanted to take a load off, skirt chase, flirt with women out in the open, and get their mojo back after a hard month of preaching and praying.

Bishop offered membership cards to men he knew personally or those suggested by current members. The monthly fee was $100, which took care of security, a hearty buffet, adult beverages, quality music and most of all, anonymity. Privacy was at a premium. There were only two things that caused someone to lose their membership cards to Mojo Mondays. Association was revoked if a man's side chick showed out or his wife showed up. Those two infractions resulted in ministers getting tossed out permanently. These were firm rules, no exceptions.

Outside the barbershop, luxury cars were parked next to the cement walkway. Shiny Lexus coupes, Lincoln Navigators, S-Series Mercedes, a sporty Tesla and a couple of Bentleys were guarded by paid security guards. Mickey Bombay stood watch outside the front door. His towering presence squashed a multitude of altercations. He didn't like roughing up important men who got out of line. It didn't happen often but at times whiskey treats in the middle of the afternoon made members act out of character. When it was necessary, Mickey stepped inside to pull their coats and regulate the drama. He reminded members to behave or be gone. It was already a delicate situation to tip out on wives in broad day light. Being told to calm down by a six-foot seven, three hundred and sixty pound former pro-football defensive lineman was hardly worth the argument.

Inside of Bishop's, on Mojo Monday, the shop windows were covered with black plastic to darken the room and set the mood. The deejay spun club music and slow jams while couples mingled and had their fill at the open bar. Today's catch was catfish fillets and crab cakes. The buffet was catered by Bishop's older sister Ophelia, who loved seeing wealthy men eat and watching the shenanigans that were sure to play out before the last piece of catfish was gone.

"Make sure to keep the fire can under that pan lit," Bishop said. "Nobody likes cold fish and it stinks up the place."

Ophelia was seventy-three years old and figured she had been on this earth too long to be told what to do by her only surviving brother. She parked her meaty fists on her wide hips and cocked her head to the side, disapprovingly. "Get on away from here, Bishop. If something starts smelling up the place, it won't be on this side of the table."

His attitude changed when the door kept opening with additional guests. "We gonna be packed all day," he said, with a warm smile. "I can tell."

"I brought some yard bird to put out when the fish is ate up," Ophelia informed him.

"Side chicks and chicken? Sounds good to me," Bishop teased, with a chilled glass of Hennessey in his hand. He surveyed the room as more members strolled in, arm in arm with women who they wouldn't be caught dead with outside of Bishop's private soirée. Women who partied for a living and offered up whatever they had to for expensive party gifts were common at The Mojo, as the barber often called his setup. Retired strippers and call girls with the day off also enjoyed the comforts of this makeshift hedonistic bazaar.

Slim Woody brought his bottom dollar prostitute as a reward for bringing in the most dough and keeping the other girls in his stable in check.

Felicia, who the fellas called Leasha, was built like a shake dancer past her prime. She was the color of dark chocolate and wore a straight blonde weave that reached her shoulders. Leasha's huge breasts sagged a bit and hips stretched the seams of her tight blue jeans but her smile was magical and her wicked whispers had customers doubling back as soon as their paychecks cleared the bank. Her tragic flaw, other than making poor career choices, was talking entirely too much about things better left unsaid.

Three pastors from the north side traipsed in. Two of them had young women barely out of high school in tow. The third minister shuffled in behind his very pregnant twenty-five year old mistress who paraded around like she was princess of the palace. Tuesday Sudderth was a single mom and bet heavily on the promise her boyfriend made on giving her the First Lady of his congregation title, as soon as he divorced his current wife, Donna.

"Have a seat, baby," Minister Josiah Turnbolt said, quietly. "You're going to make somebody nervous."

Tuesday, sauntered back and forth in a long printed sun dress and clog heels as if she didn't hear what he said. "I'll sit down when I get good and ready, Jo," she replied eventually. I don't like the way that girl over there is looking at me."

Josiah, a sharp dresser and slight in size, walked over to his intended bride and wrapped both arms around her waist as far as he could. "Come on now babe, we talked about this on the way over here in the car."

She threw her nose in the air and pouted. "I don't know why we have to keep coming here anyway. None of these brothers in here want the real thing. They're just speculating. I can't wait until I'm Mrs. Turnbolt then we won't have to come back here no more."

Seated on the sofa near their loveseat at end of customer's row, Slim had been half-listening to their conversation but noticed Leasha was ear-hustling the entire thing. "What's going on with that pregnant girl that won't sit her butt down?" Slim asked his date.

"Other than her being young and stupid? She won't sit her pregnant butt down," Leasha answered. "She really thinks he'll change once her name goes on the marriage license."

"Oh yeah," Slim said, looking at Tuesday's chubby face and breast cleavage. "She's young and tender is all. She'll learn though."

"Oh but to be young, dumb, gullible and stupid," Leasha said, in retrospect.

"Heyyyy look who it is," Slim hailed loudly, as Orlando and Mosley came through the front door. "The luckiest sucka who ever shook a pair of dice."

Leasha did a double take. She adjusted her bra and cooed softly. "Come on over here daddy. I'll show you why Jesus rose on the third day."

Tuesday was looking at Orlando too, although she did not appreciate Leasha's comment. "It certainly wasn't for any of that worn out coochie that you've been slinging around for years," she said, turning to face the prostitute. "Quality recognizes quality. You don't stand a chance with a rich man like that."

"Trick please," Leasha spat, preparing to stand up. "Bet I know more about pleasing yo' man than you do, honey."

"I got this, Leasha. Chill out and let it go," Slim Woody said, then leaned towards Josiah Turnbolt to whisper some valuable advice. "Hey man, no disrespect but you gotta check your girl, bruh."

"I'm sorry y'all. She's hard to please with the baby coming and all," Josiah said. He shot a stinging glare at his pregnant mistress. But she returned it with one of her own.

"You don't have to apologize for me," Tuesday hissed, angrily, then plopped down on the cushioned bench.

She began to cool herself with a decorated accordion fan then started up again. "Who do they think they are, all boo'd up in this barbershop like it's a bed and breakfast or something. Child please. I'm hungry, Josiah. Get me some fish!"

Josiah got up to head towards the buffet table, believing he was in an un-winnable situation. Orlando met him by the table to offer some friendly advice. "

Hey Josiah, Tuesday is really coming along, huh?"

"Yeah man, she is and getting meaner by the day," Josiah sighed.

"What is she, about eight months?" Orlando guessed.

"That and a week," Josiah added, as he piled catfish onto a Styrofoam plate.

"You still going to marry that girl?"

"I aim to, yeah," the young preacher answered, affirmatively.

Orlando stuck out his hand. "Give it to me, then," he said, with a regretful tone.

"What's that?"

"Your Mojo Monday card. Hand it over," Orlando demanded.

"Why Orlando?" he answered, panicked at the thought. "Tuesday's doing too much I agree but it's nothing that I can't shut down. Watch this here." Josiah turned toward Tuesday as she traded unflattering glances with Leasha. "Hey baby, ease up now and relax before we get asked to leave." He smiled at Orlando as if all of his troubles were over. "See there, told you."

"You act like I want to be here in the first place," Tuesday howled back. "Last month, the chicken was dry and the sweet potato pie was runny."

Slim Woody grimaced when he saw where this was headed. Bishop wiped his mouth nervously and hoped Ophelia hadn't heard the comments about her cooking. Unfortunately, she had.

"Who is this blowed up bimbo over here criticizing my food?" Ophelia argued.

"Who you calling bimbo, ma'am? You must have me mixed up with one of these hoochiefied heffas sitting over there," Tuesday replied.

Orlando and Josiah watched the women battle back and forth with their words until the wiser of the two men made it plain for the other one.

"Look at your girl, Jo'. She's showing out like a spoiled brat. It's obvious she doesn't want to be here. Even worse, she doesn't want you coming here without her if and when y'all do get married."

Josiah contemplated the scenario then dug deep down in his pocket. "But what if you have Tuesday all wrong, man."

"JO-SIAH!" Tuesday screamed. "This chick is over here talking about *I ain't this and you ain't gone married me.* This place is fool's paradise. Oomph! More like a fool's factory. Ain't nothing but foolish women up in here and fool-hearted men chasing them all the way to the bedroom."

Bishop stood up from his chair then headed straight for the young minister. "I can't have this up in my place, Josiah. You know the rules," he leveled, plainly.

As Bishop walked by Tuesday to address her man, she flashed a satisfied grin. Orlando held out his hand, again. This time Josiah placed a plastic red card in it.

"Even a fool in paradise can see when his hoe wants to be treated like a housewife," Bishop said, authoritatively.

"*Hoe*," Tuesday wailed, loudly. "The woman who made those nasty, doughy, hush puppies is a hoe."

Ophelia stepped around the food table to stand her ground and defend her food quality. "Somebody hold me back before I give this little girl the whooping she's been asking for."

"Hey, wait a doggone minute!" Josiah said, wrapping foil over the plate of food he'd just made. "We're leaving y'all. I'm sorry. Tuesday, get your purse. I am so sorry for this disturbance."

He wrestled Tuesday out of the front door just as Bombay stepped inside to shut down the disturbance.

Orlando put the membership card in his pocket for safe keeping. "See. Told you," he said, to himself, feeling totally vindicated.

People laughed at the exhibition and most of them found it hard to believe how Tuesday behaved. The deejay played a chorus of that famous Ray Charles hit. "*Hit the road Jack, and don't you come back, no more, no more, no more, no more. Hit the road Jack.*"

Mosley had been observing the catastrophe waiting to happen from the second barber's chair. He walked beside Orlando then gave his appraisal of the way things turned out. "Well, that's one way to get kicked out," Mosley said. "Long way around but effective, nonetheless."

Big Ray walked in with a slow stride wearing his signature uniform of faded jeans and an oversized polo shirt. "Hey everybody. What's up?" he said cordially, then slapped hands with Bishop's protégé. "What's good B-Boy?"

"Trying to come up," Byron answered. "You know how it do, Big Ray."

"Keep it legit," Ray answered. "Prison ain't nothing to fonk with." He signaled to Bishop that something was up that needed to be discussed discretely. Bishop read his eyes then sat his glass of liquor on the counter, above the drawer he kept his pistol in.

"I'll get the speaker?" he said, in a hushed tone.

"Nah Bishop," Big Ray answered. "No need to involve heat into this. I got security for a reason, so you don't worry. Plus I got Mickey Bombay out front and two of my goons covering the back."

Two of Big Ray's toughest bouncers stood guard over the alley and managed who came in through the back door. Only clothing vendors, shoe boosters and jewelry merchants were allowed in. It was merely a precaution but one that worked.

Orlando saw the soft exchange between Bishop and Big Ray, his Mojo Monday event planner. Without alarming Mosley, he nudged his friend slightly. "Something is up deacon. You strapped?"

"Always, when I'm watching your back."

"Might not be anything but watch yourself."

"I have the say and it's okay for now," Bishop said to Ray. "But if there's any foolishness, shut it down and we'll worry about the clean up later."

Big Ray nodded his agreement then exited through the front door just as calmly as he entered. Who was allowed to enter was completely his call, one that the old man hoped he didn't regret just making. Ray knew better than overriding Bishop's decision, considering it was his private event and establishment.

Mosley got his hands on a sports magazine then took a seat near the door and waited. Orlando suddenly felt in the mood to pass the time another way when Slim Woody's top money earner started making eyes at him.

"Come over here, sugar," Leasha said, what she'd been thinking since Orlando walked in. "You sure are a pretty fine thing."

"Not nearly as fine as you," he replied, with one eye on Slim. "I'm Orlando, good to meet you." Pimps were often quite particular about their street inventory, especially if they were off the stroll at the time. Some men even fell in love with their workers, as oddly as it sounds. Orlando wasn't sure if Slim was treating the woman to a walk in the park or putting her out to see what she could hook. Orlando had no intentions of getting involved with Leasha but having another ally might come in handy later.

"I noticed you didn't have a date when you showed up," she said, still looking him over sensually. "If you're not waiting on anybody, I'd like to say some thangs to you, if I may."

"What do they call you," Orlando asked, knowing she had a street name.

"They call me Leasha but you can call me anything you want to," she answered, in a come-hither tone.

"Hey Slim, is Leasha on the clock or purely freelancing?" Orlando asked, to acknowledge he was preserving protocol with her boss.

"She on her own today. Trying to show her the finer things in life. It's time to celebrate. Leash done set a sales record for making that magic and that money," he replied. "I was thinking of getting a plaque and putting her name on it like they do at the car dealership."

Leasha laughed at the outrageous statement and so did Orlando, who was now eying the front door. "Let me whisper something in your ear," she said, hoping he would oblige.

Orlando smiled then leaned closer to her.

Leasha, caressed the back of his head while she made a proposal that shook Orlando. His eyes grew wide then he pulled away and stumbled backward jokingly.

"You got me reaching for my wallet. Want me to dump it out right here or will you take a check?" he cackled.

"Whatevers clever. As long as it spends, you can get all the way in," she answered, loud enough to advertise.

"Whooooaaaa, shiiiid," someone heckled from nearby. "It's about to get real up in here."

When the front door opened, few people seemed to notice. Bishop, Mosley and Orlando were three that did. Big Ray came through first, followed by St. Nick with Boojie and Posha on his arms. The same bodyguard who previously worked for Slim Woody, strolled in after them.

"Like I was saying," Leasha continued, "whatever you're blessed with, I can get with. Know what I'm saying?"

"Hold on Leash," Slim interrupted, gesturing toward the front door. "Looks like a new member is getting his card."

Orlando looked on as if he couldn't believe his eyes when they met St. Nick's, then he looked passed the man he'd rather not ever see again to encounter Posha's steely gaze. She pretended that Orlando's presence didn't mean a thing her. Boojie's initial expression was altogether different. She smiled warmly at him then hit her sister with a promising grin.

Big Ray brought the new arrivals to the center of the room. "Listen up Y'all. We have a potential member for Mojo Monday. I present to y'all St. Nickolas Boudreaux, a businessman, club and restaurant owner. Bishop is cool with his membership offer." Ray handed Bishop a stack of bills with a $2,000 bank strap around it.

"Bishop is cool with the dues. If anybody got something to say about this man not being a part of this thing y'all got going here, say something now and get it out of the way or forever, and I mean forever, hold your peace."

None of the men who had heard of St. Nick wanted any parts of denouncing him to his face. Orlando had plenty of objections but thought it better to let this play out, on his terms. Slim refused to make eye contact with the gangster but couldn't help wondering how his old bodyguard, Tony Tubbs, had connected to someone with a tough reputation and penchant for violence like St. Nick.

Slim sneakily brushed an index finger across his lips to quiet Leasha. Her gift of gab often made an appearance at the worse times. Slim did not want it to happen when a new comer, with looser morals than his, was near enough to make him sorry for bringing her.

Bishop didn't get any push back from Orlando, which is the only person he was really concerned about, so he raised his glass.

"To our newest member, St. Nick. May your drinks be strong and your days be long. We're all friends here until we ain't. Only two things to lose this card, your side chick shows out..."

"Or your wife shows up," Big Ray said, joyfully.

"Get your Mojo on," Bishop said, to the group standing in the middle of the floor.

"That's what's up. Pass me another drink," said one of the north Dallas ministers, who arrived with Josiah. "Mojo, baby!"

Orlando walked casually to the beverage table and poured two glasses of champagne from a half-full bottle, while St. Nick and his guard showed the ladies around the room. When the bottle was empty, Orlando sat it down then turned around to hide it behind him on the table.

Mickey Bombay watched from the front door, just as Big Ray ordered him to. As the new member and his entourage approached the beverage table, Orlando handed a glass of bubbly to Posha then one to Boojie.

"Ladies," it's always a pleasure seeing you. He leaned in to kiss his old girlfriend on the cheek. Posha smiled agreeably then Boojie jutted out her cheek as well. Without seeking permission from St. Nick, Orlando planted a brotherly kiss on her.

"Such a gentleman," she said, before sipping from her wine glass.

"Ain't nobody said you could run your lips all over Mr. Boudreaux's woman or his business partner. I ought to make you apologize," Tony said, as he stepped up to challenge Orlando. Before Tony knew what hit him, Orlando had whipped that champagne bottle off the table and smashed it against the body-guard's head.

"Ooooooh!" Byron yelled, utterly shocked.

Everyone in the shop awed at the swift and violent way Orlando ended a scuffle that he didn't start. Slim and Leasha were excited. Boojie was turned on, Posha and St. Nick were surprised that To-ny-the-bodyguard was disposed of so easily.

"I don't like him," Orlando said, to St. Nick. "We had a run in before and he keeps coming out on the wrong end." Posha pulled Boojie out of arms-length to protect her, in the event that the squabble escalated further.

"Come over here, Sis," Posha said, to Boojie. "Let them work this out amongst themselves."

"I don't like you Nick, not at all," Orlando said, with resolve behind his words. "Maybe you feel the same way about me. This place belongs to a friend of mine. Let's agree to respect it, unless you feel some type of way about what happened to your muscle," Orlando added, referring to the guy lying on the floor.

Spectators looked on pensively, wondering if Orlando and St. Nick would go at it in the middle of the barbershop. Bishop was hoping it didn't come to blows, or worse.

"Who, Tony? As soon as he comes to, he's fired," St. Nick huffed, without a care in the world. "And no, I can't stand the sight of you one bit, Orlando. However, this is a place of relaxation so I'm in no mood to cause a ruckus."

Eventually, Tony began to stir on the ground. He woke up holding his head with his right hand. "Which one of y'all hit me while I wasn't looking?" Tony asked, with a pound of attitude.

"You looking now?" Orlando asked, then kicked him in the face. "You should have known better than to come back in here after our first disagreement."

Big Ray told his two bouncers to carry the man out through the back door and put him in the car but St. Nick objected. "Hell no, don't do that. He's terminated. Take him out with the trash."

The beefy bouncers grabbed his arms and legs then dragged him out.

"Dayyyyum," Slim Woody jeered, "there he goes again. Bye Tony, the worst bodyguard in the history of the world."

When the strong men reached the alley, they realized there was nowhere to put him so they raised him off the ground and into the large blue dumpster he went. A loud thud was heard on the inside.

Back inside of the shop, Leasha was enamored with Orlando after she witnessed him in action. Boojie was also quite taken with the pastor, much to Posha's dismay.

"Watch your moves little girl," she said. "These grown men play for keeps."

"I see what's going on and I like it," she answered, pulling away from Posha. "Can I have another drink?" Boojie said, waiting on Orlando to answer.

"Why don't we let someone else attend to that," he answered, evenly. "Enjoy the event. Good seeing y'all again." Orlando smiled in passing. "Mosley, let me holler at you a minute."

Leasha was studying St. Nick and Orlando's interaction with the ladies. She looked at Slim with a peculiar expression. "Can I talk now, daddy?"

"Might as well. I'm damn sure speechless."

"Why you didn't tell me they get raw up in here? I thought it was gonna be mostly persnickety Negros and the women who fall for that sort of jive. This right here," she said with her finger pointing toward the shop, "is some Hoes and Housewives of the Pulpit Pimps. This is ratings gold and all they need is about three cameras rolling nonstop to make it a hit, Slim. Oh yeah, you can bring me back here every month. Ain't even got to buy me nothing when the mobile bazaar begins either." Leasha pulled out her phone to text someone what she witnessed.

"Put that phone away and hold that thought. Here come the first vendor." Slim sat up on his chair and rubbed his hands together. "What they got? Dresses, pantsuits and whatnot? See, you get to pick out something nice to nuzzle them thick yams of yours."

The first clothes merchant brought in racks of department store labels, all with tags still on them, the selling had officially began. Women in the barbershop snapped to attention then eagerly sorted through rows of garments. Meanwhile, most of the men drank, amused themselves with their women's excitement for name brands and new fashions.

Most of the women wanted everything they saw but Posha and her younger sister sat comfortably on the loveseat sipping while the other women went straight at it. Spending money wasn't anything new to them but spending someone else's dough, neither of the Holywater sisters had gotten used to that. They had access to money, their own, and appreciated how hard it was to make it so the sisters remained still and observed as their contemporaries swarmed like locusts.

Big Ray witnessed the merchant taking back a dress when one of the men disagreed with the price. Watching this, Boojie felt sorry for the woman who had to return something she really liked.

"Ooh he cheap," she grumbled to Posha, when the young woman had to be wrestled away from a pair of low-rise crop jeans with embroidered pockets. "I know where she can get them for a hundred and fifty, on sale. I'll pull her to the side and put her on some real game."

"Don't go getting involved in these people's business Boojie," said Posha. "Mind your own."

"Next!" Big Ray announced, then clapped his hands twice overhead. Shuttling people in and out took some planning and foresight. No two sellers were in at the same time and neither could stay unless someone wanted to spend money on their wares.

Leasha sipped on a whiskey sour as the first wholesaler gathered his wares to leave. "Wonder if he would move faster if I made my butt clap? There was not one stitch of that mess in my size."

Orlando stood near the front door seething as St. Nickolas and his guests enjoyed the spectacle. "I ought to run down there and slap a fat knot on his fat head."

"You find out what he might be up to?" Mosley asked, as he picked at fried fish on a small plate.

"You mean why he set up shop in Dallas?" Orlando questioned, for clarity.

"I'm wondering why he's posted up in Bishops', knowing this is where you hang out?"

"You think he knew that?" Orlando asked.

"My wife even knew that," Mosley replied, sorely.

Orlando gave it some thought. "Well, guess I'd better go over there and kick up more aggravation than Nick expected. I'm tired of avoiding conflict since it appears that's what St. Nick is after."

"It's about time," Mosley said, with a grin the devil would have envied.

"Go to the car and bring back the envelope that's stuffed in the spare tire compartment in the trunk." Mosley spun on a dime then headed for the car. Orlando headed in the other direction, looking for trouble.

The next merchant wheeled in nine-foot long racks, aligned with an assortment of high end shoes. His assistant rolled in two carts with his more expensive brands on display. The Italian sales-man was proud of his assortment of Jimmy Choo, Badgly Mischka, Sigerson Morrison, Giuseppe Vanotti and Sophia Webster mules, pumps and boots.

"Nothing but the best," he said. "For the beautiful ladies. Only the best."

Leasha's mouth watered when she looked at the exclusive pairs on the cart. "How much for those silver slides with the fancy heel?"

"Roger Vivier, waxed leather pumps. Very nice, very exclusive. The curved heel is something new and all the rage in Paris this season. Retails for eight hundred."

Leasha's mouth fell open. "You know how many dicks, I mean, hands I gotta shake for eight hundred dollars? It might be the big shiggity this season but maybe I need to see what was all the rage *last* season." Everyone laughed, including the seller.

"Prices are all half off today."

"So, I only have to suck, I mean shake half as many hands to get those shoes?" She gave Slim a look he had to appreciate.

"That's a lot of time on your knees, baby girl," he told her, earnestly. "Them is old rich lady shoes anyway. Check for something to enhance your money making potential."

"Oh that's different," Boojie said, with her eyes on an interesting red pair of booties. She got off of the bench to get a closer look.

"A good choice, miss," the merchant said. "Giuseppe Zanotti. Platform lace, peep toe pumps are big in New York. Only three-hundred."

"You have a size eight, I'll take them," she said, with a satisfying smile, as Nickolas shelled out the cash.

"Those are cute," Posha commented, as she left the bench to join Boojie at the shoe racks. "I was thinking about getting those."

"B-Boy, run get me another drink while I look over a few things," Boojie said, dismissively handing Byron, the young impressionable barber, her glass.

Before he returned with a fresh cocktail, Boojie had purchased the pair of red floral lace booties for $150, a pair of Versace platform pumps for $370 and five-inch Manolo Blahnik snake skin pumps for $775. She took a long sip from the tall rum and lemonade that Byron made, then tipped him with a twenty dollar bill and caught her breath as St. Nick reeled off nearly $1,300 without blinking.

Other women picked out gifts in their boyfriend's price range as Orlando looked on with great interest. He was biding time and waiting for the big ticket items to come in through the back door then make all the trouble he could drum up for St. Nick. Orlando remembered how bratty Boojie acted when she didn't get her way. He had seen his share of young women in his time, prettier than they had a right to be and never satisfied with the trappings their good looks delivered. They always wanted more. *Always.*

"Next!" Big Ray shouted, when the vendor on deck was slow coming through the door with a rack of designer handbags.

As soon as high-end purses were in position, every woman in the room left their escorts sitting alone. Each of them checked price tags then peaked inside to note the number of zipper compartments and snap closures. Leash nabbed a two-tone blue, tall leather and suede, media tote bag. When she told Slim it was only $200, he smiled.

"So that's only a hundred, right?"

"No, sir," the salesman answered.

"All of the bags are priced as marked."

"Can't blame a brother for trying. I like that bag for you Leasha," he said with a hint of pride. "Yeah, that's nice." Slim Woody leaned forward to pay the man then crossed his legs like his good deed for the day was done.

"I do like this," Posha said, with her hands inside of a black leather bucket bag by Furla. "Three hundred and twenty-five. Yes sir, I'll take it." She rolled off several bills then handed them over. "Boojie Queen, watch how I rock this Furla. And no, you can't borrow it."

"Psst, whatever. It will be mine in due time. Like everything else you have," Boojie said, as she eyed Orlando and playfully licked her drinking straw with the tip of her tongue.

"You're getting way out of your lane, lil chick," Posha whispered. "Deal with what's on your plate before you start trying to sample what's on another woman's."

She was beginning to get concerned with Boojie's behavior. She didn't seem to care that Orlando used to be hers or that he was obviously into Carolyn when they were at the nail salon. Even worse, she was ignoring St. Nick, unless it had something to do with spending his money. Posha knew there'd be no stopping her sister once Boojie had it in her mind that she wanted something that was out of her reach.

When it appeared that everyone had spent all they had, Orlando asked the handbag dealer an important question that no one saw coming. "Excuse me, before you go. Isn't there other items you didn't show today? You know, the expensive bags you didn't think anyone here would be interested in paying cash for."

The gentleman considered what was asked and how to best respond without upsetting everyone in the room. "Well, we do have a few special pieces that I don't usually show *unless* someone asked for items that are exceptionally rare in a setting such as this."

"Really? He was holding back?" Boojie said to Posha, when she overheard Orlando. "Yeaaaah, so now we get to see the good stuff."

"The stuff I know I can't afford," Leasha answered.

"Sorry but I was not talking to you so, hush," Boojie murmured, with a dismissive wave of the hand. "This is baller territory. Sit down and be still."

"This child did not just *hush* me?" Leasha stood up with her blue tote in hand. "I don't have to sit here and listen to *New Titties Barbi* tell me to act like I don't exist so she can blow her man's wad."

Slim Woody didn't want words with St. Nick over this and wasn't about to lose his Mojo Monday membership.

"Cool out Leasha. Whatever you're thinking of doing, don't do it."

"These is all natural," Boojie said, with an eye roll that suggested Leasha wasn't worthy. "Probably too old to 'member when yours sat up perfectly like this."

Leasha's blood was boiling and everyone could see that she wanted to wrap that new bag around Boojie's neck. "I didn't live this long to be hushed by no teeny-bopper bitch."

"Heyyy, hey now," Byron stepped in and pleaded. "Ladies take it easy." He didn't like the way Leasha shot back at Boojie but he didn't want both of them to get kicked out either.

"I want to see the bags" Orlando said, firm enough to put something else on Leasha's and Boojie's minds other and squab-bling.

"Sir, please show us what else you have so we can get this over with, move the furniture back, turn up the music, and step on the dance floor."

"That sounds nice," said the merchant, who was still cautiously pessimistic that anyone in the building was willing to spend more than $1,000 for each item. "Okay, there are three remaining pieces." He pulled out a new purse then displayed it to their guests. "Here is an *Iconic* two-toned black leather and silver chain, cross body bag. It's twelve hundred dollars." When no one bit, he put it aside and pulled out another bag. He heard mumbling and witnessed some interested parties but still not one willing to pay the high prices.

"Secondly, here we have a Saint Laurent Souple bag," the merchant announced. "Its fine leather and crocodile embossed. It goes for thirty-seven hundred." He waited to see if anyone cared to purchase it but the price was steep.

Orlando chuckled a little when Boojie whispered to St. Nickolas but all he could do was shrug apologetically.

"All the cash I brought is sitting in those boxes right there," St. Nick informed her, while motioning toward her stack of shoe boxes put to the side.

"I see," the wholesaler muttered. "Then I'll just pack up. Thanks for your purchases."

"Show me the last one," Orlando demanded, when all of the air was let out of the room of supposed big ballers and shot callers. Now they seemed like a bunch of men whose side chicks wanted more than they were prepared to fork over.

When the salesman pulled the last bag out of a gray mesh wrapper, it got Slim Woody's attention. "Is that real silver?"

"Looks like platinum," Bishop chimed in. "I don't even want to know how much that cost."

"I do," said Boojie. "I've never seen anything like it."

"It's actually clear," the gentleman answered. "Although, it refracts light and changes colors when placed against a colored material." He held it against Leasha's bag and it immediately turned a light shade of blue.

"How much you want for that?" Boojie said, as she played with the golden clasp then ran her fingers along the exquisitely crafted gold chain trim.

"Well, it's a *Chanel* Plexiglass Dubai clutch with a leather threaded shoulder strap. The price is forty-five hundred."

"Damn," Slim said aloud. "That's highway robbery."

Posha whiffed at the price as well. "That's too rich for my blood."

Bishop shook his head when none of the ballers in the room agreed to dole out their hard earned money for such extravagances. It appeared the merchant was correct in assessment of the audience's inability or reluctance to purchase his exclusive wares.

As he began to put the expensive bags onto the cart, Orlando reached in the envelope and pulled out two stacks of $100 bills.

"I'll take the last three," he said, assertively. "That's twelve hundred for the Iconic Micro Grommet. The crocodile number is thirty-seven, if I remember correctly. And the lovely Chanel bag is four-thousand, five-hundred. That's ninety-four hundred total but I believe that nine thousand ought to square us, seeing as how you weren't all that forthcoming with your best items," Orlando haggled, cleverly.

The merchant took the money, stuffed it into the pocket of his sports coat and nodded appreciatively. "I humbly apologize and do believe nine-thousand will be more than sufficient. Thank you, Mr. Clay."

The audience remained glued to the high-dollar purchases. When it was all said and done, they were glad that Orlando saved their reputation as a group. Each of them applauded the interaction and gamesmanship that the pastor utilized to square things all the way around. "That's how you do it," Bishop co-signed. "Yep, that's nothing but class."

"Show off," St. Nick said, to Posha.

"Yeah, but you have to admire Orlando's style," she argued. "Wow, nicely done."

"Please gift wrap the Cross Body Iconic and deliver it to my house," Orlando ordered. "Got a niece who never asks for anything. She'd like this." He handed the man a card with his home address written on the back.

"Will do, sir. And the other two?" the merchant inquired, noting Boojie's reluctance to hand it back.

She was deflated and St. Nick was thinking how it made him look like a pretend gangster who had come up short in his woman's eyes.

"Sorry Boojie Queen. I'm tapped out," he said. Maybe next time."

"No, I think this time is good enough," said Orlando. "You falling in love with that bag reminds me of a bony young thing named Bonita I once knew. She had a thing for Wonder Woman house shoes. Never could walk around the apartment without them on her feet."

Posha swallowed hard when she thought back on the times she and Orlando had, teasing Boojie about her ridiculous affinity for those ratty shoes.

"This isn't house shoes Orlando," Posha said, in a way that begged him to reconsider coming between her sister and St. Nick."

"I think we've been here long enough," St. Nick said, as he stood up. "Why'ont you hand that purse back to Orlando and tell him no thanks."

"Whut? No way, I'm keeping this bag," Boojie said, to her boyfriend. "Don't be mad at me just because an old friend wants to treat the Boojie Queen to something special. I appreciate you Nick but this purse is coming home with me. Even if you get in your feelings and decide not to."

Bishop bit his bottom lip so he wouldn't laugh out loud as oooh's and ahhh's rang throughout the barbershop as Boojie put St. Nick in a bad situation. Eventually, he did the only sensible thing he could, make a practical business decision.

"I know y'all go way back, Orlando. Even though you know good got-damned well just how wrong this is, what you're doing. I'll pay you for it, the next time I see you." St. Nick took a few steps to leave then stopped and turned around. "Boojie, Posha, let's go. Orlando, I can't allow this to happen a second time. You do understand that?"

The pastor simply stared him down until Nick and his entourage exited the shop, leaving Boojie's tower of shoes behind.

It was quiet as they exited through the front door until Leasha hollered after them. "I guess you'll be sending for your things?" she clowned, in an aristocratic tone. Slim Woody tried to tell her to keep it down but she was having too much fun admiring her $200 purchase.

"Who are you giving that bag to?" Slim asked. "Must be somebody pretty high on your list."

Orlando looked the crocodile printed bag over and smiled. "Here you go Leasha," he said, handing it to her. "I'm sure you wouldn't feel good about spending your hard earned money on something like this so I'm gifting it to you."

"Really, Mr. Orlando? I can have this?" Her eyes filled with tears and wonderment.

"If Slim doesn't have any objections."

The friendly neighborhood pimp put his hands up and shook his head. "Cool with me, pastor."

"He don't own me, sugar," Leasha answered, standing to receive the gift. "He's my part-time pimp." Leasha hugged Orlando and didn't want to let go. "Nobody's ever done anything like this for me before, well not without having to get my knees dirty first. Thank you."

Slim was beaming with pride too. "I told you Leasha. You ain't never seen nothing like Mojo Mondays. Told you I know good people. Gangsters, pimps, and preachers. Good people."

17

PANTY PATROL

Tuesday started slow and easy. Orlando pulled himself out of bed after celebrating how he made St. Nick look like a chump in front of Boojie Queen, Posha, Slim and the other Mojo Monday guests at Bishop's. Mosley had come over that evening and sat around for hours drinking and laughing at the way St. Nick's hands went inside of his pockets to buy the expensive purse for his sweet young thing but they came out empty. Now that morning had arrived, Orlando was paying for all the laughs and everything that came with it.

He had the handbag he'd purchased for Jessika wrapped in fancy pink gift packaging before he left the barbershop then placed it on the kitchen table. Orlando assumed that Jessika would have opened her gift the moment she saw it but the package hadn't been touched. With a number of pressing errands on his agenda, Orlando left a note on the table to call when she took a break from her on-line classes at UNT Dallas.

Mosley used his key to enter Orlando's house when his knocks went unanswered. "Hey! Pastor Clay," he yelled. Mosley passed by Orlando's office and dipped his head in. He saw two medium sized boxes on top of the desk. "Pastor," he called out, while venturing into the kitchen. There was a pink bag on the table which seemed odd to Mosley because he was sure Jessika would have ripped the package apart as soon as she laid eyes on it.

More confused than concerned, he called Orlando's number on the phone. "Pastor Clay, this is Deacon Mosley. Call me when you get this." As he was about to turn and leave, the deacon heard a noise in the garage. He reached underneath his sports coat and pulled a semi-automatic pistol from his hip holder then leaned his back against the wall.

When the door opened, Orlando walked through it while looking down at his cell phone. "Hey deacon," he said nonchalantly, "I just got your call. What's good?"

With his gun drawn and pointed at the ground, Mosley shrugged. "Nothing. I guess."

"Huh. Then why are you walking through the house with your gun out?" Orlando asked, curiously, while walking past him towards the office.

Mosley put the gun away then looked into the garage. He couldn't remember his friend being so casual, about anything before. When he found Orlando coming back down the hall with a box in his hand, the deacon gave him a puzzled look.

"Pastor Clay, I thought you were a burglar."

"Why didn't you shoot me?" Orlando teased. "Grab that other box off my desk if you don't mind." Mosley went in and picked it up then met Orlando in the garage where his friend was putting boxes in the rear compartment of his Mercedes SUV.

"If I was to come across a burglar in your house, I'm shooting him," Orlando informed his favorite deacon. After he'd held in a laugh long enough, Orlando chuckled at Mosley's confusion.

"Relax friend, you couldn't have shot me anyway. Your safety was on."

"Nah, I was cocked and ready."

"I'm sure I saw the safety on."

When Mosley took out his piece again, he held it up to inspect it. As soon as he took his eyes off of Orlando, the pastor grabbed the gun in one smooth move then quickly maneuvered it away from him.

Mosley was stunned. "Whoa, why'd you do that?" he asked, like a kid at a magic show.

"What if you shot Jessika by mistake? Walking around a man's house with your weapon out is very dangerous." Orlando had Mosley's gun and his undivided attention. "If you do happen to find yourself up against a dangerous situation in a close environment, hold your pistol out in front of you like this." He stuck out his arms then motioned for the deacon to do the same. "Yeah, that's it. Remember, any weapon should be an extension of your body."

"Can I have my gun back now?"

"Will you shoot me?" Orlando joked, then handed it back with the barrel down. "I have to do some running around but I'd like you to follow me over to the W Hotel."

"Brother Breedlove come back in town?"

"Ha-hah-hah! Nope. The church leadership sent us another knuckle-headed minister to look after and I, for one, am tired of babysitting men after my job."

"Good, I'll meet you over to the hotel."

"I'll need to turn some corners later," Orlando informed him.

"What you want me to tag along with you, and the next man up, for?"

Orlando pressed a button on the way out of the house raise the garage door. "Maybe you could shoot him."

"Very funny. I'll pull the Bentley out front and see you over there," Mosley said, with a question stuck deep in his throat.

Orlando went to open the Mercedes SUV door then paused. "What? I'll set the house alarm," Orlando said, when he noticed Mosley was pondering something.

"Mind showing me that trick some time, pastor?"

"You sure? I've seen a few men get shot trying to pull it off." Orlando squeezed the key fob twice. When it chirped, the alarm was set. "If you want, I'll walk you through it. Lots of YouTube videos have been made about it. Some of them are pretty good." He smiled when it was obvious that Mosley had already begun to wonder how good those instructional videos could have been.

"I want to learn it from you. That was unreal," Mosley responded, genuinely in awe.

"Smart man. Let's go."

Mosley thought about removing a pistol from a man's hand without getting shot in the process. He imagined doing it all the way downtown. When they arrived at the hotel, Orlando pulled the Benz into guest parking. Mosley told the valet driver to keep the Bentley close so they parked it against the curb.

As the men approached the entrance doors, two very attractive women came walking out like fashion models on a swanky runway.

Mosley, and every other man noted their curves and confident struts. Orlando could have recognized their moves from a mile away although he'd experienced them both up close and interpersonally.

"Mosley, play it smooth. I know these girl but can't remember their names after cuddle puddle. I think I called the shorter one *This*, and her tall girlfriend *That*."

Mosley asked, "And they put up with it?"

"There was a whole lot of drinking and fondling going on under the sheets," Orlando whispered, as the women drew closer. "I don't think they even noticed."

"Hello Ladies," he said, from a few feet away.

The shorter one, put on a smile but kept it moving. The five-ten ex-basketball star stopped on a dime.

"Hello yourself," the taller one said from behind designer frames with tinted lenses the color of sunshine.

"Looks like you girls are up to old tricks," Orlando joked, with the utmost respect in their craft.

The Puerto Rican hottie circled back around to check out Orlando, when she realized who he was. "A girl's gotta eat, Preacher Man."

"Ahh, so you do remember me?" Orlando said, with his signature grin. "Thought I had become invisible to beautiful women all of a sudden. Isn't that how it looked, deacon?" Orlando, gestured to Mosley.

"I'm sorry, I haven't had the pleasure of making you ladies' acquaintance," Mosley said, cordially. "Deacon Mosley at your service." He smiled at them like he was running for office.

"Oh, a gentleman," the Latina said, returning his smile with one of her own. "I'm Tickie. Nice to meet you."

"Meme," the amazon, answered. "That's what I answer to, if you want me to come." She looked at Orlando, as if she wanted to be called that by him on the regular.

Mosley had been standing around, admiring the view. He wasn't accustomed to chatting it up with glitzy stripper call-girl types in front of five-star hotels so he just went with it.

"It's been known to happen, I guess. A nice looking man, like my pal here, loses a step and can no longer get a pretty girl's attention like he used to."

The women laughed at Mosley's backhanded compliment for his friend. Orlando smiled to himself. He knew that was the deacon's attempt to get in some ribbing for what happened back at the house.

"You still got it sweetie," Tickie said, to Orlando. "Just been a long night."

"Whew, and a longer morning," Meme agreed, high-fiving her girlfriend.

Orlando grinned when he imagined the ladies taking turns climbing up a seven-foot basket-baller's pole. "Y'all catch a hoopster in your snare this time?"

"Mmm-hmmm," the Latina moaned, sensually. "We snatched a live wire out of the club last night. He's a bible thumper like you."

The smile on Orlando's face fell on the ground. "T. C. Manning?" he said, flatly.

"Yeah, that's him," said the tall one, with long hair swept over the top of her head.

Mosley had heard about the Los Angeles minister, who was known to be a bigger womanizer than Orlando, but Manning was married.

"That's who we're here to see?" he asked, a bit concerned about the visiting minister, who had a vast following and more than decent TV ratings.

"I heard he was having some troubles on the west coast," Orlando said, as an afterthought.

"Maybe they ran him out of town," Mosley guessed, aloud.

Orlando didn't reply, he thanked the girls and said goodbye in a way that said he wouldn't mind bumping into them again. Once he and Mosley walked inside the lobby, Orlando stopped near the house phone. "T. C. Manning is as shrewd a business man as he is a biblical scholar. I saw him perform an old school tent revival some years ago. Over fifty souls gave their lives to Christ that night."

"In one night?"

"If Pastor Manning is leaving LA, it's his own doing. Nobody's runs that man out of anywhere."

After they called upstairs and got the room number, Mosley pretended to take a man's gun away several times until Orlando gave him a hard look to cut it out.

"Room 818," Orlando said, as he knocked on the door. "If these wall could talk, huh?"

Mosley stood behind the pastor, looking over his shoulder as the door swung open. There was a bare-chested fifty-five year old with coal-black hair looking at them.

"Hot damn! Hello gentlemen. Hell, if it isn't the honorable Orlando Clay in the flesh." He reached out to shake hands but Orlando pulled out a cell phone instead.

"Hold on, Minister, I got to take his call." Orlando put the phone to his ear then entered the suite with Mosley wondering what was going on. There were women's panties on the sofa and at least three empty bottles of champagne on the coffee table.

"Yes ma'am. I'm here now. No ma'am. Okay. I'll surely tell him that." Orlando put the phone back in his pocket.

"Who was on the phone? Sister Betty Burlington?" Minister Manning asked.

"Afraid not. That was your wife. She said to run off any of those wicked women I find and send your slippery, no account ass right back home in a jiffy."

Mosley was appalled until T. C. Manning doubled over with laughter. "Ha-ha-ha-ha! Hallelujah! That was a good one, Clay. You had me going."

"That was a joke?" Mosley asked. "For real?"

The older man laughed out again. "Let me show you how funny that was. Oh dear, come on out and meet the boys."

A slight-built dark skinned woman in her mid-forties came out of the master suite in a short floral house dress. The color of milk chocolate, Mrs. Manning was attractive and had obviously undergone her share of nips, tucks and augmentations. Her lips were fuller than natural, cheeks plump with an artificial filler and her breasts were larger than normal for a women her size.

"Honey, these are the brothers from MEGA. They dropped by to say hello," the visiting minister said, fondly. "Fellas, meet Dr. Duchess Manning. The Mrs."

"Ma'am," Mosley replied, while trying to avoid gawking at her firm nipples poking through the dress.

Orlando wasn't so bashful. He took a good look at the woman's breasts. Since she was showing them off without a bra, he figured it was permissible. When he saw the twinkle in her eyes, he knew that it was.

"Sister Manning," he said, behind a grateful expression. "Good to meet you."

"Wish I'd known more company was coming," she said, looking at the remnants from the wild orgy the night before. "I would have tidied up a bit." She casually picked up the panties as if they were socks then shook her head disapprovingly. "I'm sure we'll meet again."

Orlando offered a soft smile when nothing else on earth seemed appropriate. Mosley tried hard not to imagine the minister's wife sandwiched in between the strippers he'd met down stairs. He wanted to ask whose panties those were on the sofa and how to go about arranging an open relationship where your wife was cool with it.

"Yes ma'am," he said, instead.

When she walked into the other room, Orlando stole a peek at her behind then patted her husband on the back. "Brother Manning, you lucky dog," he said. "That's not the same woman you were married to when I saw you preaching a tent revival in Biloxi."

"That was my ex-wife Gladys. Rest her soul," he said sadly.

"Sorry to hear she passed away."

"No, she's very much alive I'm afraid. Lives in Atlanta with most of my money."

Orlando laughed. "Then I'm *really* sorry."

Mosley was thrown off by everything he'd seen and heard since coming through the door. He needed to sit down so he took a seat on the sofa then immediately sprung back up. He didn't want to get anything on his pants.

T. C. Manning was tickled at Mosley's behavior. "Hee-hee-hee," he chuckled. "Man, you have to be careful. The maids haven't swept through the place yet."

Orlando felt like he'd overstayed his welcome.

"Looks like you're still getting settled in. Let me know when you want to get more acquainted with the city and I'll swing back by to pick you up," he said, then glanced at his watch. "Come on Mosley and let this living legend get back to... whatever we interrupted." He tapped Mosley on the arm, moving him closer to the door.

"Ahhh, I'll be alright," Brother Manning answered. "I know some people."

"We're on the welcoming committee so it's a part of the show," Orlando told him.

"You're a fine preacher. I will not allow you to trot us around town and have me feeling awful about taking your job."

Suddenly there was a knock.

"Probably my tour guides now. You mind getting that?" T. C. Manning asked Mosley.

The deacon opened the door and stood still. You could have knocked him over with a feather when he saw St. Nick and Posha standing in the hallway.

"Uh, come on in," he said eventually.

Orlando stepped back and sighed when they made their way inside. "Nick. Posha," he greeted them curtly.

"Pastor Manning, how the hell are you?" St. Nick hailed, with a hearty handshake. "Slimming down I see." Then, the gangster stared down Orlando. "Like gum on the bottom on my shoe, I swear," he said, as if it were a sick joke.

"We've got to stop meeting like this," Posha told Orlando. She stared at him as if she had actually grown tired of their chanced runs in.

"Good seeing you again, too," he replied, half way out the door. "Come on, Mosley."

"See you around, Pastor Clay," Manning said, to end their visit. "So, I see you found the hotel okay Nickolas," Minister Manning said to St. Nick. "Let me get some clothes on so we can talk business."

The door closed but Mosley's mouth was hanging open. On their way to the elevator, Mosley gazed at Orlando in disbelief. "You don't have nothing to say about what just went down back there?"

"Where would I begin, deacon?" Orlando asked, then pushed the down button. "Huh? Where in the hell would I begin?"

Inside the elevator, Mosley tried to make sense of it all. "We see two of the finest strippers, slash party girls, in Dallas, who spent the night and better part of the morning in that minister's suite? A minister whose doctor-wife is very likely a panty thief?"

"Among other things."

"Yeah, big-tittied is one of them other things," he marveled. "Did you see those fun bags?"

"I did."

"And to think that small man satisfied all three of them women up in that bedroom."

"And on the sofa," Orlando reminded him.

"Yeah, that too."

"I'm sure T. C. Manning took some breaks and watched the girls go at each other a while," Orlando smirked knowingly. "That's the way I'd have gone about it."

"I'll bet there's a play book for that sort of stuff," Mosley said, with a straight face.

"Sure is. With pictures and everything."

They stepped off the elevator laughing as Mosley shook his head briskly like something was stuck in there.

"Then it got real strange when Nick and your old girlfriend rolled up on the scene." He stopped at the valet stand while Orlando kept walking towards self-parking. "You give any thought to them four getting into something, you know, more than business up there in that fancy hotel room?"

"Not until now I haven't," Orlando told him. "I'll catch up with your later."

"Where you going?"

"To the hospital to see Numbers then to another place."

Mosley tipped the valet attendant then nestled behind the wheel of Orlando's Bentley. He sat in front of the hotel for a while and watched beautiful people come and go. Since he didn't have a particular place to be, he took his own sweet time getting there.

When Orlando stepped off the hospital elevator on the floor where Number's was recuperating, it was a circus. News cameras were setup on both sides of the door and anxious reporters waited patiently out in the hall for their turn to interview the hero. Orlando maneuvered his way inside of the room only to be combatted by an over protective nurse, who was pale and freckled with fiery red hair and obviously overwhelmed.

"Excuse me but all you media types have to wait outside," she said curtly.

"He's not with them. That's Pastor Clay. He's a friend type," Numbers said, with a smile hugging his dry lips.

"You tell her, Numbers. How are you feeling my friend?"

He sat up a little taller in the bed and nodded that he was okay. "Good as can be with barbequed knuckles," Numbers chuckled.

"You look well. Your face is healing nicely," Orlando complimented.

"Doctor said it was first degree burns, blisters, and such on this side," he gestured to the right side of his face. "Mmmm hmmm."

"I know you have to be here a few more days before they can release you. Is there anything you want or need in here?" Orlando asked. "I want you comfortable as can be until it's time to bring you home."

"I don't need anything unless you have three extra fingers," he said, then laughed at himself.

"Numbers, that's not funny."

"Yes it is."

"Mr. Ashland tells that joke to everybody who ask if he needs something," the nurse informed Orlando. "And then they laugh it up."

"Yes we do," added Numbers.

Orlando turned his back to his friend so he could whisper to the nurse. "Have those reporter been here all day?"

"Only since his funding campaign hit a million dollars. Been like buzzards over a slaughter house, circling for a few hours now," she replied quietly.

Orlando turned towards Numbers. "I have to go but have someone call me if you need anything."

"Other than a few extra fingers?" the patient howled, hysterically.

"You're still on that?" Orlando asked, with a laugh on his lips as well.

"It's still funny," Numbers answered. "Plus you fell for it two times."

"Anything else I need to know? That's what I'm asking?"

Numbers thought real hard before he answered. "Naw. All the reporters want to know what I'm gonna do with a million dollars."

Orlando looked passed the doorway where the news crews were standing around. "That's a good question. What you tell them?"

"I'm gonna put it with my other million," he replied, nonchalantly.

"Isn't that the sweetest thing?" The nurse cooed and comforted him when she heard his simple reply, thinking he was a poor man coming into a mountain of new riches.

"Yes ma'am, like candy." Orlando placed his hand on his friend's shoulder. "Be well. I have to go."

"That niece of yours can put together piles of money even faster than you," Numbers surmised. "Must've taught her good, pastor."

"Jessika did this on her own."

"Tell her to come see me. She's the angel who didn't go back to heaven."

Orlando looked puzzled so the nurse filled him in on the bad news. "The burn unit couldn't save the little girls they brought in from the car fire. One had a chance until bacteria set in her wounds."

"Thanks, I didn't know," Orlando admitted to the nurse. He had been so occupied with the business end of life that he hadn't kept up with local news.

"One more thing, Pastor Clay," Numbers whispered.

"Yeah, what is it?"

"Somebody ate my jello."

"Okay. I'm sure we can get you another one."

"Somebody ate it *every day*," he said, motioning towards the nurse suspiciously.

"I did no such thing, Mr. Ashland," she chided playfully.

"Let's get this hero as many desserts as he wants. Put it on his tab. He's got a ton of walking around money coming in."

When Orlando exited the room, reporters fought to get inside. He smiled about all of the media then wondered how much Jessika would have gotten a kick out of it. She had afternoon classes so he expected a call later. She was good about checking in, unless somebody was having a sale or somebody's boyfriend was acting up. Jessika was hyper focused then but what nineteen-year- old college girl wouldn't be.

18

SAPIOSEXUALS

The house read 2053 Mimosa Lane. Orlando pulled over against the curb a few houses down from the dark red brick two-story home that Carolyn lived in alone since her husband died. She'd kept up the house and yard and even added some colorful perennials in a flower bed out front to liven it up. The black shutters were beaten by the Texas sun and beginning to fade but other than that, the house was very attractive.

Orlando wasn't all that convinced if he wanted to go through with the thoughts playing around in his head. Using a business opportunity to get closer to Carolyn had crossed his mind before but now that he was sizing up the situation, her vulnerable state and the fact that she was becoming more open about her interest in him, he didn't feel right about it.

He punched her name in his cell phone then thought better of it. She answered before he could disconnect the call.

"Hey, this is Orlando. I sent some boxes over to your house by courier. Should be there any minute. Will you be there to receive them?"

"Hi there, Orlando," she said, cordially. "Yes, I'm home."

"Okay then. Call me if you have any questions."

"Will do. Thanks." She hung up the phone abruptly, without any closing salutations.

Orlando looked at the phone peculiarly and had a brief conversation with himself. "Guess that's that. Oh hell," he said to himself, when realizing Carolyn might not be in the beautiful house of hers alone. "What if she's already entertaining when I knock on the door? What if he's somebody I know? That would suck. What if a man comes to the door without a shirt on like Reverend T .C. Manning? What if the half-naked man *is* Reverend Manning. Man, get out of your head," he said, looking at his reflection in the rear view mirror.

He found himself knocking at Carolyn's door, caught between a rock and a hard place. He'd been riding around all day with boxes of receipts, tax forms, and revenue statements prepared by his previous accountant, just itching to drop a few lines. Standing next to three boxes on the porch, like he'd rather be somewhere else, Orlando flashed an awkward smile when she opened the door. "Hello. It's the courier ma'am. Where should I put these boxes?"

Carolyn looked out the door and smiled when she saw her pastor instead of a delivery man. "Uhhh, where did you call from, around the corner?"

"No. Down the street. Like a proper stalker."

She laughed and looked passed him again, as if she still expected to see someone else. "Well, please come in. Bring the boxes into my husband's office."

Her husband's office? he thought. Orlando felt lower than before. "I'll put them in here and be out of your way as quick as I can."

He felt wrong for being there under false pretenses and even worse for staring at her butt when she turned around in black leggings. The way her pink short-sleeve sweater hung off one shoulder had him feeling guilty about wondering how that blouse would look on the floor, next to her bed. Before he allowed that image to take up residence in his head, Orlando picked up the boxes and then followed Carolyn inside.

"Why, are you in a hurry," she asked. "You just got here. Besides I wanted to ask your opinion about a few things from a man's perspective."

"I'm a man. So, that would be cool I guess," he said, visibly thrown off by her invitation.

"Unless being a minister makes you feel some type of way about being here with a single woman?"

Orlando placed the last box on the floor by the large maple desk. "No, I'm okay with it," he replied. "We're just two adults talking, right?" When he looked around the office, a knot formed in the pit of his stomach. The room was a shrine to Carolyn's late husband. There were pictures of the former pastor on every wall. His face was everywhere, all eyes looking directly at Orlando. "Uh, do you have some water?"

"Do you mind if I have wine while we talk?" she asked, then walked away.

"I guess not," he answered to himself. Carolyn was already off to the kitchen to get her glass of vino. Seconds later, Orlando followed her into the kitchen area.

"Look," he said. "I don't know about this. I don't feel right being here with somewhat dishonorable intentions."

"Intentions? To see me naked?" she asked, knowingly after sipping from the wine glass.

"Wait, what?" he answered, with a guilty expression. "Where did that come from?"

"You telling me that you haven't thought about getting me alone, maybe today, and seeing me naked?" she asked, then drew in another sip of merlot from a long stemmed crystal goblet and watched Orlando squirm.

"Can I have one of those?" he asked.

Carolyn poured a glass of wine for Orlando then waited on an answer.

He drank a big gulp, while looking over the rim of the glass at her, wondering what he'd gotten himself into. "Well, now that I'm pressed and since you put it like that. I-I got confused," he stammered. Orlando wasn't as prepared as he thought to move in on Carolyn but she was adequately equipped to take him down, if she wanted.

"It's a very simple question" Carolyn added. "Do you want to see me naked, Orlando?"

The pastor shifted his weight to the other leg to stall then he cleared his throat. "Huh-hmmm. Are we being brazenly honest? Or can I fudge the truth a bit?"

Carolyn smiled then let it fade away before answering. "Let's agree to be brazenly honest to one another for the rest of this visit, at least," she replied, earnestly. "We're still in the flirting stage of this, whatever this is, and it's far too early to start lying to each other so…" Orlando smiled comfortably for the first time since he arrived.

Carolyn looked back at him oddly. "Finally, the smile that drives women crazy, makes an appearance," she complimented.

Orlando said, "Opinions vary, believe me, but thanks just the same." He sipped on the wine then looked at the bottle on the granite counter top. "Smooth. What is this?" he asked.

"Ménage à Trois," she said, with a hint of flirtation.

"Really? From a local winery," he guessed.

"Local Walmart," she said, giggling at him as the wine began to take effect. "It's good though, huh?"

Orlando nodded and laughed along with Carolyn. "Yeah, very good," he admitted, as their eyes met in a meaningful way, for the first time since he walked through the door.

"See. It's alright to relax on *my* turf," she said, leading him into the den. Orlando picked up his glass and walked closely behind Carolyn.

She took a seat on the sofa, a light-brown cloth lounger with faint maroon checkered squares that you wouldn't pay attention to unless you stared very hard at the pattern. Orlando didn't notice the design when he eased down on it, next to Carolyn. His eyes were steadied on the prize.

"*Your turf?*" he asked, after running her words through his mind for the third time.

"Yes, in this magazine article, it said to observe how a man acts when comfortably in his own confines and how differently he *reacts* when he's in yours."

"You've been researching?" he asked, interested in her findings.

"Psychology is my hobby. I wanted to study it in undergraduate school but my parents weren't having it. Said, I needed a career that paid enough to eat real food in case I couldn't snag a husband."

"Ha-ha-ha! That's funny," Orlando laughed. "Yet insightful."

"So you agree with that?" she asked, feeling the pastor out.

"Is this the first question, from a man's perspective?" he answered, cleverly.

"No, just small talk," Carolyn said, as if it meant nothing at all.

"It's chit chat?" he asked, after another sip of wine.

"Casual bantering," she answered, thoroughly enjoying their game.

"I see. Just a little, witty repartee between friends?" Orlando offered.

Carolyn licked her lips subconsciously then smiled nervously. "Yes, casual word play."

"Ask me that question again," he said, with a better understanding of what Carolyn was up to.

"The one about you wanting to see me naked," she asked, feigning innocence.

"That's the one," Orlando nodded, with another appearance of his killer smile.

"Would you? Like to? See me naked?" she questioned, while leering at him suggestively.

"Yes. Buck naked," he said, with a subtle kiss on her lips.

"Oh my. Orlando Clay is kissing me so sweetly." She picked up a glass and drew in another swallow to finish it off, without taking her eyes off of him. "Let's go in there and talk some more," she said, getting up from the sofa then heading toward the master bedroom.

"I hope you got some time because I've got plenty to say," Orlando teased.

She stopped at the mouth of the bedroom then turned toward him. "I have very high expectations that you do know exactly what to say to make a lonely girl giggle in all of the best ways possible," she whispered, in his ear. "It's been a minute since I had a *long*, meaningful conversation."

Orlando planted another soul-stirring kiss on Carolyn's lips that moved her deeply then he followed her into the bedroom. The evening sky was pitching a veil over the sun as he placed his wine glass on the nightstand then slid both arms around Carolyn's waist.

"You are so beautiful. I always wanted to tell you that."

Carolyn moaned as she pressed her behind against him. "You're intoxicating. Even when you're preaching. So damned sexy."

Orlando slowly ran his stiff tongue along the ridge of her neck then nibbled on her exposed shoulder. "Yeah, this is nice. Touching you, like I imagined." He followed the curves of her hips with his fingers tips, lightly stoking them.

"You know how to make a woman feel necessary."

"You're exceptionally necessary to me."

Carolyn turned around to face him. "Am I just another chick on your hit list?"

"Where'd you hear something like that?" he asked, with a wrinkled brow.

She lifted up his shirt then pushed her hand down his pants. "Rihanna, I think. Or was it Nicki Minaj? I get their songs confused."

Orlando's eyes widened with surprise. "You could never be on anyone's list Carolyn. There's no box to check for a lady like you," he squirmed, then eased her hand out. "There is no compartment, type, or category to put you in."

"Is that how you see me?" she asked, kissing on his neck. "What about your other women?"

"Other women? You have no competition," he replied, returning the favor with eager nibbles on her neck and ear. "If that's the question, *you* are the answer."

"Do you want me?" she panted, while pressing her lips against his.

Orlando felt the smooth red wine mixing in with the rampant passion that caught him off guard.

"Yes," Orlando answered, honestly.

"Who else?" Carolyn asked, while penning him against the door with hot, wet kisses on his chest.

Orlando kicked his shoes off then unfastened his belt. "Are we still being blatantly honest?"

Carolyn giggled sensually then breathed in his expensive, sandalwood-scented cologne. "My God you smell good. Yes, of course. Be honest."

"Listen to me, closely," Orlando whispered, licking her lips slowly and tasting them. "I don't want nobody else but you, *right now*." He held his steely gaze as Carolyn thought about his amazing confession.

She laughed heartily then fell deeply into his strong, welcoming arms. "So you're saying, at this very moment, I'm the only one for you?" she asked. "What a guy?"

"I know, right?" Orlando agreed, sarcastically. "I keep telling people that."

Orlando pulled Carolyn down on to the king-sized bed with a quilted cushioned headboard. She opened her legs longingly then popped up as if something had poked her from underneath the mattress. "Whooo! Wait! We can't do it on the bed."

"You got a bathtub?" he said, jokingly.

"Yeah but that isn't it." Carolyn looked terribly apprehensive. "It's, you know. Me and my deceased husband Jerome's bed."

"Oh, I get it. Yeah-yeah that makes since," Orlando understood. "You got three other bedrooms though."

"We don't have to go that far," Carolyn answered, throwing the pillows onto the floor. "Lots of room down there."

Orlando snatched the comforter and top sheet off of the bed then laid them down on the floor like a magic carpet. He took his time kissing and touching and tasting everything Carolyn had to offer. She screamed without an ounce of shame, clawed and cried each time she came and arched her back to longingly to receive every inch of pleasure Orlando gave abundantly.

She needed.

He held nothing back.

She cared.

He shared.

They both fell into something that neither expected so soon. Two hours and sixteen minutes later, they both came crashing back down to earth and reality from a magical ride that neither of them would ever forget.

Orlando held Carolyn close to him as she laid her face against his chest.

"Thank you for making me remember how it feels to fly."

"I wanted you to get everything you needed. I guess flying qualifies too."

"You did all of that," she said, pulling the bed sheet over her breasts. "Is it too soon to ask how long we're going to carry on like this?"

"Hmmm. Until you say stop."

Carolyn tried to see further down the road but the way forward was hardly clear at all. "What if I don't ever say stop?"

"A lady of your caliber, you will eventually tap out," he explained. "And I will understand when you do, no matter how bad it hurts me."

Orlando was the son of a preacher who saw lots of pain wrapped up in relationships that stalled somewhere in the middle. He witnessed more than one man marry the wrong woman for the right reason. And, too many times he observed women putting their lives on hold and waited for men that would never be theirs. Orlando had seen it all up close. People growing old and bitter while watching their crushes move along without them. He wouldn't wish either of those scenarios on his worse enemies.

She felt perfectly natural against Orlando as if they had been together before now. It caused her to question his comment.

"How can you be so sure? You've had problems with women like me?"

Orlando chuckled softly. "Women who have everything except for the right man in their lives, want that more than anything. That obsession can destroy them when nothing else can make a scratch. What's for you, will be yours. Won't ever have to force the real thing."

Carolyn kissed his chest then crawled on top of him. "Can we talk about this again after you catch your breath?"

"I could go another round," he answered. "This time not so fast. We got all night."

"Uh-uhhh, you can't stay the night. Neighbors will talk if you're still here in the morning."

"I don't care what people say. Let 'em talk."

"That's because you're a man," she said, between soft smacks on his neck and ears. "A man who plays by a different set of rules than other…"

"What, respectable preachers?"

Carolyn began to grind on his stiff erection. "Ooh, damn. More like other reasonable men in your position is what I was going to say."

"I see," Orlando whispered, "and I apologize."

"Keep it right there, Orlando. I want to fly again."

"Okay but could you put your pearls back on this time?"

"Maybe next time," she moaned, on the down stroke. "Gotta keep you coming… back for more."

"I can dig that," he agreed, while squeezing her behind. "All of that."

"Yeah?"

"Mmm hmmm."

19

TAKEN

Orlando noticed from the street as he drove closer to his home that no lights were on inside. The house was unnervingly dark inside. The 5,000 square foot house looked like a lifeless, darkened box. He expected to see Jessika's 3 Series BMW parked in the middle space of their three-car garage but it wasn't there.

Orlando pulled the Mercedes SUV into the far left space very slowly. He was more concerned than angry that his adopted niece hadn't been in contact all day. Now that it was almost 10:00 p.m., he was getting upset with himself as he made his way into the house. Something seemed off when the pink gift package hadn't been opened. Orlando also considered ringing her phone endlessly until she answered but his scheme to get next to Carolyn claimed priority over his bothersome attack strategy on Jessika's phone and privacy.

He tried to remain calm when he opened the door, flicked on several lights then cleared the security alarm. As soon as he walked into the kitchen, the large pink bag was exactly where he'd left it. Orlando smiled nervously. Although it was unusual for Jessika to be away from the house for long periods of time, she was a responsible young adult.

There had to be millions of explanations why she had been out of pocket. She could have decided to spend the day with a girlfriend or classmate and lost track of time. Suddenly Orlando began to pace the floor. He took out his phone and pressed send under her name.

He heard her voice mail pick up after three rings.

"This is Jessika. I'll call you back when I'm not doing something fun. Ha-ha!. I'm only joking. Leave a message."

When he heard the beep, Orlando thought long before he spoke.

"Hey Jess, this is me. I left a voice message and a few texts. Call me as soon as you get this. Talk to you soon. Bye."

He disconnected the call then looked at his phone with disgust.

Orlando circled the kitchen island for several minutes while running scenarios around in his head. He didn't know who to call. Didn't know any of the people she hung out with because she was a homebody and didn't venture out much. Orlando was excited when she took on the Go Fund Me project for Numbers. It was a huge break out moment for her. He was happy to see her blossom and could not have imagined the level of success the campaign had reached. With that in mind, he punched in Jessika's blog spot about the promotion to see if she'd posted anything lately.

He skimmed over a dozen shout outs from girls her age and guys flirting. There were also requests for more information and tons of well-wishers. What was missing, were responses to the comments from Jessika spanning over the past thirty-nine hours. Orlando felt the knot swelling in the pit of his stomach. He realized that he hadn't seen her since Sunday evening and it was now Tuesday night. How could he have allowed that much time to pass without seeing her, hearing her move around upstairs or checking in with her on the phone? He was rife with anger then. Mad at himself for giving a nineteen-year old enough space to let her slip away, Orlando hollered, "Got Daaaammit!"

He was hyperventilating at the thought of something happening to her hours if not days without him knowing anything about it.

"Think man. Think," he repeated. Okay, okay, okay."

What if she was hanging out with some friends and met a boy, he thought. Jessika was nineteen and pretty. Sooner or later it was bound to happen, he reasoned. But what if she met an overly aggressive boy or older man. What if Jessika was with someone who hadn't allowed her to use the phone? Once that thought entered his mind, Orlando imagined the worse. Without wasting another second, he raced up the stairs to Jessika's room. Her bed hadn't been touched. There was no signs of her back pack or purse.

He returned down stairs nervous and somewhat distraught. He thought of calling hospitals but knew there was a call he had to make first. Orlando called the phone company then waited until a polite customer service representative answered the phone but the pastor needed answers fast. After jumping through a few hoops, he finally demanded a customer service manager.

"How may I help you?" the manager asked.

"Yes, I'm a customer and need to know the last time my niece used her phone. It's on my account," he said, trying to remain calm.

"One second please, Mr. Clay. Okay, I see the additional number now."

"Can you tell me when the last time was she made a call? I can't get in touch with my niece, Jessika."

"I am searching the records now. Yes, here it is. There have been incoming calls from several numbers but no outgoing calls from this line since Monday around noon."

"Can you give me the last number she dialed, please?"

"Yes, I have it," she said evenly. "Sir, it's the same number you're calling from," the service manager informed him.

"Oh God," he said, helplessly. "Can you notify me if this number is used again?" He felt the air evaporating from his lungs. "I need to know where it is."

"I can tell you approximately where the phone was when last in use," the manager said, affirmatively.

"Please, ma'am. I need to know," Orlando pleaded.

"The call was nearest to west Redbird lane and South Westmoreland Road cell tower."

"I know that area. And you're sure that phone line has been dormant since then?" he asked, not sure he wanted to know the answer.

"Yes. There have been no text or internet applications activated. No data usage what so ever. I'm sorry."

"Thanks," Orlando said, with a voice so small it was barely audible. "Thank you for the information."

Orlando sat at the middle barstool with his head hanging down. He called Mosley and asked him to come over right away but neglected to say why. As soon as he hung up, Orlando called area hospitals to see if they had a young woman admitted in the past thirty-nine hours with a head injury. He assumed she must've been seriously injured if the administrators weren't able to ID her or reach family members.

Mosley came rushing through the door when Orlando was in the kitchen talking to a hospital admissions nurse on the phone.

"No, it would have been in the past day or so. She's a nineteen year old. Black. About five-six. A hundred twenty-five pounds. No, no tattoos. Yes, I'll hold."

He gave Mosley a pitiful look that shook the deacon.

"She's missing Mosley," Orlando said, with more fear on his face than he wanted to show. "Jessika is missing."

Mosley was speechless. He sat down on the stool next to Orlando and listened intently as the phone conversation continued.

"Yes, thank you for checking. I know where to go from here," the pastor said softly.

He stood up then slid the phone into his pocket. I'll be right back. Call and tell Paula you're gonna be home late tonight."

Orlando disappeared into his home office. He opened the wall safe and pulled out a chrome-plated semi-automatic then grabbed a hand full of black plastic bank cards. He couldn't sit still and wait another moment before getting out of that house to look for Jessika.

When he returned to the kitchen, Mosley was on the phone with the Dallas County morgue. "Yes sir, she's nineteen. Biracial. Five-six to five seven. She would have been around one hundred and twenty or so pounds."

Orlando swallowed hard when he heard Mosley say the words, *she would have been.* He looked away with his head lowered while the deacon held on silently, awaiting word.

"Uhhh-huh. You sure? Thanks," Mosley said, into the phone then he clicked it off. He looked at Orlando and shook his head. "They got a girl down at the morgue but that wasn't her, pastor."

"Let's go to where her phone was last used and look around. I can't sit here another second. Jessika is out there somewhere. In a ditch maybe. I'm going to find her and bring her home," Orlando vowed. "She's been gone almost two days and I didn't even know it until tonight. What kind of man doesn't know when his only family is in trouble?"

"We'll get to the bottom of it pastor. Jessika is out there and she's expecting us to help. That's just what we'll do," Mosley reassured him.

They left the house with all of the lights on. Orlando wanted her to feel safe, in the event she did come home while they were out. Before they pulled away from the house, Orlando shared with Mosley where Jessika's phone had been used last and which hospitals he'd called so far. They rode a while before another word was said between them.

"Pastor, we need to get the police involved if she don't turn up tonight," the deacon said, finally, without taking his eyes off the road.

"We can cross that bridge if we get to it. Meanwhile, I'll reach out to someone who can make a few inquiries without getting everybody alarmed."

He typed a quick message then pressed send before putting the phone away. *I need you to call me. Emergency.*

The Bentley glided down I-67 then exited on Red Bird Lane and headed west. What was Jessika doing near that intersection, Orlando wondered if anyone saw her leave from there, if someone took her or if she willingly went along. There were too many questions and so far no answers. As they drew near the intersection Mosley recognized a BMW sitting alone in a parking lot.

"That could be Jessika's car over there," Mosley said, as he turned left then pulled into the lot beside the BMW.

When Orlando saw the UNT Dallas sticker in the rear window and a metal necklace with a wooden cross hanging down from the mirror, he knew it was Jessika's car. "Let me check," he said, then stepped out onto the cement. The pastor's heart rate quickened, afraid of what he might find. His mouth felt dry and as he took steps towards the vehicle.

Upon circling to the driver's side, there was no broken glass on the lot, no spilled purse with remnants belonging to Jessika on the ground. Orlando breathed a momentary sigh of relief. There were no retail stores close enough to video tape that corner so Orlando hoped there was something left in the car to provide a clue.

He unlocked the door with a spare key then looked inside. There wasn't a thing out of place but he saw something sticking out from beneath the passenger seat. He pulled it out to inspect the long white bandage that was spotted with dried blood.

"On no," he said aloud then hurried to the rear of the car.

Mosley hopped out of the luxury sedan quickly when he feared what was written on Orlando's face.

"Pastor, let me open it up," Mosley offered. He wouldn't have wanted to be the one to find either of his children dead and stuffed in a trunk.

Without answering, Orlando popped the trunk open. His eyes narrowed when they found her backpack perfectly placed in the center of it. He unzipped it to find a laptop, Jessika's purse and her cell phone.

"They took her Mosley," he said, while staring at the opened backpack. "Somebody's got Jessika."

Mosley wanted to argue that Orlando's niece could have been somewhere partying but she wasn't the type of person to drop out of her life and disappear.

"What if somebody stole Jessika's car and she's somewhere trying to catch a ride home?" he asked, with the hopes of coming up with something to help them avoid the obvious.

"If someone stole this car, they wouldn't have left a nice purse and a six-hundred dollar cell phone behind. Naw, this was a pro. Didn't plan on leaving any clues. He left one though. I hope it's enough." Orlando folded the gauze then put it away in his pocket.

Mosley had to resign himself to the same facts that his friend had come to deal with already. Jessika's car was abandoned, her purse was in the trunk and her cell phone was inside. It looked like a professional job. Other than the blood spotted gauze that Orlando found under the passenger seat, the operation went off without a hitch.

The pastor returned to his car and sat down in the passenger seat. "You know we have to find her before whoever did this gets what he wants," Orlando said, staring endlessly through the front windshield. "The longer people go missing, the smaller the chances are of getting them back. Too many things could go wrong, deacon. Kidnap victims starve to death, choke on food, suffer heart attacks, fall down stairs and break their necks too. The list goes on and on,"

Orlando informed his friend. Snatching grownups was not a science and most takers did it wrong. Getting what they went after was the only good outcome. Anything less than that was an utter and complete failure.

Orlando lowered his head to ask God to intercede. He prayed for a good outcome. "Father, it's me. I'm coming as humbly as I know how. I pray that you're listening and that you still care about that happens to my family. Father, I'm begging you to be with Jessika while she's in the hands of a dangerous person. So much hurt and harm could come to her and I can barely stand thinking about it. Please God, forgive me of my sins or ignore them long enough to help me find my family. She's the last one I got left. God, help me. That's my plea father. I come asking your protection. Not for me Lord as I would gladly give my life in place of Jessika's. I'm saying it right here, right now, take me if it means saving that poor girl from a horrible death. Keep her encouraged and filled with hope. Tell her that I'm here and looking for her," Orlando said, as his words turned into quiet whispers. "I ask it all in the name of the Savior, your son Jesus. Please hear my humble cry. Amen."

"Amen pastor," Mosley cosigned. "Let's figure out a way to get Jessika back."

"If she's hurt, deacon, a lot of people are gonna die over this."

"Amen to that too."

After discussing their next move, Mosley was heading to Orlando's house to wait for a call, which was the way most kidnappings worked. Although, that was only if they wanted money in exchange for Jessika's return. The deacon pulled over at a service station to gas, not knowing how many miles they would have to travel before coming up on some valuable information they could use.

While Mosley was handling the pump, Orlando's phone rang. He looked at it then answered casually.

"Hey, Vera."

"It's been a busy night. You in trouble?" the detective asked, more so for practical information than infatuation sake.

"No, I'm alright," he said, wondering if telling a cop was the right thing to do. "Jessika is missing. That's all I can say for now." He wanted to trust the detective by providing more information. Years of police work taught him that the fewer people who knew about an operation, the better the chances were of coming out on the right end of it.

"I can't believe that. Maybe she's mad at you and staying with a friend or something," Vera offered. "You know how young people do."

"This isn't like that. Jessika isn't the type to get shook up and bolt from home," Orlando assured her. "A home is all my niece ever wanted."

"Okay. Has she been gone long enough to invoke missing person's protocol?"

"No, not forty-eight hours yet. I'm not going to report it, Vera."

"You might not have to," she replied. "Let me call her cell phone carrier and get a line on where she might be."

"I already called the phone company. That lead me to her car. It's abandoned and let me answer all of the other questions you're going to ask since you're handling me like a nervous soccer mom. There was no sign of struggle or blood splatter." Orlando neglected to mention the gauze he had tucked in his pocket.

"You call the hospital yet?" Vera asked.

"I thought of that. Nothing at the hospitals or the cold storage." Orlando couldn't get himself to say that word. Morgue.

He's uttered it often enough in his line of work but it sounded so final now that it was his family member missing.

"Well, it's still early in this sort of situation. Don't go and do nothing crazy," the detective warned.

"What you mean *don't do nothing crazy?*" Orlando responded, angrily. "I ain't nothing but crazy, over this?"

"Hey, I got to take this other call coming in. Can you hold?"

"Yeah, I can."

Orlando was fiddling with Jessika's phone with his long fingers when something spoke to him. He got an inkling to turn it on while waiting on Vera. It powered up but nothing seemed to work. None of the buttons responded so Orlando called it with his phone. Still nothing. He was looking at it peculiarly when Vera came back to their conversation.

"Orlando?"

"Yeah, I'm still here. Don't know where else to be except for home waiting. Hope for a demand call," he answered woefully.

"Just so you know, I wasn't coming at you like that but I get it. Your niece is missing. It would twist me up too but someone has to start this investigation and you're too close."

"I don't agree but there's no debating you on police matters, so I won't argue the point," he huffed.

"Oh, you want to play that game? I'm a detective whether you like it or not and a damned good cop at that," Vera shot back. "Did you get your niece's car towed to the police impound so we can test it for the perps fingerprints that might be in the system?" Vera asked. When Orlando didn't answer, she knew he hadn't thought of it. "See. Like I said. Too close.

If the same thing happened to me, you'd have put that car on a flatbed truck and dusted it for prints yourself. Tell me I'm lying?"

Orlando didn't have a leg to stand on. She was right. He was too close. Admitting it wasn't as hard as he thought once he realized how large of a mistake he'd made. "I'll go back and wait with the car before someone jacks it and muddies up the potential crime scene."

"Now you're talking but text the physical address to me instead and I'll have someone I trust to run by and tow it in," the detective said, softening a bit.

Orlando loved the way Vera took charge. The only problem was her inability to let him do the same. "Okay, then what Detective Miles?"

"Then come to the address I just sent you. We got a body and the victim's faced is burned beyond recognition. The call said black female, medium build. I'm sure it isn't her but come on by so we can rule it out."

"Jessika. Her name is Jessika," Orlando said, more scared than angry now.

"Yes, of course her name is Jessika. I understand," Vera replied, apologetically. "I'm just playing this like any other case so we don't miss anything we shouldn't."

"Thank you Vera. I'm sorry," he offered, softly. "Hey, I see the address you sent. I'll be right there."

Mosley returned to the car then started it up. While the Bentley motor idled quietly, he looked at his watch. "So where we going now?"

"To see Vera," Orlando answered, void of emotion.

"Yeah?" Mosley said, expecting more information.

"Head over there on Rugged by Kiest Park. There's a crime scene at Kiest and Polk."

The deacon remained silent as he drove along the Dallas city streets. He couldn't think of anything except reaching the scene and finding Jessika's cold dead body. Orlando read his mind then told him what he felt deep down inside.

"Don't worry yourself Mosley. Jessika is too smart to end up like her mother, thrown out on the street. She's a survivor." Orlando held that thought closely to his heart then prayed again.

Red and Blue lights flickered off of the beige brick of the A-1 Convenience store. Several marked police cars set a perimeter around the trash dumpster behind the neighborhood get-and-go mart. "Stay with the car, deacon," the pastor ordered. "Might not be too many friendly faces around here."

Every uniformed officer on the scene stared at Orlando when he stepped out of the shiny Bentley sedan. He looked passed each of them with his eyes locked on Vera, who was bending over a copse on the ground.

"Sorry, this is a homicide scene," a young white officer said, with his hand stuck out to forbid Orlando from coming closer.

"He's with me," Nelson yelled, from the inside of a black Cadillac.

"Ahh hell Vera, what's *he* doing here?" Orlando grunted.

She turned to see Nelson getting out of the front seat of his car. "I called him after talking to you," she informed him. "Knew you probably would be against it."

"Then why'd you do it?" Orlando asked, feeling agitated and betrayed.

"Because this isn't about you," Vera answered, to set him straight.

Nelson started toward them with a badge hanging from a chain around his neck. "Hey partner," he said to Orlando. "You shouldn't have come here but I get why you had to."

"So let's see what all the fuss is about," Orlando said, totally dismissive of Nelson's chatty banter. He ducked under the yellow police tape that sectioned off the area where a woman's body laid, half naked and scorched from the neck up. Nelson and Vera flanked him on both sides as they leaned as closely as possible without touching anything on the body or the ground nearby.

"Watch your feet, Nelson," Vera said, "Can't disturb the scene."

He was too busy reading Orlando's body language to hear her warnings. Nelson had been a law man for years so he knew better. When he noticed a glint of recognition in Orlando's eyes, he tapped Vera on the arm.

"What's up, Orlando?" Nelson said, slowly.

"This is not Jessika. My niece is still alive," he announced. "I can feel it."

"You're certain?" Nelson asked, thinking how it was hard to make a positive identification with her arms outstretched and clothes torn off.

"Somebody was mad at this girl," Orlando answered. "This attack was violent, not business."

Vera agreed that the scratch and claw marks on the girl's torso made it appear that money wasn't a motive. "Whoever this woman was, she fought back," the detective surmised, correctly. "Maybe we can get some of the attacker's skin under her nails and run a DNA analyses."

"The doer didn't take the cash from her wallet but there's no ID to speak of," Nelson chimed in.

Vera noticed how Orlando focused on the hand bag still clutched in the victim's hand. "What is it? You wondering why the purse is still here? Maybe the killer knew the handbag was a knock off."

"That's the real thing," Orlando said, with utmost certainty. "Saint Laurent. Crocodile embossed leather," he added, in a bittersweet way that strongly suggested he knew something. "That bag goes for thirty-seven hundred dollars on the street."

Vera shined a flashlight beam on it. "How can you be so confident about that hand bag?"

"This victim was a street walker who went by the name of Leasha. One of Slim Woody's girls. She had a mouth on her and really knew how to turn a man on with a big laugh," Orlando said, as Vera and Nelson stared back at him. "I know the hand bag is genuine because I bought it for her. No strings attached. I paid for that bag because it felt right at the time. Leasha probably pissed off the wrong somebody by bragging about it." Orlando turned to walk away from the scene and a number of cop's roving eyes.

When the pastor returned to the Bentley, he found the deacon standing inches away from the driver's side door.

"Come on Mosley, these nice people have some things to do," Orlando told him. "And, so do we."

20

TURNING POINTS

Orlando and Mosley regrouped at his house. Duke was parking his white plumbing van out front just as Nelson started up the cement walkway. When he recognized the large bald man in a tank top shirt, he sighed.

"Oh brother," he sighed. "It's too late for this, tonight."

"Hey Dude, where you going?" Duke said, with a spot-on preppy impersonation.

Grunt climbed out of the passenger side, laughing. "Do it again, Duke. That's hella funny."

"Dude. Dude, wait up," said Duke, with some extra whine poured on to annoy Nelson even further.

As Nelson turned to address him, Duke raised his hands in the air. "Don't shoot officer. I got my hands up."

Grunt reached inside of his waistband and drew a .45 caliber canon. "I wish you would pop my boy and run to the courthouse talking about, *I was scared and feared for my life.*"

"Yeah Dude, why you coward cops do that anyway?" Duke lowered his hands as he walked up on Nelson.

"Are y'all that scared of black men or do y'all hate us so much that you shoot then lie about being scared?"

"Yeah, which one is it?" Grunt asked. "Cowards or Klan in cop's clothing?"

When the front door opened, Nelson was wedged in between Grunt, who was a few feet ahead of him and Duke, standing directly behind. Orlando folded his arms and leaned against the door jam.

"The moment y'all want to stop playing dirty cops, stop and frisk, let me know. We'll be inside trying to figure out a way to get Jessika back." He leered at the men disapprovingly then casually stepped back inside.

"Please don't close the door," Nelson whispered, under his breath. "Don't close it. Don't…" he mouthed, as the door slammed shut.

"Ha-ha-ha, *Alt-Right*. You're in the chicken coop now," Grunt teased him. "Your partner left you out here to contend with us."

"You ever shoot a black man? One who couldn't fire back?" Duke asked pointedly. "At least give a brother a fair fight but nah, y'all too cowardly for that. You'll make sure he has no gun then light him up, saying I thought he had one."

Nelson took a step toward the house, he knew the men were just messing with him but a wrong reaction from him could have easily turned that hazing incident into a murder trial. "Y'all through?" he said, calmly, "Giving the white boy a hard time?" Nelson measured his words and his movements. He didn't want the situation to go from zero to one hundred real quick and in a hurry. "Would it help if I said I liked black people? Some of my best friends are actually black. You do know that."

"Whut?" Duke said, with a look of disbelief. "Is you for real?"

"This dude is white privilege dot com," Grunt cackled. "*I'm cool with the bros*," he mocked. "I'll bet you're cool with the hoes too?"

"Answer my man's question. Which is it?" Duke asked, through tightened jaws. "This epidemic of Po-Po capping black men like they're in a bonus round, are they Cowards or Klansmen in cop's clothing?"

"And you'd better get it right." Grunt locked eyes with Nelson and backed out of arms reach when he noticed how nervous the agent had become.

"Whatever I say is probably gone piss you boys, men, off so I might as well be honest," Nelson answered. "This, what y'all got me hemmed up in, is not okay. Just like police officers shooting unarmed black men in cold blood is not okay. Most cops talk big stuff at the gun range and at the bar with their friends but most of them are more terrified to be in a physical struggle with one Black man, righteously defending himself, than two 'Bama bikers pushing meth."

"You doing good so far. Keep going?" Duke demanded.

Nelson was mad. Mad for being put in such a compromising position. Mad at the state of race relations in America. Mad that distrust stood between people of color and others. Nelson was mad that it was, what-it-was, with no end in sight. He imagined being a black man held at gunpoint by two white officers trying to decide if they could blast and get away with it. He considered his anger, and safety while answering the question.

"Police officers are humans. Some are good and bad just like in every other line of work. Some of them are unprepared and lack the training to do what they get paid for. Some do the job because they love it. Others join the force because they can't pass the fireman's exam." Nelson sighed hard when no one laughed at his joke.

The front door opened again, this time much slower than the last. Orlando walked onto the porch carefully then stood and watched with bated breath. He didn't know how their game turned into something cold and dark. He was not about to pull off Duke and his best friend only to have Nelson shoot them once their guards were down. Not that he knew it would happen exactly that way but it wasn't worth chancing. Orlando stood still, silently praying that cooler heads prevailed and that Nelson could talk his way out of a jam that wouldn't end all three of the men's lives on his front lawn.

"Don't know why we're at each other's throats," Nelson continued, "it's been going on for too long. I'll say this and be done with it. You want to shoot me or beat on me after I'm done then hell, maybe I got it coming." Nelson lowered his head as if he were praying. Then, something totally unexpected poured out of his mouth. "Eric Garner was murdered by a group of thug cops who choked him to death. That was wrong. Michael Brown was an unarmed black man and murdered in cold blood. That cop was most likely scared of an ass whipping so he took the bitch way out. That was wrong. Ezell Ford, shot to death by two cops. He was unarmed and murdered. That was wrong. Tamir Rice, a twelve year old boy murdered by a Cleveland police officer who thought the child's toy was a real gun.

Would the cop have murdered a white twelve-year-old child in broad day light, even if he was pointing a real gun at them, I doubt it. So, that was wrong. Terence Crutcher, who was unarmed and gunned down on a Tulsa, Oklahoma highway by a female officer who shot him while he was surrounded by other cops. That was wrong."

Nelson took a deep breath then swallowed hard again. "Black men are dying at the hands of white cops and mostly white juries are letting them get away with it. You can march and sing and pray. But, until more blacks start sitting on juries and start sending white cops to prison for murder, the problem will not stop."

The federal agent kept his hands raised and still as he choked back his swelling emotions. Grunt still assumed the firing position but his heart was no longer in the simulation they initiated. Duke had a sole tear racing down his cheek.

"Philando Castile. Alton Sterling. Sandra Bland. All murdered," Nelson added. "In every case, the officers were dead wrong. Stephon Clark was shot up in his grandmother's backyard in Sacramento. Imagine, what would have happened if it was Stephen Curry of the Golden State Warriors instead of Stephon Clark, that took nearly ten bullets for having a cell phone. What the cops did was wrong. Every time. Without question. Dead wrong."

Duke turned away then wiped his face. Nelson was a bundle of nerves as he watched Orlando go back in the house a second time. He understood that Orlando was a black man who had to be on guard every time a police officer pulled him over. The strain must have been difficult to bear, even for a man of color with uncommon wealth. It wasn't anything a white man ever had to deal with but

Nelson tried to imagine how it felt. Knowing that he never could know the fear or anger black men like Orlando had to contend with, hurt him deeper than any bullet could have.

"So, we all good here?" Nelson said, eventually.

When Grunt put his gun away, Nelson had his answer.

"Yeah, we good man," Grunt said, with a ton of regret. "I didn't know you was all *Black Lives Matter* and stuff."

"You need to tour around the country giving speeches to your country ass cousins," Duke suggested, seriously. "Tell 'em to put those tiki torches down too before they set all those white robes on fire."

When all was said and done, Nelson walked into the house first. Orlando and Mosley observed closely to see if he had been beaten or busted. There wasn't a nick or gash on him anywhere. Just as Mosley pushed out a sigh of relief, Grunt crawled in the house on all fours. Duke came stumbling through the door behind him. He fell over holding his crotch.

"Omph! Man! I thought we were cool," Duke groaned.

"Just because I know right from wrong and I'm wise enough to call it out when a gun is pointed at my head, don't make me no pussy," Nelson said, seething mad for being handled like a dirty cop.

Orlando looked at the young men groveling around on the floor in pain. "Does that make it even, fellas?" the pastor asked. "Please say it does. We don't have all night."

Grunt nodded his consent.

"Yeah," said Duke, with two hands still cradling his sore testicles.

"Yeah, I guess," Nelson hissed regretfully. "But they'd better not tell anyone what we talked about out there or we'll go at it again."

Orlando flipped Jessika's cell phone over and over in his hands. He had seen about all he was willing to take from the others.

"Now that y'all got all of that raging testosterone out of your systems, let's talk about the situation that brought us together tonight."

"That's just fine with me," Nelson agreed. "We should have called the Feds hours ago. This is what they do."

"Get the FBI involved? If I wanted to get Jessika killed yeah, I'd get them on the phone," Orlando huffed. "We don't need the keystone cops screwing this up."

"Why don't you tell us how you really feel, Orlando," Nelson sighed.

"I feel like crap," Duke said, as he shuffled into the restroom.

"I can't feel my balls," Grunt whimpered.

Mosley shook his head at the entire affair. It was misguided aggression for sure. Each of the men upset that Jessika was taken and neither of them could do a single thing about it. It had to hurt but he was concerned their anxiety would come out sideways and have them looking to hurt one another. Hopefully, they had figured out what had them going off on each other. Hopefully.

"Sooner or later the phone is gonna ring, with somebody on the other end demanding piles of cash," Nelson said. "Then what?"

Suddenly Orlando's cell phone buzzed on the coffee table directly in front of the sofa. He leaned over to check it out as Nelson walked to the center of the room to get a good look at it too. The screen read: *Jessika*.

"It's coming from Jessika's phone but I'm holding Jessika's phone," Orlando said, with his and her phone in his hands. "What the hell is going on?"

Grunt sat up on the loveseat when he heard Orlando's conundrum. He waved frantically until the pastor looked his way.

"Answer the one that's ringing and toss me the other one."

Orlando threw him the phone, encased in a plastic Tiffany blue cover. "This is Orlando," he said, into his cell. Initially, no one spoke and then a man's voice came through muffled.

"We got your sweetie pie. Seventy-five thousand for the girl's kidneys or we let her die."

"Hey wait. Wait a minute. What do you mean her kidneys? Orlando shouted, louder than he meant to. "Man, you'd better not hurt her. There will be no place you can hide!" The phone went dead and left Orlando scrambling for something to hold on to. "Hello! Hello!"

When he slammed the phone down on the table, Nelson eased into a high-back chair. A look of bewilderment shrouded his face. "Well, that went well."

Duke came out of the restroom pulling a wedgie out from his behind. "What I miss?"

"The phone rung. The pastor's cellie, not this one," Grunt said, in a slow way that meant he was putting some mental energy into it. "This is the girl's phone, the one that called your uncle's."

Grunt inspected the phone by holding it up to the light and shaking it. When Orlando held out his hand to ask for it back, the smaller man shook his head. "Not yet."

Nelson laid his head back against the head rest. "This is not good. Where are you going to get seventy-five grand, Orlando?"

"Don't worry about money. I got money. I just need Jessika back in one piece," he said, pacing the floor. "These fools talking about yanking out her organs. What kind of games are they playing?"

A text message came through on Orlando's phone. The name read: *Jessika*. Again, everyone in the room seemed surprised, except Grunt. He was fidgeting with the phone and looking for a way to get inside of it.

Orlando read the text aloud. "$75,000. Each!"

Mosley frowned and sneered at the message. "That ain't fair, asking double the money?"

"You said you got money," Nelson reminded Orlando.

"Yeah but they don't know that," the pastor argued. "Unless, they bugged my house."

"Ooh they got an app for that," Grunt told them, with a raised brow. "Yeah, Defrib My Crib. Watch how it works." He pulled up the app then nodded successfully. Everyone watched as Grunt put Jessika's phone down on the table then pointed his phone towards several directions in the room.

Orlando wasn't sure Grunt's actions were warranted but the pastor didn't want to take anything for granted. He watched the man circle the den until his phone beeped when he approached the lamp on an end table. Nelson was noticeably agitated as it beeped erratically when Grunt held his phone beside the gray lamp shade. When he reached inside of the shade and pulled his hand out, a small circular listening device was pinched between his fingers.

"Damn. They're bugging my home too?" Orlando bemoaned, angrily. "They're no small outfit. This bug looks military grade."

"More like government grade," Nelson said, with a grimaced expression.

Orlando leapt to his feet. "You got something to do with Jessika's kidnapping, Nelson?"

When all eyes were on the special agent, awaiting an explanation, he came clean. "I didn't have time to keep tabs on you and chase down leads on Saint Nickolas' business ventures so I…"

"And I thought y'all was friends," Duke said, in a funky tone. "Can't trust nobody these days."

"Ain't that the truth?" Grunt agreed, as he placed his phone down on the table. As soon as it sat next to Jessika's cell phone, it went off with a series of loud beeps again. Grunt picked up Jessika's phone then slammed down on the table hard. It broke into several pieces. He wasn't surprised to find another listening device hidden in it. However, he didn't expect to discover the SIM Card had been removed.

"You didn't have to do that," Nelson told him. "Obviously they cloned Jessika's phone number and took the card out. I could have told you that."

"Really, you knew that before now?" Mosley questioned.

"No, not before Baby Hulk smashed the phone but I could have guessed," Nelson said, defensively.

"We still have to run more scans throughout the house," Orlando announced. "You disappointed the hell out of me Nelson. Spying."

"It was the only one. And I was looking out for you too. Sort of," he explained. "You know I was following orders, partner, and I wasn't going to tell them anything if I learned something about your newly found wealth.

"They're the government. They already know where the bodies are buried," Orlando replied.

"Whose bodies?" Duke asked. "Not if I can help it."

Grunt searched the rest of the house with his phone app but came up empty. "That's the only one in the house. Tricky Dick Rockefeller was telling the truth. This time."

Another text came through as the men sat around scratching their heads and passing judgment on Nelson. Orlando read it carefully. "You found my little listening buddy. Not bad. Now find $150,000 by five o'clock tomorrow or we sell her parts to the highest bidder."

"Partner, this is going wrong. Ask for proof of life," Nelson suggested. "Ask now before they hurt her trying to play doctor."

Orlando typed in his response. *I can get it but need more time. Give proof of life.* Orlando knew if it appeared he had ready access to the money they demanded, the amount they demanded would have continued to rise until they bled him dry. Orlando's phone buzzed again with an incoming call alert. He hurried to answer it.

Nelson took out a small note pad and pen. *"Put it on speaker phone."*

"Hello. Jessika? Jessika?"

"I'm here, Uncle," she said, with a groggy voice.

"Did they hurt you? Are you okay?"

"Yeah. Like a pack of powdered donuts."

The line when silent then a text hummed in instantly. *"You got PROOF. Get me CASH,"* Orlando read. "This is bad," he said.

"No, this is very good," Nelson debated. "She's alive and they want to exchange her for money; which you said you had access to." The exasperated look on Orlando's face was perplexing to Nelson.

"They're hurting Jessika in some way. Maybe even raping her," he added, sorrowfully. "Powdered donuts is her way of telling me she's in trouble. See, at the foster home where she grew up, there was sexual abuse from some neighbor boys who held her down, laughed and shoved powdered donuts down her throat so she couldn't scream out."

"Poor girl," said Mosley. "That's a shame."

"That's why Duke found those boys, one by one, and gave them what they gave to Jessika. Lots of unwanted sexual attention."

"And bags of powdered donuts to choke on while their assholes were being torn out," Duke said eagerly. "It wasn't funny to them then. Not one of those jokers laughed."

"Damn Duke," said Grunt. "But you didn't like it though? Right?"

"Are you crazy? I didn't use my own personal dick. I paid the Slyway Gay Crew to snatch those boys up and run a train through them."

"Slyway Gay Crew?" Nelson asked.

"Yeah, a bunch of gay dudes who run a shopping mall boosting ring," Grunt answered. "They don't act like sissies so they're gay in the sly way. You know, the muscle bound, steroid homo-thug, types."

Duke thought back a few years. "I did watch the entire *jam* session though. Surprisingly, enjoyed it too. No homo."

Grunt was visibly disappointed and rather skeptical as to exactly how much Duke enjoyed the male rape retribution. "So, you say. You got video?"

"Hell naw, man! That would be gross. Just stop it, Grunt."

Mosley couldn't shake their conversation out of his head and think about the interaction from the kidnappers.

"Didn't they say, we got your sweetie pie? Bring the money or we let her die?"

"That means she's already somewhere cut on and laid up," Orlando reasoned.

"Or let her die," Nelson repeated. "It might not be up to the callers whether Jessika gets returned or not. They didn't say they'd kill her. Maybe they'll just leave her somewhere if you don't pay on time."

"To die? I don't think so Nelson. We're going to do whatever they say while looking high and low for anyone who might have seen Jessika." Orlando began to run a counter-intelligence operation in his head, like he'd done dozens of times to trap law-breakers who thought they could outsmart him. "Duke, I need you and Grunt to hit a couple of spots tonight. Turn over a few rocks and see if something interesting springs up. Talk only to shot callers and let them know there's a fifty-thousand dollar reward if my niece is found alive."

"Most people will sell out their whole family reunion for fifty grand," Grunt said, with messages already going out from his phone.

"Deliver the word in private Grunt. This is personal," Orlando added.

"What if somebody was on the setup team and washed their hands of the kidnapping since then?" Duke questioned.

"No questions asked. None whatsoever," Orlando answered.

"Don't you think you're playing with fire?" Nelson asked nervously, as Grunt and Duke walked out the front door on a mission. "I mean, once word about the reward hits the streets, it's going to get back to the kidnappers."

"That's what I'm counting on. They won't have a safe place to lay low. I don't want them getting an ounce of sleep," Orlando explained. "I need them tired and making mistakes. Maybe they'll slip-up and let Jessika escape or send us a message somehow as to her whereabouts."

"I'll head out and check with some people who'll only feel comfortable talking to a man who looks like me," Nelson said.

"What, skinny, with an overbite?" Orlando asked, jokingly.

"Exactly. I'll skedaddle and let you know if I hear anything worth reporting back."

"You sure about this?" Mosley asked, when there wasn't much else to say.

"If your boys came up missing, I'd do the same thing to find the men who took them."

Mosley didn't have to think about it. He rose to his feet and looked Orlando square in the eyes.

"We taking the Bentley or the 'Benz truck?"

21

STOMPING MAD

At two in the morning, customers poured out of *Twisted Kisses*, Posha's strip club. It was the perfect time to have a sit down with the owners. With Mosley's long strides behind him, Orlando gave a stern look at the bouncer who tried to frisk him the last time he came to see Posha. The bearded man, who smelled of reefer held his hand up to stop Orlando then saw the deacon walking with deadly serious purpose.

"Not this time, brother," Orlando said, as he motored past the doorman. "I don't feel like being frisked tonight."

"Alright, *OG*, calm down," the bouncer replied, then lowered his arms.

"Move," Mosley demanded, with a stiff forearm to the man's chest. "That wasn't no *OG*, he's a pastor."

"Damn. All that ain't even necessary. Most of the preachers I ever met were original gangsters back in the day," he said, boldly, once the other men were already inside the building.

Dancers were scattered in several places as the house lights came up. Men stood up and headed for the door, adjusting themselves and cussing about all the money they'd spent on lap dances.

Orlando caught the deejay's attention. The wild-haired college student acknowledged his pastor then signaled towards the manager's office. Orlando nodded thank you to his faithful church member then sidestepped a few drunken patrons on his way to see Posha.

"Move man!" Mosley said, to an inebriated middle-aged man in a Hawaiian shirt, trying to hold onto a chair that swiveled.

When he let go, the chair fell to the floor and the flowered-shirted man went down over it like a ton of bricks. The deacon didn't stick around to see if the man had hurt himself or broke his neck for that matter. Mosley saw Orlando twist on the door handle so he took off through the club to join the pastor.

"Who do you think you are?" Posha shouted. "You're not the law anymore and you can't be busting up in here like you still got a lock on me." She moved decisively nearer to a thick-necked guard counting money.

"You heard the lady, playa," the dark squat-built man said, with authority.

"So, that's how it's gone be, huh?" Orlando fired back. "Then let me break it down for you so you can't play the grieving sister when this all goes south."

"If you're here to talk about any business between you and St. Nick then leave me out of it."

The guard stood up and moved Posha out of the way. "Don't make me get ig'nant."

"Too late for that," Orlando said, knowing what the man's next move would be.

When the guard went for his gun, Orlando snatched it out of his hand then raised it to beat him over the head with.

"Noooo!" Posha screamed. "Don't you dare hit, Fredrico. He's just doing his job. Your business is with me, not my staff," she said, with her finger pointed at Orlando.

Orlando gave the declawed guard a harsh look that backed him up. "You heard the lady. Its best you left now. You do not want to see how *I* get ig'nant."

The guard waited for a sign from Posha. "What you looking at me for?" she asked. "The one who took your *big bad gun* told you to get out."

Fredrico lowered his head in shame then slinked out of the door with his tail tucked between his legs. Mosley eyed him until he was out of the room then he closed the door.

"Bye, Fredrico."

"Now that I got you alone, don't you even want to know why I barged in here without giving you the respect of calling first?" Orlando asked, as a thought came to him. "Or maybe you already know why I'm here."

Posha looked past him at Mosley. "You got *Black Moses* with you so it must be over some mess with you and my business partner."

"Actually, I was coming to see you, about something that's near and dear to me," he answered, in a softer tone. "It's a life or death situation and had to be said in person."

Mosley didn't object to being called Black Moses but he was put off when Posha sat on the desk then crossed her legs to expose more of her upper thigh to Orlando. Mosley twisted his lips when she grabbed her old boyfriend's hand like it was time to kiss and make up.

"If it's that serious, then go ahead."

"Jessika is missing. Somebody took her. I'm guessing it was yesterday."

"That girl you adopted? Ozone, you got to get her back," she said, using the pet name she'd reserved in the past for their alone time.

Orlando looked back to see if Mosley was paying attention but his backup was standing near the door pretending to master the gun-grabbing maneuver. He hadn't heard a word.

"So, you didn't forget calling me that when we were, you know, intimate."

"Driving each other crazy? No, I could never forget that. You got some ways, dude," Posha said, with a twinkle in her eye.

"From what I remember, you do too."

Orlando felt Mosley staring a hole in him so he snapped back to business. "Can you help me find Jessika? I can't let anything happen to her."

"Yes, of course. What you want me to do?" she asked.

"If you were to hear something, call me no matter what time it is."

"Really?" she asked. "Okay. I will if something comes up, then."

"Yeah, seconds can be the difference between me brining my niece home or getting an undertaker involved. I don't like undertakers."

"Me neither, their hands are always cold and clammy when they touch your booty," she stated, from prior knowledge as a stripper.

"Thanks for over-sharing, I wouldn't have known that."

"Sorry."

Orlando pulled away from her clutches and headed for the door.

"Thanks Posha, for understanding. And helping if you can."

She wanted to say more but didn't.

Orlando wanted to stay longer but couldn't.

It was better for the both of them to stay away. Their synergy was dynamic whenever they connected sexually and something usually ended up broken. The last time he left her bed, her heart was in tatters.

"Pastor, what was going on in there?" Mosley asked, as soon as they exited the parking lot in the pastor's black Mercedes SUV.

"Animal magnetism," he said, softly. "And two people who broke a lot of beds, lamps, and windows."

"Windows?"

"Posha has a thing for doing it in the backseat. She kicks like a mule once she gets going. It's nothing, really." Orlando tried to shake off his memories of backseat bouncing with Posha but it was a fun ride. "Hey deacon, take I-35 to the Tollway and forget I ever mentioned anything about Posha."

Mosley tried to remain silent but couldn't hold his tongue. "If you say so but just to be clear, I can't think of nothing else but parking and sparking a hellcat like Posha."

"Here's something to contemplate since I'm betting that these so-called kidnappers aren't transplant doctors. Who would they go to for medical attention if something went awry while trying to remove body parts?" He looked out of the window in a far away gaze. "Doesn't matter who performs organ surgery, there's always lots of blood and a number of mistakes waiting to be made."

"What are you thinking now? Calling on some emergency rooms?"

"There's a woman I know. She does high quality patchwork

for people who can't show up at the hospital with gunshot and stab wounds. Too many questions asked and too many forms to fill out."

Sheyla McElroy lived on the outskirts of town on a small ranch just south of DeSoto. She was a board certified surgeon who lost her medical license when a patient died on the operating table. The good doctor drank herself into a shameful early retirement. Spending the past six years as a country veterinarian, who also dressed and closed human wounds, Sheyla worked all hours of the day and most of the time with a slick and nimble scalpel. When she had too much to drink, her hands shook like the ratty screen door on her modest wood framed house.

When Mosley pulled in front of the yellow two-bedroom weather beaten house, Orlando told him to flash the lights three times, two more, then one and wait. After the deacon did as he was told, the house lights came on and flashed three times, two more, and then one last time.

"That means the doctor is in and sober," Orlando said, as he smiled like the fun was about to begin.

"She's a *real* doctor?" Mosley asked, from the front porch.

"Real enough."

When the door opened slowly, Orlando pushed it all the way and walked in cautiously. "Come on deacon. Let's dive in."

The house was small and built by Sheyla's father with his own hands. That explained the uneven floor and rustic bare walls. The big room was just off the kitchen. It had a tall metal table, used for working on dangerous men and wounded animals. That's where Sheyla stood, sipping from a coffee cup.

"Didn't think I'd ever see your sorry butt again after you went all big-city preacher," she said, with a hint of playful resentment.

Sheyla was around fifty-years-old but she looked much worse for the wear. Her thick, gray, curly hair and deep wrinkles made her appear a lot older. She wore jeans, boots, and plaid shirts as a rule but the former doctor was all woman.

Many years ago, Sheyla patched Orlando's broken ribs and deep lacerations when he was bushwhacked, beaten, stabbed, and left for dead. The former agent had gotten too close to busting a team of armored truck hijackers. By the time he realized they were on to him, it was too late. Someone found Orlando dumped by the side of road. They drove him to Sheyla's back door, knocked then drove away fast.

She fixed him up and nursed him back to health, a little at a time, until he had the strength to move around on his own. Sheyla liked it best when Orlando was incapable of navigating under his own strength. She liked it an awful lot.

"You're still as feisty as ever," Orlando said, with a humble grin.

"Who's the sidekick?" Sheyla asked, with a wondering eye.

"That's the deacon. I call him Mosley."

"Hey there Mosley," she said, looking him over thoroughly. "Pour you a cup of coffee?"

Since he didn't smell any coffee brewing, Mosley declined. "Naw, I'm good. It's a little too late... for coffee."

"It appears that both of you fine gentlemen are upright and in one piece so why have you darkened my door at this wee hour?"

"It's about a girl," Orlando answered.

"Isn't it always?"

Orlando laughed when he thought about it. "This time, it's a young girl. My niece is in trouble."

"You know I don't do abortions Orlando. Gotta draw the line somewhere."

"She's not with child Sheyla, she's been kidnapped." When the surgeon heard that, she sat her cup down on the table as Orlando continued. "Yep, taken. And the men who did it said they want seventy-five grand for each kidney."

"What? I thought kidnappers were supposed to threaten bodily harm *until* the family paid the ransom."

"Not these guys," Mosley said, "they're altogether different."

"So where do I come in?" she asked.

"If somebody comes around talking about organ removals, call me. These people either took the kidneys out or are planning to soon, from what I can tell, and then try to sell them back to me. If they get into some trouble and come running here for you to fix her, I need to know about it right away."

"Wait, wait, wait," Sheyla said, as if she had just connected the dots and remembered something that might be important. "When did your niece go missing?"

"Couple of days ago?" Orlando answered, anticipating the doctor's answer.

"Usually men come around here getting gunshot wounds and busted hands looked after but yesterday, two homeboys showed up unannounced with blood dripping down their fingers. They wanted to know if I had some organ transplant books. One of them asked if I ever extracted any livers or kidneys before."

"How old were they?"

"Old enough to know better, if that's what you're asking," she answered.

"Two men? Shot in the hand?" Orlando asked, curiously.

"Nuh-uh, pinky fingers were missing," she answered. "Damnedest thing too. Both men were short a finger on their left hand."

"Duke and Grunt," Mosley said, quietly.

"These men didn't bring in a girl with them?" Orlando questioned. "A pretty light-skinned thing about twenty years old."

"No but now that you mentioned it, there was a girl who stayed in the car with a third guy. Couldn't tell how old he was but older than the other two for sure."

"Was it these two knuckleheads?" Orlando asked as he pulled out his phone and showed the doctor two pictures of the men who tried to steal his Bentley.

"Bingo! Winner-winner, chicken dinner," she cheered. "So you already know the kidnappers? Won't be long before they're back here again."

"If we find them first, they're taking a trip. Bullet train, straight to hell," Mosley informed her. "Won't be no coming back from that."

"The girl," Orlando said, "does she look anything like this?" He showed Sheyla a picture of Jessika at her high school graduation in her cap and gown. She was dressed in light blue and red, with a made up face and long flat-ironed hair.

"I can't say for certain but that does look a lot like her. Except the girl outside had that wash and wear hair."

"Crinkly, like the mixed girls on those rap videos we used to watch together?"

"Yep, about like that," she answered.

"I don't guess you know where those guys whose hands you wrapped went?"

"Yeah, I do. They went away from here after paying four Ben Franklins and two Ulysses S. Grants."

"They paid five hundred and left?"

"Didn't even stick around for a table dance," she joked. "And I was giving them two-for-ones."

Mosley laughed at the thought of Sheyla bouncing her saggy buns up and down for a couple of hardened kidnappers. "You don't say? Two-for-one, huh?"

"Come back when you're all by your lonesome and I'll drop it like it's hot."

Orlando shot a judgmental glare at Mosley then kissed Sheyla on the cheek. "You can't handle her two-for-ones, deacon. Better men than you have tried and failed."

"You should know, honey," she said, as the men walked out her door. "Don't be a stranger." Sheyla sipped bourbon from her coffee cup and reminisced about better times, when men like Orlando used to drop by late at night for a much different reason.

Back in the car, Orlando yawned heartily. "It's almost four o'clock. I'm hungry. You hungry?"

"I could eat," Mosley said, nonchalantly. "Any particular spot in mind?"

"What do you say we go by this after hours joint on the south side?" Orlando looked at Mosley to see if his friend caught his hint.

"Yeah, I've been meaning to try that place."

Mosley hooked a U-turn. He jumped on I-35 then zoomed around the downtown canyon on Interstate 30.

That time of morning, the streets were empty so they arrived at the Craw Daddy Breakfast Bar as the late night crowd soaked up rounds of alcohol with greasy burgers, scrambled eggs and stacks of hot pancakes.

Orlando answered a call from Duke as Mosley parked the car out front. "It's late nephew. I really appreciate you turning over a few rocks."

"Is that you who just showed up at the breakfast bar?" Duke asked, quietly.

"Yeah, you must be inside?" Orlando asked, while craning his neck to see into the restaurant.

"Waiting on some hot wings, French toast and eggs over easy," said Duke. "Me and Gee are sittin' in the first booth on the left."

"Mosley just drove me out to Sheyla McElroy's place. Guess who was out there yesterday asking about surgically removing livers and kidneys?"

"Who?"

"Those two car jackers whose wings you clipped."

"You lying Unca'? They graduated to people-jacking now?" He paused for a second to think about it. "Those dudes can't be behind this. Not by their selves."

"We'll come in and grab a table. Don't act like you know me. This is St. Nick's place and it might be wise to go incog-negro."

"Yeah, I've seen him here before but not tonight. One more thing before you come up in here," Duke said, then covered his mouth with a plastic menu. "There's a motel on I-35 like when you're on the way to DeSoto. Lots of teenage girls are getting strung out there."

"I'm still listening," Orlando said, patiently waiting on something that made an impact from where he stood."

"Word on the street is, they're moving some meth through there. St. Nick is leasing out half of the rooms."

"I hear you, Duke. I'll take a rain check on the high protein breakfast. Meet me at Bishop's later. Ten o'clock sharp. St. Nick has been getting under my skin. Maybe it's time to rub him the wrong way for a change. Tell Grunt to deliver a few of his little critters to the restaurant. Customers hate that sort of excitement but health inspectors love finding big old rats in the fresh food bins. He put his hands on my tailor to send me a message. Now, I'm sending one back to Nick," Orlando groaned. "I like that tailor. Besides, civilians are off limits. I'll make sure that the wanna-be Godfather learns that, the hard way."

"Grunt's gonna enjoy puttin' in that type of work tonight. I'll tell him. Later Unca'."

"Later nephew."

Orlando hung up then apologized to Mosley for passing on a meal but something more pressing needed to be addressed immediately. He dialed his old partner right away. "Nelson, call me when you get this," Orlando said, then ended the voice message.

Mosley watched Orlando staring down at the phone as if it had all the answers. "What's wrong, pastor?"

"St. Nick is involved in this somehow. There are too many coincidences. Boys, who he says are missing in action from his crew, are hemmed up somewhere with Jessika. St. Nick is renting out half the rooms at the motel that's moving methamphetamine. Nelson's got to know something about this. He's had eyes on that fat clown since he hit town."

"What's the next move?"

"Go home. Get some sleep. Tomorrow is going to be a big day."

22

DON'T SHOOT THE PASTOR!

Nelson stood outside of Bishop's barbershop. Big Ray, Slim Woody, Mickey Bombay, Duke, Grunt, Bishop, Ophelia, and his protégé Byron were already inside. Nelson was invited but he dare not go in and join the others without Orlando's presence. He was a government special agent, which meant a cop by any street standards and if that wasn't bad enough, Nelson was white. Regardless of his smooth way of talking and stylish clothing, he was an outsider, someone to be feared, distrusted and handled with a long stick when it came down to it. Hence, Nelson's lonely pose under the front awning when Orlando arrived.

"What's up? Didn't think you'd ever get here," Nelson said to Orlando, then nodded hello to Mosley.

"It's only a few ticks past ten. Why didn't you go in and hang out with the brothers?" Orlando asked, in a sly joking manner.

"Seems like me and the *bruhs* always get along better when you're around. Besides, I am a law man and need to remember that some people got a legit reason to hate me."

"Not us," Orlando said, as he passed Nelson by to push the shop door open.

"Not yet," Mosley chimed in, to make his own stance known.

"You sure about that?" Nelson asked, following behind Orlando.

Once they were inside, all of the men said hello to Orlando then looked at Nelson suspiciously, wondering why he was allowed into their sanctuary. Why was he allowed to share in their plan?

"From where I stand, sure looks like generations of hate to me," Nelson said, to himself.

"Hello everyone, thanks for coming. Y'all know Nelson, my ex-partner from when I was with the government. He's part of the solution, not the problem, so treat him like a light-skinned cousin on your momma's side," Orlando ordered, sternly.

"Ha-ha, ain't that something," Ophelia said, from her seat in the third barber's chair.

Rig Ray chuckled at the request. "Ha! Not my momma. On my daddy's trifling side of the family, maybe."

Slim Woody slurped from a jar of Tennessee whiskey and diet coke until he was ready to trust what Nelson had to say. "Law is supposed to protect and serve. Where was the protection when Leasha got her face burned off, huh? Somebody tell me that," Slim whined, miserably.

Orlando stepped up. "We know you're hurting Slim. Leasha was well liked and the way she died wasn't fit for a dog. But, we needed you here today for your street knowledge about the pimp game. You know that none of us here agree with how you make a living but everybody's got to eat, including the girls on the street so keep calm and hang on for a minute."

He waggled his head a few times as if he was trying to argue without words. Eventually he waved his hand in agreement.

Slim Woody wasn't a pimp by trade and actually not much of one at all. His workers signed contracts, had company-sponsored health-care, and walked off the job whenever they wanted. Other men who treated their women harshly, even smacking them around, often referred to Slim as *The Supervisor* because he didn't threaten his workers with physical harm. He cared for the female hustlers in his employment and considered each of them his friend. Slim mourned the death of Leasha because it was senseless, violent and final. He agreed to listen and keep his mouth shut unless there was something significant to add. In the meanwhile, he was drowning his sorrows one sip at a time.

Nelson looked at Slim's head bobbing up and down, riddled with grief. He measured his words before addressing the bereaved man. "I was there when they found Leasha. Orlando made a proper identification of the body. She was thirty-three years old and her toxicology came back negative. A woman her age, drug free, made that decision to hook on her own. Many young girls are snorting meth now and doing whatever their pushers tells them to do. It's an epidemic. We got to turn this around, fast."

"Okay, listen to Nelson. He's been doing this sort of thing a while and he's one of the best at it."

"Thanks Orlando," Nelson said, then addressed the others. "I've been traveling from Los Angeles to the back woods of Ala-bama and the southern most parts of Louisiana. I've busted illegal pharmacies, meth labs and funeral homes laundering money from drug dealers. There isn't much I haven't seen but there's some new tricks on the scene. A start up business takes a lot of capital, a whole lot of money, and there are new crews springing up all over the south wanting a piece of the pie. Only thing is, there's one pie. People are getting creative."

Nelson looked at Orlando to see if it was alright to continue into the gory details of street life. "Go ahead, we need to know what we're up against," Orlando said, decisively.

"There's something we called a *Drug Dealer's Special*. It's a body part buyback program. If a small time hustler can't repay his distributor for a delivery, his momma gets a kidney removed. It's sold on the black market to hospitals when the money doesn't come in on time. What law enforcement is dealing with just got uglier," he said, before Big Ray jumped in.

"Man, you can cut that crap. Tell us how what's going on affects us."

"I'm so glad you asked. There has to be a transplant doctor involved or at least a trained general surgeon who knows how to successfully remove organs without killing the patient." Now everyone was attentive and listening to every word. "Doctors are making $50,000 -$100,000 off the books, whether the patients make it or not. And I don't have to tell you, African Americans are last on the donor lists because human bodies are more likely to be compatible with organs from the same race. Color matters in the transplant business. Now, it's on Dallas' doorstep."

Mickey Bombay crossed his thick arms, scowling over the news. "You saying people are snatching body parts in D-Town?"

"All of the dead girls, black and brown girls, you've been reading about in the papers. Most of them have been cut up, in surgical ways," Nelson informed them.

"Good Lord," Ophelia sighed. "Those poor babies."

Nelson took a deep breath then pushed through. He knew what was coming next.

"All of those young women were selected for eyes, kidney, livers and knee ligaments. Most of the women likely died on the operating table because most doctors aren't willing to perform this sort of thing and risk life sentences if caught. Some fools think they can watch how surgery is performed on YouTube and pull it off successfully."

"Why do they burn the girls after they cut on them?" Ophelia asked.

"To destroy the evidence," Bishop said, to his sister.

"Hell, that's what I would do," Duke admitted.

"Bruh, what you mean *would*?" Grunt said, shrewdly.

"What was that Grunt?" Nelson asked.

"Nah dude, we're good over here," he backtracked, then he and Duke gave Nelson a Wakanda Forever style double-fist across-the-chest salute.

Orlando stood up and tapped Nelson on the shoulder. "Thanks partner but this is where I step in." He made eye contact with everyone in the small barbershop, then he told Byron to ensure the door was locked because he didn't want any interruptions. "Here's the situation so listen close. If you hadn't heard yet, my niece Jessika was taken a couple of days ago. The kidnappers have already asked for seventy-five thousand to return each kidney." Orlando read the pain and disbelief on their faces before continuing. "I am willing to pay the money but there's no guarantee they'll release her alive."

"What do we do then?" Big Ray asked.

"Whatever my Unca' says," Duke replied. "Go ahead and tell 'em Unc' how we get our fam back."

"I was just getting to that. The last call Jessika made was not far from Kimball High School. Her phone was cloned and they took the SIM card. On the way over here, I called the cell carrier again.

The men who took her are using Jessika's SIM in another phone to order pizza and porn on cable. The calls came from the Motel on 35 and Camp Wisdom."

"Let's get over there and blast those fools," Grunt demanded.

"We can't, y'all can't do that," Nelson said, hesitantly, "and I'll tell you why. There are underage prostitutes on the scene. Some are runaways. Others are sex slaves. FBI and DEA are running a joint task force to address the problem."

"Damn that man, I thought you were part of the solution," Slim Woody spat. "It might sound funny coming from me but saving those girls can't happen too soon."

Nelson shook his head. "You're not even supposed to know about the sting they have set up for tonight."

"Jessika could be dead by then Nelson," Orlando said, with all sincerity.

"If she's even still there, Orlando."

"Do you mean even if she's still alive?" the pastor asked, coldly.

"All hell just broke loose," said Grunt, as he looked at the live stream on his cell phone. "Local news just blew the lid off our secret."

Bishop turned on the TV. There was a full-sized photo of Jessika spread across the screen. The crawler underneath her picture read *Good Samaritan Missing. Whereabouts unknown. Family pledges $50,000 for safe return.*

Bishop turned the TV off then whipped his head around towards Orlando. "This is gonna get that girl killed."

Orlando agreed. "We can't let that happen. Duke, take Grunt and block the rear exit. I'll call Vera on the way to meet us there. Ray, you and Bombay stop anyone from leaving out the front entrance."

"What if there's trouble?" Big Ray asked.

"I got bail money," Orlando told them. "Just stop anybody from leaving that motel."

"You can't ruin months of work, not even for a chance to save Jessika. Just think of all the other girls we'll save if every one of the bad guys who are tricking them out gets captured in this sting. Just wait 'til tonight," Nelson pleaded. "You'll have police backup and everything."

"I can't wait! And, you ought to be ashamed for asking me to," was Orlando's reply. "When I was an agent, sometimes I had to decide if I was an agent or a black man first. I don't have that dilemma anymore."

The men dashed out the door in three teams of two. Big Ray and Mickey Bombay tore out of the parking lot in a raised Toyota Tundra truck, leaving white smoke behind. Grunt loaded his shotgun in the passenger side of the van while Duke fumed angrily down Wheatland Rd. Mosley pulled into traffic heading south. Orlando sat quietly in the backseat of the Bentley, wiping down two chrome-plated widow-makers. Mosley didn't bother the pastor by asking details of what to do once they arrived at the motel. He was all in, down for whatever it took to get Jessika back alive, and that was sufficient enough for both of them.

When they reached the location, both of the other teams were sidelined and forced to sit still across the street in the parking lot of burger joint. Sheriff's patrol cars, Drug Enforcement Administration vehicles and numerous other unmarked Federal vehicles had blocked off all the exits. Officers were sent room to room with tactical precision, clearing possible threats. Others were making arrests, taking prostitutes into custody, rounding up low level dealers and customers.

"What's... what's all this?" Orlando asked as Police sirens and flashing lights seemed to fill the airspace between Orlando's car and the building he needed to get into. "Where's Big Ray and Duke? Mosley go around and pull up on the grass. Drive over the curb," Orlando ordered.

"Those cops won't like that, pastor."

"They don't give a damn about a young black girl. Jessika could be in one of those rooms bleeding out for all they know."

"Okay, then. Hold on!" Mosley wheeled the Bentley around a city cop who was directing him back onto the service road.

"Hey, don't go that way!" the officer yelled after Mosley. "Hey! Stop!"

Several police officers raced toward him to cut the car off from advancing further into their perimeter. "We got a breach!" one of them screamed, into a response radio clipped to his chest. "Dark Sedan. I repeat. A dark sedan. Dang, I think it's a Bentley!"

Two sheriff deputies knelt on the grass, ready to open fire, just beyond the street when it appeared that Orlando's car was in route to jump the curb and head for the parking lot where police officers were detaining and arresting numbers of hotel guests.

"Stop the vehicle!" someone shouted, over a patrol car speaker. "Stop!"

"Go around the other side," Orlando demanded. "Damn them."

Mosley glided the car through the adjacent burger-joint's parking lot then swerved to miss Duke's van. Big Ray waved his hands vigorously for him to pull it over and give up but Orlando had other ideas. Bystanders screamed and pointed when they realized what the luxury car was doing.

"This is getting hairy, pastor, they got us boxed in." Just as Mosley swung a right to give up, a black Cadillac pulled in front of him. The Bentley skidded to a stop, mere inches from Nelson's driver side door.

He climbed out through the window, like a NASCAR driver, when his door couldn't open against the Bentley's front grill. "Don't shoot!" he screamed. "Dammit, don't you shoot!"

Everyone was looking on, watching a dozen police officers, with their guns drawn, racing towards the cars that nearly collided. Nelson waved his arms and flashed his badge to show that he was one of them. Unfortunately, they weren't having it.

Nelson raised his hands in a defensive manner when he recognized they hadn't heard a word he said. "Don't you shoot," he repeated. "Unless you want to go to jail, don't you shoot at us!" He placed himself between the driver's side window and the police officers who stopped ten feet away but still took shooting stances.

"I'm a government agent. Kinda a big freaking deal too so don't shoot at me," he told them. The men in this car are unarmed," he said, to allow the occupants of the vehicle time to disarm themselves. Once Nelson heard the glove box slam shut, he knew it was alright to let the cops advance.

"Step away from the vehicle," he heard someone say, as they walked closer with their guns pointed at him.

"I will *not* step away from the vehicle. Unless you want to end your career gunning down a GOVERNMENT AGENT, stand down.

Outside of the burger joint, no one moved until two boys, who worked there, recognized the man in the back seat of the Bentley. Orlando was their pastor and the man who'd given them the whipping of their lives in the church's office a few weeks ago, for the shenanigans they pulled in the choir hall.

"Oh snap, that's the pastor in the Bentley."

"Why those cops pointing guns at him?" the other boy said. "They must think he stole that whip."

"HEY, DON'T SHOOT THE PASTOR!" they yelled, in unison.

"HE DIDN'T DO NOTHING! THAT'S HIS CAR," Marcus hollered.

"Look y'all, they're gonna shoot Pastor Clay!" another bystander complained, loudly. "Everybody get your phones out. We're going viral with this right now."

"Yeah, put your cameras on them," Nelson said. "Everybody, get your phones out. Let's go viral. Maybe this time the cops will go STRAIGHT TO JAIL," he shouted, loudly in the police officer's direction.

When more than thirty people in the crowd began to live stream the standoff, one by one the policemen begin to holster their weapons.

"I got this covered," Nelson told them, to convince the more stubborn ones to let it go. "There's nothing to see here," he teased, in the same dismissive tone they use to disperse crowds and send civilians away.

Orlando took notice of the boy's role and couldn't have been more proud, then he noticed Grunt sitting in the van with his shotgun pointed at the remaining officers. Orlando shook his head slowly, telling the impressionable young man to back down. Reluctantly, he obeyed.

Vera marched up to the Bentley and looked inside. "What the hell, Pastor? Deacon? Are y'all trying to get shot?"

Orlando got out of the car then peered over the top of it. "We're trying to get inside there. The people who took Jessika made a lot of calls using her SIM card from this location last night. I know we caused a fuss but I got to get up there to look for her."

"There's protocol for clearing each room first," Vera said, angrily. "Of course you know that."

"Yes, I do and I'm sorry Vera. Jessika could be in there dying while we're out here talking about some got-dammed protocol," he fussed, heatedly.

"Okay, I can get you up there but only after the room has been cleared by County Sheriffs."

Orlando's brow raised when he replayed her words. "Room? You found her?"

Nelson relaxed finally. He'd heard over the police radio that a woman was Dead On Scene from possible stabbing. "You can't go up there. What if your niece is in one of those rooms?"

"I'm only interested in one room," Orlando answered. "The one where they found the girl's body."

Vera sighed sorrowfully. "When will you ever stop acting like a cop?"

"When I no longer have to do a cop's work for them," the pastor said, self-righteously.

"You do realize your hastiness is the cause for all of this attention?" Nelson asked Orlando. "We had it on lock. Could have busted twice as many perps. Maybe even a shot caller or two but as far as I can tell there's a large and very expensive net full of minnows, not good for anything but bait for bigger fish." Nelson looked at Vera then threw his hands up. "You take him up there. I don't want to hang around here another minute. Hurts my heart to see good policing go to waste like this."

"Thanks for the pep talk you gave to your contemporaries Nelson, you saved them a lot of lawsuits," Orlando said, from a high-minded position. "It wouldn't have turned out right for them."

Nelson hopped back in his car then closed the door. "Boy, did you get it wrong this time, Orlando. I saved you a lot of bullets and this community from burning down to the ground. What did you think was going to happen after your *Super Fly Shaft* routine? Cops are suspicious of black men in two-hundred thousand dollar cars, especially in this neighborhood." Nelson drove his car in the other direction as fast as it would go then disappeared around the corner.

When Orlando turned to find his men in the crowd, he waved them off the scene. He quickly told the boys, who had been instrumental in turning the crowd against the officers, "Thank you for your leadership. Well done, young men. Now get back to work before you lose those jobs."

"Alright pastor. We won't let nothing happen to you," Derrick said, with pride.

"Yeah, we need good men like you helping us to do things right," Marcus explained, to the best of his ability. "At least try to be better than before," he added.

"Go on now. See y'all at church on Sunday," Orlando said definitively.

"Yes, sir."

"See you Sunday."

Up on the second floor, investigators were inside of room 256 tagging everything that wasn't nailed down and dusting for prints, as if there hadn't been hundreds of people partying in those scummy rooms during the past few weeks alone.

"Remember, you're only here as a courtesy of the Sheriff's Department, don't touch anything, step on anything, or breathe on anything."

"I got it, Detective Miles. I got it," Orlando answered, with his hands raised.

Orlando followed Detective Vera Miles into the room slowly. It was filthy, decorated in early tragedy. The walls were all painted in dingy tones of off-white. The carpet was worn to the padding underneath in some places and all of it smelled of stale smoky residue. There were clear empty bottles of antiseptic alcohol spilling over in the trashcan, beer bottles on the table, several blood soaked bathroom towels on the floor and deep red blood stains on the sheets that covered the victim.

Vera nudged an investigator's arm while he was taking crime scene photos of everything. "I think we're ready," she said, in a way that indicated they were ready to have the sheets pulled back from covering the victim's face.

Orlando could see by the color of the girl's leg, sticking out of the covers that she was too dark to be Jessika but since he was granted a look, he took it.

"Dear Lord," he said, peering down at the receptionist from Posha's nail shop.

"This isn't your niece but you know her?" Vera inquired, curiously.

"Yeah, she worked at Posh Nails. Her name is Teresa. They call her Reesie, I think. You can contact Posha Holywater to get this kid's full name and emergency contact information." Orlando noticed there were a number of clear plastic wrappers near the bathroom door.

Vera took notes then followed Orlando's eyes to bathroom. "You don't think it's odd that this is the second victim of violence you've identified in the last two days?" she asked.

"If you put it that way, yeah. Very odd. Weird even," he answered, still looking towards the back end of the bedroom. "This is all wrong. Reesie was a quiet, shy type. She shouldn't be caught dead in a place like this, Vera. Anyone clear the bathroom yet?"

"There's a Post-It on the door so yes, someone has checked it out already."

Vera followed him across the room. He opened the door carefully with his elbow, just enough to peek his head in. When Orlando saw the clothing on the floor, his breathing quickened. A pair of white shorts were laying near the cruddy bathtub filled half way with water that had turned pink and several pounds of melting ice chips floating on top of it.

"Those shorts," he gasped. "She was here Vera. Jessika was here."

"How can you tell? That style of shorts is very popular. I almost bought a pair myself but I'm not hitting the gym like I used to."

"This is where they kept her, on ice in this tub. Oh God," he moaned, uncontrollably. "We missed her Vera. They were right in this room and we missed her."

"You're coming unglued, Orlando. It's time to get you out of here." She marched him down the stairs and past the manager's office until he stopped on a dime.

"Wait, the video tapes. A place like this has video, right?

Look at those cameras," he said excitedly." He pointed up towards the stairwell where two cameras were attached to the wall, facing in opposite directions.

"Sorry but that was the first thing I checked when arriving on the scene," the detective informed him.

"Sorry? What do you mean sorry? Let's go in the manager's office and view the video."

"I already went in there to secure the video footage but there wasn't any. Drug dealers are notorious for snatching the incriminating footage when they make a run for it. The manager said those are dummy cameras used to scare off robbers not for filming cheating husbands or restless housewives," Vera explained. "Those video cameras don't work."

"Nothing makes sense, Vera. The kidnappers bring Jessika to the only motel on the planet with no video surveillance then they rush her away from here minutes before we show up. It's like they knew we were coming."

"Your old partner called in the reinforcements."

"Nelson?"

"He said you and some homies were about to blow this sting wide open. The brass made a decision to move in and get what we could. Nelson's going to be in hot water over taking down this location before the feds were ready."

Orlando frowned at the entire situation. He felt guilty for sending the police agencies in early but it did prove that his niece was alive. At least there was that. He couldn't save Reesie. Jessika was wounded but she was alive.

Seconds after Orlando was back in the car with Mosley,

Orlando's phone buzzed. When he saw Jessika's name flashing, he answered it hurriedly. "Hello? Jessika? Hello?"

"This is on you, *Pastor Money Bags*. What happens to the girl from here on out is on you."

"Tell me what you want. Where are you?" Orlando demanded, desperately.

"Not where you think. The commotion you caused just raised the price. Double the money by nightfall if you don't want Jessika home, piece by piece."

"Hey, don't do that! I'll get the money. Hey!" Orlando yelled.

The man on the other line disconnected the call. Orlando cussed and screamed in disgust.

"They're going to kill her, deacon. I'm sick and tired of being lead around by the nose and one step behind. There's a Judas among us. I don't know who it is yet but somebody I trust must have tipped them off."

"Take me by my office at the church. I've gotten a ton of texts and missed calls from Sister Burlington. I hope she's not offering her help. I have enough problems already," Orlando complained.

Deacon Mosley agreed. "Mmmm Hmmm. You do have those, pastor. Mmmm Hmmm."

23

ANGEL AMBUSH

The church parking lot was busier than normal for a Thursday afternoon. There were audio and video trucks, Internet cable company vans and a cream-colored Rolls Royce in the assistant pastor's parking space. Mosley pulled in next to it.

"Guess I know what this is about," he said. "Least I don't have to worry about T. C. Manning dinging our car door."

"That would be the least of our worries. Damn," Orlando griped.

Orlando walked into the business suites at M.E.G.A. It was buzzing with white people, white people that he hadn't seen before in their business suits, jeans and designer button-down shirts with their sleeves rolled up. They were huddled in groups, standing around discussing M.E.G.A. church business and the best marketing strategies to push out the new church's new upscale persona.

"We in the right place, right?" Mosley asked, looking over all the movement and visitors.

"There's something janky going on," Orlando replied, as he stood outside the pastor's office.

Mosley gave him a peculiar look. "What you waiting on, pastor?"

"Deciding if I want to know what's on the other side of this door or not." He opened the door slightly then pushed it all the way open. There were boxes of hymnals, a portable plastic wardrobe armoire, makeup kits, and two tall swivel stools.

"I know you didn't have anything to do with this," Mosley said to Orlando, with a puzzled expression.

"I did," Sister Betty Burlington answered, from the hall way. "I tried to tell you what was going on Brother Orlando but you didn't return any of my calls or texts.

"*Orlando?*" he repeated, with a subtle grin.

"Well, there's been some significant changes here at MEGA."

"In two days?"

"Time waits for no one and I made it clear that you were on borrowed time."

Orlando heard what Sister Burlington was saying. He didn't like the way it sounded. "Okay, I'm here now. Let's hear it from the horse's mouth."

Mosley wanted to laugh so bad it hurt but he thought better of it. "I'll go stand outside." Before the deacon could exit the room, Sister Betty Burlington stopped him.

"No, you need to hear this too deacon because it concerns you as well. I know there has been no love lost between us Brother Orlando. The leadership here has met with Minister T. C. Manning and he accepted our terms."

"That's what this is all about? Booting me out or letting T. C. turn this church into something unrecognizable, something new?"

"Not new, different," she answered proudly. "It's all but said and done. We meet with the lawyers next week to finalize everything but what you see going on around here it the beginning of the next chapter of MEGA. We're going global and introducing this congregation to things I've never imagined."

"With that new pastor you're signing up, you can say that again," Orlando joked. "You're going to see everything and I do mean *everything* in due time."

"Unfortunately, neither of you will be around here to witness any of it." Sister Burlington sashayed to the other side of the door, after she was quite satisfied in setting them straight. "One of the first orders of business is to remove you as Interim Pastor, cut Brother Mosley from the Deacon Board and eliminate Sister Carolyn Drew's position as CFO."

"You're firing me?" Mosley asked. "Can you do that?"

"Wait, what's this about letting Sister Carolyn go? She's been here since before the split that almost broke this church in half. She's a great accountant and you know it."

"Maybe so but one of the points of contention in the new pastor's contract is bringing in his own chief financial officer. Besides, Sister Carolyn is a bit too chummy with you. I've noticed y'all together. People are talking."

"Do you hear yourself?" Orlando said, with a measured voice. "You're handing the financial well-being over to a man who just bankrupted a larger congregation in Los Angeles?"

"Mere rumors," she replied.

"That you can actually verify on Google."

"Be that as it may be *Brother Orlando*, I go out of my way to dismiss hearsay and busybody gossip."

"Unless it applies to me?" Orlando was at a loss for words.

There was so much he wanted to say and none of it appropriate. After a deep sigh, he looked the pastor's office over again. Suddenly, it didn't appeal to him anymore.

"I've been chasing the men who abducted Jessika for the past couple of days. Not that it matters to you because it's a family thing. I hope you get exactly what you deserve by making this move. But MEGA deserves better. I know that and you should too."

"Good luck getting your niece back, since family seems to be more important than being here when repeatedly summoned."

Orlando walked away but Mosley was close enough to Sister Betty to smell her tired, stale breath. "This great man has given so much without asking for a single thing in return. There will come a day you'll be begging Pastor Clay to come back."

"But it's not *today*," she whispered, with a slight chuckle. "Tell Sister Paula, I said hello."

Mosley followed Orlando into the auditorium. Crews of construction workers mounted camera hitches, multiple plug-in outlets, and recessed lighting. "Well, I see they're putting my salary to use in ways I never intended," said the pastor.

The deacon didn't want to believe it. "You don't think they'll stop putting money into the Oak Cliff Born & Raised college scholarship fund that you started?"

When a troop of professional praise dancers strutted in with gym bags and bottles of water, Orlando sucked his teeth in opposition to what was happening right before his eyes. "I recognize a couple of these girls from the Shake Shack. Looks like T. C. Manning has definitely brought the circus to town."

"And the church leadership had already found another constituency to put through college," Mosley joked.

It was easy to see what Minister Manning was up to. He wanted to dazzle the congregation with bright lights, cameras and action while fleecing them in order to stuff his own pockets. Orlando was concerned the most about members who wouldn't mind it a bit, as long as they were entertained on Sunday mornings. Even though there was no way to stop it, he wasn't the type to sit and watch the train wreck happen without warning the passengers.

Mosley wasn't looking forward to telling his wife that he had been unceremoniously demoted for nothing more than his loyalty to Orlando, who Paula didn't seem to care for in the first place. Going back to working a nine to five never agreed with the deacon but he had a family to feed. As soon as Jessika turned up, in whatever capacity, he was prepared to tell Orlando thanks for the opportunity to drive him and of course for the laughs. Deacon Mosley imagined those words would be harder to come up with than the conversation he'd be having with Sister Mosley. He didn't know if that was fair to her but it made perfect sense to him.

Orlando received a text from Posha, asking him to come see her at the nail salon. He figured she'd heard about Reesie's body being found at the motel and wanted to know more about how it happened. When they arrived, the visit played out altogether differently than what they anticipated.

Posha sat in the first chair at the salon. The mood was somber as several of the nail techs drank wine and liquor shots from the cooler while reminiscing and sharing selfies they had taken with Reesie.

"Hey Orlando," Posha said, saddened by circumstance. "There's something I should have told you the other night at the club."

"I'm sorry about Reesie. My condolences," he offered. "Want to go and talk in your office?"

"A lady cop is in there interviewing Yuma. Reesie followed that fast chick around, getting into whatever she said and did."

"Yuma? Isn't that your lil' sister Boojie's BFF?"

"Was, Boojie said Yuma was getting into some other type business that she wasn't down with so they're only some-timey now."

Orlando was beginning to understand how a shy reserved girl like Reesie could have been introduced to tricking at a cheap motel.

"Did Yuma put Reesie onto that fast life?"

"Reesie was young and didn't know better. She thought that fast life was the real life. You hear me?"

"Yeah, I do," he said, with another notion pushing its way to the front of his mind. "You think St. Nick had anything to do with Yuma turning out that dead girl?"

"He didn't say stop if he did watch it happen." She looked at the closed manager door then whispered to Orlando. "Nick might have something to do with that kidnapping business too. He's been having a lot of secret type conversations and your name is coming out his mouth too often to be a coincidence. I made a mistake signing up with him to do business. I hate when you're right. And you've been right, a lot."

He read Posha's body language and facial tics. If she was pitting Orlando against St. Nickolas, he couldn't see it written on her face.

"Are you working me, Posha? Huh? You hyping me up to make a move on St. Nick so you can break free from those new partnerships you signed with him?" the pastor wondered. "All I got to do is go where you tell me to find him, get into another argument and kill him. Is that it?"

"Heeell no and don't ever ask me that again," Posha shot back, insistently. She was pissed at his accusations. "Don't put it pass me to look out for my sister and try to save her from a miserable life with that ex-con but this ain't that. Not yet, anyway."

"Sorry to think that about you," Orlando said, regretfully.

"I can't charge that to your heart," she said, with forgiving eyes filled with truth. "You must be out of your mind with misery from trying to get your niece back. Just thought you should know that Nick is up to something that's got you involved in it."

"I appreciate that. Where can I find your business partner if I was to go looking for him?"

"He's at Boojie's pad. A high-rise apartment on Victory Park lane."

"The new ones over by American Airlines Center? Boojie Queen done gone uptown?"

"Hood Hollywood," Posha said, with a slight hint of apprehension.

Orlando laughed then looked at the manager's door again.

"The lady cop talking to Yuma. She say her name was Vera Miles?"

"Yep and that you were the reason she's Jenny-on-the-spot."

"How do you mean?"

"Her face got all flustered when she said your name then waited to see if I felt some type of way about it after she brought you up."

Orlando knew exactly what Posha was doing, her eyes gave her away. "Me and Vera go back a ways."

"Was she the one you dropped me for?" Posha asked, dying to know the truth.

"Nah," Orlando said, hoping to spare her feelings. "No way I'd push you aside for another woman." He was only half-lying.

Their romance was over and done with when Vera came along. She was the perfect excuse to end things with Posha that were already finished.

The smile she gave him let on that she didn't believe it no matter how badly she wanted to.

"Here's the address," she said, then wrote a door number on the back of his hand with an acrylic marker. She knew Orlando still had left over feelings when he allowed her to scribble on him without hesitation or complaint. "See you around, Ozone," she said, affectionately. "Got a funeral to plan. Reesie's people ain't got the kind of money it takes to do it proper."

"She was a good kid. I'm very sorry," Orlando said, before leaving the nail salon.

Orlando didn't tell Mosley what he learned inside of the nail shop, only that he needed to have a word with St. Nick and he knew exactly where to find him.

"Is that it, what Posha wrote on your hand?" Mosley asked, looking at the numbers on Orlando.

The pastor smiled and nodded asserted. "Yep. I watched and let it happen."

When they pulled into the apartment building's parking garage, Nelson met them at the elevator. Mosley looked at Orlando for answers but he was surprised as well.

"Special Agent, Nelson Brown," Orlando said. "Are you the welcome wagon or a private security detail for the fat slime ball upstairs?" Orlando asked.

"Neither, Orlando. I came straight here when you walked into that pretty lady's nail shop. I knew you'd turn up here sooner or later with this address written on a napkin or some such so I came over and waited." Orlando tried to hide the door number written on the back of his hand but Nelson had already seen it.

"Bah-hah-hah! Damn man, what does she have on you to get away with something like that? Hope it's not a *permanent* marker?" Mosley was a tad bit embarrassed for his friend but refused to show it. "So why you here then?" the deacon asked Nelson.

"I wasn't talking to you," Nelson answered, "but since you asked. I'm here to keep the peace and save my investigation into Nick Boudreaux. Y'all ruined the DEA and Sheriff's joint task force that the Dallas PD is still pissed about because they learned of it on the back end. Please don't mess this up for me."

"Alright, I won't make waves but I am going up and have a say with your suspect. If he ramps things up, I can't control what happens after that."

Mosley pressed the 'Up' button on the elevator. "Maybe this is a good time for you to leave, special agent. What y'all call it when you don't want to admit to knowing something?"

"Plausible deniability," Nelson answered, reluctantly.

"Yeah, that. Run and get you some," Mosley suggested, then stepped on the elevator.

Orlando jumped on and looked at Nelson standing alone on the ground level as the doors closed. "You still don't trust Nelson?" he asked Mosley.

"Question is, do you?" the deacon asked.

Orlando knocked at the door then stood to the side, so he wouldn't get hit if someone started blasting through the door. He was still thinking about Mosley's question regarding Nelson when he heard footsteps approaching.

"Stay calm and don't shoot anybody," Orlando whispered across the doorway.

"Then how are we playing this?" Mosley asked, as confused as he was concerned.

"So don't shoot anybody *unless* you have to," Orlando clarified.

"Oh okay, got it," Mosley said, satisfied with those instructions.

Boojie opened the door in skimpy pink workout shorts and a bedazzled sports bra. She smiled when Orlando stepped in front of her, as if it was a friendly visit.

"Ohhh Nickolas. You got company, boo," she sang sweetly.

The way she said it, told Orlando they already knew he was coming. When Boojie turned and walked back into the apartment, Mosley held his pistol behind his back and checked out her wiggle box.

"Put that thing away," Orlando hissed. "They're expecting us."

Mosley did as he was told and returned the pistol to a side holder then pulled his shirt tail over it. He walked in more at ease than either of them should have been.

The furnishings looked like they walked into IKEA and bought an entire apartment display. A yellow leather sectional took up a larger portion of the front room with Aztec wall art and southwestern-style rugs on the hardwood floors. The theme was put together well but lacked imagination, Orlando thought.

"Nice place you got here. I'm surprised Posha hadn't come over and done her thing to it," he said.

"She wanted to but this is *my* spot. I do what I want here."

The visitors weren't offered a seat so he stood in the middle of the room. When St. Nick came out of a bedroom with a fog of weed smoke trailing behind him, it was clear that he wasn't alone in there.

St. Nick walked to the refrigerator then pulled out a long neck beer. He twisted off the bottle top and took a swig.

"I heard you wanted to talk to me," he said, from the kitchen area. "So talk."

Boojie smiled as if it was a game she liked. She had no idea how close she was to standing in the path of mayhem and murder if the bomb dropped while she was directly in the middle of the two men.

"Y'all hungry," she asked. "I'm a good cook."

"They won't be here that long," St. Nick answered, for his visitors.

"Posha told you we were coming?" Orlando asked, knowing the answer.

"Yeah. I told her it was a good idea when she came up with it," St. Nick said, as the back bedroom door opened and three thugs came out holding heat.

Mosley raised his hands when it was clear St. Nick's boys had gotten the drop on him.

Orlando turned and smiled. "It's alright deacon. Sometimes in life you get caught up in an angel ambush."

"A which?" St. Nick asked, before pouring more imported beer down his throat.

"You never heard of an angel ambush? The story goes there were sentries responsible for patrolling on the outskirts of Heaven to make sure no one sneaked in. At some point they were tricked, bound, gagged, and disguised as part of the devil's henchmen. They were mistakenly charged with overthrowing Heaven then tried by St. Michael, the arch angel himself and was summarily cast out of Heaven along with Satan."

"Is this real?" one of the gunmen asked.

"Shut up!" St. Nick told him. "Can't you see this Holy Man is talking?"

Orlando had St. Nick' attention for the time being so he stayed with the tale he heard as a child. "Well, those innocent angels were never able to clear their names. Angel ambush is the worst kind of trap, one that can only be sprung by someone you trust. You can't see it coming and can't do anything about it."

"I'll let you men talk amongst yourselves," Boojie Queen said. "All of a sudden, I feel like I stepped out of my lane. Excuse me, y'all." She whispered something to Nick then sauntered off to the bedroom and closed the door.

"She told you that nothing better happen to me?" Orlando asked him.

"How'd you know?"

"I saw her grow up, Nick. She's not as ruthless as she thinks."

"Yeah, I've been working on that. Men, put your guns down," he ordered. "I knew you'd be coming for me when they took your niece from you. I didn't have nothing in on that. However, I do have a man on the inside. He runs with them every now and then. He takes them drinks, smokes and lately meds and food too. They'll eat anything from that Coach's Box off Camp Wisdom and Main."

"Sonny Dreadlocks or Hollywood Harris?"

"Oh, you know the renegades who took the girl? They've been on the move since they left my crew and started doing things I wouldn't sanction. Kidnapping is bad for business and a stupid business to be in. The margins are huge if you get away with it but not too many people are that smart or lucky enough to get away clean."

"You saying you know where they are?" Orlando asked, hoping St, Nick did and was willing to share it.

"For fifty gees, I'll find out today where they ran off to. Maybe for a hundred thousand, I'll even help you round them up."

"You snitching now, Nick?" the same gunman asked, with a foul look on his face.

"Excuse him, y'all. He's my cousin. My auntie's youngest son. Remind me never to do business with family again but hey, what you gonna do?"

"I want her back, Nick, today," Orlando said, sternly.

"That's why I'm offering a proposition you can't refuse. Bring me the ransom money and I'll be the go between. You pay me fifty grand, I tell you where to find them. You pay me their ransom quote and I deliver, with a fifty-thousand dollar handling fee for my troubles."

"That's a lot to think about. I'll send along Mosley to make sure things get done right," the pastor countered.

Mosley's eyes widened. He hadn't planned on hanging out with gun-toting dope heads.

"Your call," St. Nick answered. "Long as you let me know early enough to put my inside man in the know."

"Why you doing this, Nick? I know you can't stand me," Orlando said, as curious as could be.

"Three reasons," he replied, without having to think about it. "True, I wish you were dead but I like money and people say you got lots of it. You're too connected in this city. I can't kill you and get away with it, yet."

"What's the third thing?" Orlando asked, with an attitude.

"My life stopped when you busted me. I did five years, federal time and that's day for day, no early release. My son got clapped up on a basketball court. My wife started sucking dick to feed her coke habit. I thought my life was a bitch until I heard your wife and kids died in a hit and run."

"And," Orlando said, while contemplating if St. Nick had something to do with it.

"No, I didn't reach out and have them touched from prison, if that's what you're thinking." St. Nick glanced around the room before he offered some powerful information that could have easily exploded in his face. "Yeah, I knew it was bound to happen but I didn't do a thing to stop it once the word was out to get it done."

"You know who killed them?" Orlando said, moving closer to Nick, until one of the men pointed a gun at him. "I knew in my heart it wasn't an accident."

"Yeah, I know who put the hit out but it's not for me to say. Least not yet. What I will say is you and me are a lot alike. Both lost our people. Me and you both did time. Mine from a jail cell. Yours, locked in your own private hell."

Orlando couldn't refute St. Nick's claims, neither of them. "It appears we have a deal," he said. "I accept your terms. You're right, we are a lot alike. Now, I can't kill you either. Least not until I find out who I owe a real bad death to first." Orlando wanted to say something else but didn't. "Come on deacon, we'll work out the details later. Nick, you'll be hearing from me."

"Hell, I know I will. Your pretty niece ain't doing so well from what I hear, so go on and get me that money so I can get your family back. All that's left of it," he added to rub it in.

He and his men had a good laugh at Orlando's expense.

As soon as they were out of the apartment, Mosley cleared his throat. "You really gonna put me in with them reefer dudes tonight for a ride along?"

Orlando didn't answer until they reached the ground floor. He sensed that Mosley was more afraid than he was letting on upstairs and that told him something else he needed to know.

"Of course not but I wanted St. Nick to think I was willing to do anything and pay anything," Orlando said, eventually. "He might not be pulling the strings on the kidnap but he knows who is. Let's go put some cash together and make this thing happen."

24

A JUDAS AMONG US

Orlando told Mosley to lock the door behind him as they walked into the house. The deacon hesitated before following, then came on in and twisted the dead bolt behind him. He couldn't help but think about what Sister Burlington said, him being on his way out of a job. Now, risking his life on the back of that disappointing news had him reconsidering a lot of choices he would never have given a second thought otherwise.

Mosley walked into Orlando's plush office and stood still as Orlando pushed his large desk against the wall. He didn't know why the pastor was shifting furniture until the area rug was pulled up. It revealed a wooden trap door, with two metal handles.

"Hey, give me a hand," Orlando said, when he yanked on the trapdoor. There was metal handle that wouldn't lift the heavy wooden door until Mosley lent his muscle.

"Uhhhhggh, yeah that's it."

When the door swung open, Mosley's eyes widened. He saw stacks of bills wrapped in plastic, two AR-15 rifles and an assortment of antique handguns.

"You planning on going to war with those killing machines, pastor?"

"Never know what might come down the pike. Semi-auto rifles are still legal, for the time being. The NRA is lining so many politicians pockets, congressmen don't care how many schools get shot up with these assault weapons. It's all about money and power."

"You think these Parkland Florida kids can make a difference? I say a prayer everyday my boys get on that school bus. Can't imagine their bodies being shot to pieces in an elementary class room. Just ain't right."

"No it isn't, Mosley. Not even close."

Orlando pulled several stacks of money out of that hole in the floor then placed them on the desk. When he heard the front door close, he pulled an assault rifle up to his chest then slowly inched around the corner to see who had entered his home, unannounced. When Orlando saw who it was standing in his foyer, he cocked the rifle quickly. "What are you doing in my house, Nelson?"

"Why you holding a gun on me like I'm a common criminal? Wait, that's an AR-15," Nelson said, alarmed with his hands moving upward in a defensive motion. "Are you going to war with some-body you really don't like?"

Orlando saw that his former partner was afraid of the damage the powerful assault rifle would cause, if the trigger was pulled ever so slightly. "Maybe I should and we'll get to that," Orlando replied, without blinking. "For the last time, why are you here?"

"Ask him how he got in," Mosley said, with a gun ready by his side.

"It was unlocked," Nelson responded, with a bold face lie. "What is the big freaking deal here?"

"I locked that door, made good and damned sure it was latched tight too," Mosley contradicted him, then aimed his pistol at Nelson's chest.

"So what, I tripped passed the lock. I wanted to know what was going on in here and why y'all sneaking around like somebody was following you."

"But you were following me in that gray Dodge," Orlando answered.

"He was?" Mosley asked, then played it off. "Yeah, that's right, I saw him too." No one believed him but it sounded good so he went with it.

"This rifle is getting heavy, Nelson," Orlando warned. "And, sprays like an Uzi with one hell of an attitude." Nelson was about to respond when the front door opened. Vera Miles came skulking in with her service revolver drawn.

"Hello Vera," Orlando said, nice and easy, with his rifle still trained on Nelson. "Come in and lock the door."

She did, then put her revolver away. "Well, this is something I didn't expect to see."

"What brings you by today?" Orlando asked her.

"I followed this joker from St. Nick's girlfriend's place when he followed behind y'all," she informed them. "I thought it was odd and because I'm an inquisitive person by nature, I wanted to know what *he* was up to."

"That's makes three of us," Mosley quipped. "What is Nelson up to?"

Vera walked over to Nelson to relieve him of the pistol on his hip holder and then she walked next to Orlando.

"Now can we discuss this like adults?" she asked. "I don't like that killing machine stocked, cocked, and ready to go wild, anywhere near me."

"After a dozen school shootings, it's got a bad rep," Orlando said, lowering it off Nelson.

"You think," Vera spat, sarcastically. "Military rifles should be *in the military*. You got something to eat?"

"I guess. Help yourself in the kitchen," Orlando offered.

When Vera took a few steps in the direction of the kitchen, she glanced into the office.

"Holy Moses!" she shouted. "Who did you rob, Orlando?"

Before he could address it, there was a knock at the door.

Everyone froze except Nelson, who found all of the activity amusing.

"This is getting rather cozy, if I do say so myself," he chuckled. "The party is just getting started."

Mosley looked out of the window. "It's Sister Carolyn, from the church."

"Of course it is," Orlando replied, in an exasperated tone. "Well, let her in?"

Mosley paused to question his orders. "With all this going on, pastor?"

"Why not? I need to know if the woman doing my taxes is a stand up individual or not, don't I?" he asked, irritably.

Nelson smiled at Orlando. "You're doing the dead preacher's wife?"

Vera nodded her head. "Yeah, he's doing her. This ought to be interesting."

Nelson and Vera knew that Orlando wanted to see Carolyn's reaction to the heavy artillery he was holding and it didn't have a darn thing to do with tax preparation. Orlando wanted to note Carolyn's reaction to what he was prepared to do if and when he caught up to the kidnappers.

Mosley opened the door to let her in. "Sister Carolyn, it's good to see you," he said, hiding his gun behind his back.

When Carolyn stepped in, holding a stack of papers, she saw the huge rifle in Orlando's hands. She screamed, clutching the documents against her chest.

"Ahhhhhgggh, what the hell is that?"

Nelson said, "The kind of gun you take out when you want to end the world, one battle at time." He smiled then looked her over thoroughly. "Howdy do. Remember me? I'm Nelson. Me and your new boo used to be partners. Lawmen, not the significant others type," he added, for clarity. "We were really good friends once and *trusted* each other."

"You want to talk about trust. *You* followed *me*," Orlando argued.

"What is she doing here?" Carolyn said, sizing up Vera.

"Orlando's ex-boo was tailing me. She's a mighty fine detective," Nelson answered. "If anybody's keeping score, here."

Vera scoffed at Nelson. "You *still* think you got a shot at getting some of this?"

"Deacon, please take this thing and put it away. I'll deal with Nelson's sneaky ass later," Orlando said, handing Mosley the high-impact rifle, then he walked over to Carolyn while everyone watched their interaction. "What you got there?" Orlando asked.

Carolyn was looking at Vera so hard that she forgot about the documents she brought over to discuss. She turned her gaze on Orlando finally.

"I have some papers to ask you about but maybe this isn't the best time."

"You know what, this is a very good time to talk about my finances." He knew it was a matter of time before Carolyn was canned at the church. Making her feel comfortable about his lifestyle had to start somewhere.

"This is very private," she said, with everyone looking on. "I only came by to tell you that I cannot represent you as a CPA."

"Why not?" Orlando asked, uncertain if he wanted all of the others to know his business. "You're great at this and I'm about to get audited, if I can't make my numbers add up."

"Orlando, I'm not going to jail for you," Carolyn said, louder and more assertively than she meant to. "You have over a million dollars."

"Really?" Nelson said, with renewed interest. "You don't say?"

"It doesn't look like that much from here," Vera remarked, with her best guess, as she eyed the stacks of money sitting on Orlando's desk.

Nelson, Carolyn, Vera and Orlando walked into the office behind Mosley. No one said a word until Orlando spoke up first.

"Look, I can explain," he sighed deeply.

"I didn't mean a million in cash," Carolyn whined. "What *are* you into?"

"Yeah, what?" Nelson asked. "Lemme see you talk your way outta this one"

"This looks like the kind of trouble that Houston mega church pastor got himself into," Carolyn chimed in, regrettably.

"Uh-huh, money laundering and wire fraud," Vera said, confidently. "The feds got Caldwell indicted over it."

"Pastor, what's up with all this?" Mosley asked, like he didn't know the money was in the office.

"Wait a minute! All of y'all need to stall that corruption talk," Orlando huffed, with an ounce of resentment. "Nelson, is that why you came buzzing around Dallas, all of a sudden? You've been in Houston taking down Kirby John Caldwell and now you're after me?"

"You didn't hear me say that," Nelson answered, and not too convincingly. "But you got some serious explaining to do."

"I didn't ever take a dime that wasn't owed to me," Orlando said, with a huge weight lifted off his shoulders. "All of y'all got it twisted. I thought y'all knew me better than that but I'm glad it finally come down to this. I've been keeping my blessings under wraps for years. Only Jessika knows the full extent of my wealth because I taught her to pay my bills and make deposits. I own twelve businesses, some with Numbers as a silent partner but most of them outright."

"Where did your windfall come from to get this empire off the ground?" Nelson asked, with an ounce of skepticism.

"Yes, I'd like to know that myself," Carolyn said, with her arms folded cautiously.

"When I was locked up on bogus charges, the government couldn't cut my pay without a conviction or they'd risk a huge lawsuit. They kept paying me for almost two years, including cost of living raises. When the FBI dropped the charges against me, I also received ten weeks of vacation pay."

Vera was losing interest in Orlando's narration of his new found wealth, especially since it didn't appear she was in line to enjoy any of it. "I'm naturally inquisitive like I said before, but at this moment I'm a lot hungrier than nosey so..."

Annoyed with her appetite and attitude, Orlando waved her towards the kitchen. "Yes Vera, eat whatever you find in there."

"So far that accounts for what, maybe two-hundred-thousand?" Nelson asked.

"Before taxes," Carolyn agreed. She was still somewhat skeptical.

"My wife, Shonda, had life insurance on me. I had a million on her too," he offered sadly. "Never thought I'd cash in hers first. I thought I was going to die when I got released from prison. No family, no job, nowhere to be particularly."

"So, what did you do?" Mosley asked.

"I drank a lot in local watering holes. I met Numbers outside of a Denny's then again while waiting at a bus stop. Neither one of us were waiting on a bus. We talked awhile and I listened a lot. I'd realized he was special that first time we met. No matter what I asked him about, he knew it. I heard some very rich convicts talk about the stock market when I was inside. They all knew a lot about picking winners. Numbers had them all beat. I said this company was growing too fast and it was gonna split and double in value or burst like a lot of dot com companies."

"You telling me you took a million dollars and bet it on a stock?" Nelson said, more excited than Orlando. If this were true, his former partner was safe from federal probes, which often started with IRS audits.

"I bet it all on Google. March 27, 2014. It split five days later. That cool million doubled during the week I was sipping on fruity umbrella drinks in the Bahamas."

Carolyn cleared her throat. "Ahh hmmm, excuse me. But your net worth is north of *seven million* dollars, Orlando."

"Seven million? Damn, how long was I gone?" Vera asked, then bit into a turkey sandwich. "Are you printing money, Orlando?"

"Whewww," Mosley whistled, then sat on the desk, near the bundles neatly wrapped bills.

"I never stopped playing the stocks. Numbers is rarely wrong about a good tip so I play every third or fourth move he suggests I make. That way the Federal Exchange Commission isn't breathing down my throat. I was going to give a chunk of my good fortune to MEGA but they just hired the devil's son-in-law as their new pastor. He's getting into something with St. Nick and will likely drag the church in at some point."

"I knew my partner was no crook. I tried to tell 'em," said Nelson.

"You didn't have to tell them anything," Orlando argued, heatedly. "There's nothing to hide. The simple truth is, I'm lazy with my tax filings at times and the IRS hates that."

Carolyn walked over to Orlando. "We can fight these threatening IRS letters?"

"Oh no, no, no. Don't you dare do that, Carolyn. It's the game they play," Orlando replied excitedly. "As long as I act scared, they'll fine me and go away. Fight it and they'll tie me up in knots for years."

"Where is the rest of the money?" Carolyn asked, with her eyes narrowed cautiously.

"Off shore, where the rich fat cats keep theirs. You could run my business instead of the church's and I'll double your salary, Carolyn." He didn't have the heart to tell her an immediate employment shift was on the way at M.E.G.A.

"I'll get back to you," Carolyn replied, blushing openly.

"I'll be here waiting," he answered, with a warm smile.

"I'll be over there in the corner, throwing up," Vera teased. "You sappy church people kill me."

"Whew, thank you Jesus. Y'all have no idea how hard it's been sitting on millions of dollars and keeping it to myself. It's been rough."

"Looks like you've been handling it just fine," Nelson concluded. "How much of it would you pay to get Jessika back?"

"Every penny," Orlando answered, quickly.

"I just thought of something," Nelson said, excitedly. "Give me your phone."

Orlando handed it over. Nelson took a picture of the bundle of cash sitting on the desk then texted it to Jessika's cell number. *Want this money? Bring my child home.*

"You think they'll go for it?" Mosley asked.

"They don't have to. The minute they reply, we'll demand proof of life again and force them to call and put Jessika on the phone. Then, we'll have Orlando's cellular carrier tell us where they're calling from. Nobody knows about this plan but the people in this room. If we keep a lid on it, we learn where Jessika is then we go get her."

Later that night, it was almost nine o'clock when the last member of the *Jessika Retrieval Team*, rolled into Bishops barbershop. Nelson was fidgety. He apologized for running behind then took a seat between Mosley and Duke.

Big Ray sat next to Grunt on the padded benches called customer's row. Mickey Bombay stood next to Bishop, who was showing off naked pictures of some African woman that was demanding money. Ms. Ophelia sat across from Byron, complaining about her feet. Slim Woody didn't make the meeting. He was still distraught over the death of Leasha.

"Apology accepted Nelson, now let's get down to some particulars," Orlando said, to the group. "We all know what's at stake here. Earlier we let those dudes get away. It's not going to happen a second time. I have money, in the event that I have to pay them off."

"Who's directing this take-back, if we see them trying to move Jessika again?" Duke asked. "Broke my heart to see them bring that dead girl out of the motel in a body bag. Could have been Lil Jay."

"It's been a long time since you called her that Duke."

"Because she hates it," he said, as everyone laughed. "That's what I'm gonna call her when we're done tonight."

"You do that," said Orlando. "But first, we're going to set a perimeter. Locate the spot they're holding her then sit on it until everyone is in place."

Mosley's foot tapped nervously. "How many people are we looking at dealing with?"

Orlando gave it some thought but allowed Nelson to speak up ahead of him. The pastor wasn't one hundred present certain he could trust his former partner but he had to. If he was wrong about the special agent, a lot of people could go to jail, or much worse.

"We have no idea how many shooters or guards they got on the payroll but I'm guessing four, no more than six. Once the word went out about Orlando's fifty thousand dollar reward, it drove them underground."

"Yeah and right into a better position for us to pounce. Quiet, let's set this thing up." A text came in on Orlando's phone at nine o'clock sharp to discuss the money drop. He stuck to the plan and asked for proof of life. Fifteen minutes later, the phone rang.

"Yeah," Orlando said, into the phone.

"Uncle... come and get me... please," Jessika whispered. "I'm cold." Her voice was frail and shaky.

"Jessika, hang in there honey. Hang in..." he muttered, before the called dropped.

Orlando stood silent. Nothing could pierce his fear of Jessika dying before he could find her.

'Hey! Hey, partner!" He heard someone say, seemingly from a faraway place. "Snap out of it Orlandoooo..."

"Hey Unca'," Duke said, with a firm grasp of Orlando's arm.

"Huh? What happened?" Orlando asked.

Nelson said, "Yeah, what did happen on the phone? What did she say to you?"

"She said please come, she was getting cold," Orlando answered, still trying to come back to himself after hearing Jessika's voice. "She's still alive but sounded weak."

He immediately dialed the phone carrier's customer service department. "Yes, this is Orlando Clay. I need an address from a phone call I just received. No, I cannot hold. This is a life or death situation." He took a slip of paper out of his pocket and wrote the address down as the service agent informed him.

"Are you sure? Thank you ma'am. Thank you."

Everyone took their phone out as Orlando looked at the slip of paper then began to write the address on it. "She said the call came from 9819 Greenspan Circle."

"Good lawd that's some Holy Hallelujah news!" Ms. Ophelia shouted.

Bishop jumped in his seat. "You scared me half to death 'Philea? What's the matter with you?"

She stammered so hard that dentures almost flew out of here mouth. "I-I-I know exactly where that is," she said, with both hands on her knees. "And Orlando should too because he owns the house at that address."

Duke stood up with an expression of awe shrouding his face. "Unca', she's right," he said, wearing a half smile. "Remember that time I kicked the door down and made that family evict themselves for being two months late on the rent?"

"Don't tell me that's the house?" Orlando asked.

"Right across the street from it," Duke answered. "Both of those places are yours."

"Well if that ain't ironic," Nelson remarked, with a twisted grin. "Hiding at your house. In plain sight."

"Tell me about it." Orlando looked at his watch. "I'll ask them to bring Jessika here for the swap. It's in a public place so they'll trust it. That'll give us time." Orlando turned to the old woman, who was beaming like a ray of sunshine. "Ms. Ophelia, thank you. Go on home and act like nothings happened. On second thought, go on over to late night bingo and have a ball." He handed her a stack of folding money. "Don't spend it all in one place."

"Pastor Clay, bad luck runs in my family." She slid the money in her bra then winked at Orlando. "For safe keeping. Y'all be careful." She exited out the back way, where her younger boyfriend was waiting in her car.

"Remember what we talked about," Orlando said, to the rest of the group, with utmost sincerity. "Big Ray, Bombay, you know what to do. Take the north end of the block. Duke, help them hem up that entire circle. Get there and sit on the house but don't get too close and spook them."

Duke said, "Got it Unc'. We out."

Grunt followed Duke through the front door with a look of resolve that put Orlando's mind at ease. "Y'all see that? Nothing's getting past Grunt with his shot gun. Nothing."

Bishop went into his office and closed the door. Byron played Candy Crush while checking himself out in the mirror. Mosley was still seated when the others wasted no time getting to their marks. Nelson gave Orlando a hard look then threw a glance in Mosley's direction.

Orlando's long sigh conveyed what he was thinking. Mosley wasn't cut out for gun battles, not when you got right down to it. He was tough but had too many reasons to deter him from going all the way to hell if circumstances called for it.

"Come on outside, deacon. Come on," Orlando insisted.

"I'll be in the can," said Nelson, feeling out of place and knowing what was to come. He went into the restroom as Mosley stood up slowly then followed Orlando out onto the broad cement walk way in front of the shop.

"We're in this pretty deep and the water is rising fast, deacon," Orlando advised, with a firm handshake. "Go home, Mosley."

"I'm in this with you like always, pastor."

"Not this time, my friend. If this goes sideways, bodies will fall."
Mosley turned around to compose himself then he faced
Orlando after pulling the right words together. "You don't think I
could protect you. Huh? Is that it?"

Orlando remained silent for as long as he could. He didn't want
to lie so he turned his back as Nelson walked out of the door.

He'd been watching from inside and felt he needed to move this
part of their relationship along. "Fact is Deacon Mosley, Orlando
don't know if he can protect you," Nelson concluded. "Nobody is
questioning your loyalty or ability. You got a family, something to
lose. Can't be thinking about that if this gets thick."

"Pastor, this how you see it?" Mosley questioned.

Orlando said, "I'd like to have you with me on this but Paula and
the kids need you brother. See you in the morning."

After Orlando watched Mosley slink towards the parking lot,
he walked back into the shop to give Bishop instructions, in the
event someone came around looking suspicious. Orlando overheard
Byron on a phone call, whispering into the phone.

"Naw man, they about to about to crash the party. Blow out the
candles and..." he said, stopping in his tracks when realizing he
wasn't alone.

Orlando took a seat directly in front of the young barber.

"Yo! B-Boy, what's up?"

"I'm cool, Pastor Clay. I'm good sir. What, you need a cut?"
Byron responded, nervously. He popped a nylon cape, inviting
Orlando to have a seat in his chair.

Nelson returned, surprised to see Orlando sitting down calmly.

"I thought we were leaving?" he said, apprising the situation.

"I thought y'all been gone," Bishop announced, when he exited the office to find them still there. "I've been in the back, face-timing a Nigerian princess. She say I can be her King and everything, if I wire her sixty-five hundred dollars. I'm gonna do it too. You know those African girls sho' know how to wrestle that tiger."

"Hold on Bishop," Orlando warned. "Me and B-Boy got us something to discuss."

Nelson noticed Orlando's steely gaze, locked onto Byron's eye as if he was tracking his prey. "Ohhh damn. Here we go."

"You know, I've been racking my brain trying to figure out how those kidnappers were a step ahead of us at the motel."

Bishop, still not sure what was transpiring, stood next to Byron like a father standing up for his son. He had been more a father in the past year since taking the young man off the streets, teaching him how to cut hair, and to run a business.

Nelson thoroughly enjoyed what he was seeing. The heat was finally off of him. "Ain't hard to stay a step ahead when you have an inside man stealing the game plan."

Orlando observed Bishop nervously wiping down his cutting tools. He stared down at the ground while cleaning a straight razor with a dry white rag. Finally, he raised his head then put a mean look on the accuser, the pastor.

"What are you saying *Mr. Clay*? This boy is like a son to me. You know that," Bishop grumbled.

"I didn't do nothing y'all. I didn't," Byron blathered, until Bishop squeezed the back of his neck then pushed him down in the barber chair."

"Keep your mouth shut," Bishop scolded him. "Grown men are talking now."

Instinctively Byron leapt out of the chair to escape. Nelson stuck out his lizard-skinned boot to trip him up. Byron wiggled to get free but Nelson grabbed and held his arm, just above the elbow to hold him still.

"Ahhhggghh!" Byron wailed loudly. Please let me go! Let me out of here!" As Nelson squeezed the young man's bicep harder, Byron winced miserably. "Oooouch, that hurts."

Nelson helped him back into the judgment seat then ripped the white barber smock and t-shirt off of Byron's right shoulder. There was fresh claw marks, dug deep into his skin. Nelson realized the same time Orlando did that Byron was not only involved, he was a murderer.

"You killed that hooker, didn't you?" Nelson interrogated, with a swift punch the gut.

"Wait, wait," Byron cried, with this hands up defensively.

"You're a killer and a spy, ain't you?" Nelson slugged him again two more times. Wap! Wap! "That poor woman had her hands up just like you do now when you took her life." Byron fought to get loose but there was no use. Nelson had him hemmed up in the barber chair.

Orlando looked on with sadness and anger in his eyes. "Leasha had skin underneath her fingernails when we found her. Don't even have to test it for DNA. Why'd you kill Leasha, Byron?" Orlando asked boldly. "Was it St. Nick who put you up to it?"

Bishop looked on but didn't have the words to step in and defend the young barber. So, he watched, and waited until it all played out.

"Wasn't no St. Nick. He didn't even know about it," Byron said, as he brooded angrily. "Boojie Queen likes me. She's always nice to me. I couldn't stand the way that prostitute got all salty with Boojie at the Mojo Monday over those high priced purses."

Nelson sat down, with his service weapon laid across his lap.

"Don't try to run again. You're a murderer and we don't have all night."

"No need for that Mr. Nelson Rockefeller Brown," Bishop told him. "Put that dream crusher back to where you got it from. We're among friends. Martin Luther King Jr. had two of his secret strategy meetings right here in this shop. He was going to start a colored maids' strike and put Dallas on the Civil Rights map."

Bishop searched the recesses of his mind to reminisce a little more. "Ron Kirk, Dallas' first Black mayor started his campaign on this very floor."

Nelson put his gun away, against his better judgment as Bishop cast a hurtful glare. Byron breathed a sigh of relief until the interrogation begun.

"B-Boy, isn't that what Boojie Queen called you on Mojo Monday, when she asked you to bring her some ice for another drink?" Orlando asked.

"Naw-Naw see. She must've heard Big Ray call me that," he argued.

"Only problem is Ray spoke to you long before Boojie and St. Nick 'nem came in. You're in good with them, huh?"

Nelson eased his gun out again, this time to stay. "You said there was a Judas among us and damned if you wasn't right."

Bishop closed his eyes briefly, to assess the moment. "If all that is true, Byron's responsible for letting those men who took Jessika get away when we had them too, right?"

"That wasn't none of me," Byron quibbled. "I smoked the hooker but I only made some phone calls to help my friends escape is all. That's it."

"Spies gotta get what's coming to them," Bishop determined, then he pressed the long shaving razor blade against Byron's throat. "How much they pay you, son? How much!"

"I'm sorry Bishop. I didn't know they would take the girl and then cut her up."

"Wait, hold up there Bishop," Orlando said, when a slight nick opened just below Byron's earlobe. "Who paid you B-Boy to keep tabs on our plans?"

Bishop begun to cry. "I took you in and raised you like one of my own. I was ready to hand this shop over to you."

"Please don't kill me. I'm sorry. I'm sorry," Byron pleaded hysterically.

Nelson picked up his gun then handed it to Orlando. "Go ahead and finish this. We should have been gone."

"Everybody hold on a minute. Just calm down!" Orlando hollered. "My team is in place. Nobody's getting off that block."

Tears ran down Bishop's cheeks. "How much did they pay you, got-dammit. How much you sell your soul for?"

"St. Nick told me to ear-hustle when y'all came in and keep him in the know about my friends who took that girl." Byron couldn't believe the other men were extremely upset with him. "Nick promised to let me run the strip club when all of this was over."

Orlando cocked the gun with a look of disgust in his eyes.

"You're too stupid to live."

Bishop gripped the razor tightly then sliced through Byron's throat before the pastor pulled his trigger. The young man clutched at his neck with both hands as blood poured down his shirt. Bishop held on firmly to his protégé as the young man kicked and gasped for breath. Orlando and Nelson looked on with stares of disbelief as life streamed out of the betrayer.

"It's almost over, son," Bishop said, in a comforting manner. "It's almost done."

Orlando's eyes blinked finally. "Nelson let's go. Bishop, I'll send somebody over to help you with him."

"I'll see to it myself, pastor. Sometimes a man needs to take out his own trash."

"Just the same, I'll see to it that Duke gets by here with a cleaning crew to straighten this up."

They left Bishop with his hands on Byron's shoulders, soothing the dead man's slumped body as only a friend would after making the hardest decision of his life. He understood what had to be done, and whose place it was to see it through. Yet, it didn't make his duty any easier to carry out.

25

NIGHT HAWKS AND HOSTAGES

Mosley sat in the dark alone. After his abrupt departure from the group, the deacon felt ashamed. He was a loyal friend with a servant's spirit but Orlando believed murder would not have rested well with Mosley's soul. Furthermore, the act of taking a man's life often came with dire consequences and lasting residue that most men could not readily dismiss. Still, Mosley, being sidelined when his friends were off doing battle for a noble cause hurt him like hell.

Paula walked into the den a few minutes after he'd been there. She felt his presence but wondered why he was in the dark. Cautiously, she flicked on the light then called out her husband's name when she saw him.

"Steven? Steven, you okay baby?"

Initially, he didn't respond. Mosley merely tossed her a fleeting glance to acknowledge he'd heard her voice.

"Hey," he sighed, in a low solitary tone.

Paula was well aware that his relationship with Orlando came with lots of concerns. Yet, she believed his work for the church was worthwhile. It was an association she tolerated at times although praise for Orlando was never high on her list. Seeing her man deflated with his head hung down was a cause for concern.

"What are you doing in here?" she asked, with her hand rubbing the back of his head. When he didn't answer, she pressed.

"Aren't you supposed to be out with the others, helping to get Jessika back? That girl must be terrified."

"Pastor didn't give me a choice," Mosley brooded. "Just said to go home."

"*And you left?*" Paula's mother asked boldly, from the doorway. She had been listening quietly and didn't think of intruding on their intimate conversation but she felt compelled to jump in then. "What was Pastor Clay thinking about you to say that?"

"He wasn't thinking about me, per se," Mosley answered, looking at his wife.

Paula couldn't stand the way he looked at her so she turned away.

"Can't believe I'm saying this. I agree with mama," she admitted, in an obvious bind. "You got a family honey and Pastor Clay is as much of it as we are. Maybe you should have stayed with him regardless of what he had to say about it."

Paula hoped her words made a difference, after seeing Mosley's spirit broken into pieces. When she turned back to see if her validation elevated his mood in any way, the deacon was already gone.

Inside of Orlando's rental property, Jessika laid dying. She spent most of the day floating in and out of consciousness in that gray-brick house with maroon shutters. Huddled under a dirty bed comforter, Jessika was tired, shivering with chills and suffering from severe dehydration. Excruciating pain rifled through her entire body. She ached all over, in the front bedroom of 9819 Greenspan Circle.

Nelson parked his Dodge Charger between Duke's plumbing van and Rig Ray's giant Toyota truck. They all stood behind the vehicles peering down at the house where Jessika was being held, which was difficult for them. Someone had previously shot out all the streetlights to darken the immediate surroundings. It was an old military tactic that drug dealers adopted as a survival strategy against the police.

Orlando listened as Duke laid out the landscape for them. He knew the neighborhood very well.

"I use to kick it with this chick who lived right over there. She had this yorkie that kept digging under the fence when she let it out in the morning to pee." Duke pointed at the alley behind 9819 Greenspan. "There's a row of bushes back there, all against the back of that house. You can't see three feet from the inside past all the leaves. That means they can't see you coming in through the back until it's too late."

"That also means we're going in blind," Orlando responded, pensively.

"I didn't say it was a *perfect* plan," was Duke's somewhat defensive reply.

Nelson looked through infrared binoculars towards the enclosed end of the street. The x-ray vision they provided allowed him to see human images moving around in the house. Through the lens, he saw two bright images upright and standing side by side.

"Two jokers are in one room shooting the breeze, looks like."

"You get good night vision with those?" Grunt asked, with heightened interest.

"There's another two bogies in a second room and someone lying down in the smaller room on the front side."

The thermal reading was low so he knew it was Jessika. "Yeah these Night Hawk Binoculars are infrared and thermal tested from 20 below zero up to 110 degrees in the desert heat. These are the best instruments the government has to offer for situations such as this," Nelson bragged.

He looked over at Grunt expecting to see him in total awe. Instead his eyes found the plumber's assistant looking through an exact pair of Night Hawk Binoculars. "Nice, huh?" Grunt said. "Got 'em off Ebay."

Orlando opened the brown leather satchel, which was stuffed with stacks of money wrapped in clear plastic. Beneath the bills was a small .38 caliber pistol.

"You're really giving those assholes all that money?" Big Ray asked. "Why don't all of us bum rush the house, light those fools up and take a nice trip afterwards. Get some bikini freaks and something to sip in the sand. I know I need a vacation, pastor."

"Sounds fun, Ray, but Jessika and a few of us could die down there," Orlando advised. "Let's talk about a vacation when we make it back. It'll all be on me. Just make sure y'all blast anyone that comes this way. No exceptions."

"Hell yeah," Big Ray said. "Y'all be careful. We got it on this end."

Orlando followed Nelson down the alley and behind the gray brick house. They peeked through the tall bushes Duke told them about, in order to see the back door next to a huge barbeque pit.

"I wish I brought a key for that door," Orlando whispered.

Nelson flashed a devilish grin. "Who needs a key?"

Since Nelson had recently broken into Orlando's house, he had no qualms about breaching the lock on this one.

Within seconds they were inside, with a satchel full of money. Nelson was armed with his government issued semi-auto. Orlando had a .44 shoved in the back of his waistband and a surprise in the bottom of the bag.

Once inside the house, Nelson pointed at the room to the left then held up two fingers, for the two bandits in there. Walls in the house were thin, mostly plasterboard without insulation. He and Orlando heard the men discussing what their plans were for spending the money after delivering Jessika.

"When we get this paper, I'm buying me a drop top six-four with three wheel motion," he said, imagining himself in a 1964 convertible automobile with hydraulics. "You can laugh if you want to but I always dreamed of rolling in something west-coast gangster style like Ice Cube and 'nem did back in the day."

"What if we don't get her to that preacher before she dies?" the other voice said.

"Then we show up with her body, tell the preacher she's asleep then blast his ass and take the money while he's trying to wake her up."

Jessika laid in the next room, staples closing up the wounds from a botched kidney removal. She overheard the men's conversation but had no idea her uncle and his former partner were even closer than her abductors. As grave fear washed over her, Jessika tried to get up and run but didn't have the strength to climb out of bed.

Nelson heard the kidnappers growing impatient.

"Let's go ahead and pack the girl up then get out of here," one of them said. "We'll get to the drop point, make the swap, take the money and then kill everybody in Bishop's barbershop."

"Yeah, one of those bastards took off my pinky finger, I don't care if that chick croaks a minute after I get paid."

Jessika mustered up enough energy to slide off the bed. She cringed in pain when she hit her head on the floor. The men in the front room heard the thud it made. One of them got up to go and check it out. It was Sonny Dreadlocks from Big Ray's gambling house.

Suddenly a phone began to vibrate. The two men in the next room thought it was one of theirs until they realized it wasn't. It was Orlando's cell phone and he couldn't get it to stop buzzing. Nelson couldn't believe it was happening.

"Really? Man, shut that thing up," Nelson demanded.

St. Nick was calling Orlando on redial about the money swap they had agreed to. Now that he'd crawfished on their arrangement, it was coming back to haunt him.

"It's St. Nick," Orlando said quietly, then glided the phone on the kitchen floor away from them. It landed next to the stove, about ten feet away.

When Dreadlocks stepped into the room where Jessika was kept, he found an empty bed and the window opened.

"Ain't no way that sick bitch climbed through the window," he said, to himself.

"No, I did," Mosley replied, from behind him. As the kidnapper turned toward him, Deacon Mosley smashed him over the head with his gun. Sonny Dreadlocks fell hard onto the floor. His body landed next to the closet, where Jessika was huddled up in pile of dirty clothes.

"We've been looking everywhere for you," Mosley assured her.

"Hold this gun, point and squeeze if you see another overgrown rat that you don't like." Jessika held the hard metal pistol in her hands nervously. Her tired eyes grew wide when she almost dropped it. "You got it?" Mosley asked kindly, then he took off without awaiting her reply.

After giving Jessika his only weapon, Mosley walked to the doorway and looked out. Two men from the front room were coming toward him. One of them had a pistol in his hand. The deacon took a deep breath then walked out of the room with both of his hands tucked casually in his pant pockets.

Standing with their backs against the wall, Orlando watched Mosley walk casually out of the bedroom. Orlando brushed Nelson on the shoulder. "It's the deacon," he whispered.

"Hey! Whoever's in that kitchen, come out now!" a strong voice demanded.

Nelson exited the small area first. He came out with his hands up, his gun in a surrendering position. Orlando took his time sauntering into the den area, purposely showing the weapon in the small of his back.

Four men surrounded them. They were angry for the intrusion and shocked that a rescue effort was taking place.

"Now ain't this something," Hollywood Harris said, as he laid eyes on Orlando. "The big-time pastor came to save the day. I would applaud you for your attempt to jump us but I can't BECAUSE MY HAND HURTS!" he spat, while holding up his left hand with a medical wrap around it.

"Sometimes that's the cost of doing business," Orlando said. "Things don't always go the way you plan."

"Plan? Cutting off my pinky finger shouldn't have been the part of no plan," he whined. Man, give me your gun."

One of the men walked behind Orlando and pulled the weapon out. He watched the pastor cautiously, back away then hand the weapon to Hollywood.

"Now I got one. It ain't no fun till the rabbit has a gun," Hollywood joked. "I ought to shoot you for coming into my hideout."

"Let's get the money and go," the voice from behind Orlando suggested.

Orlando recognized it but couldn't place where he'd heard it from. "Before I hand this money over, I want to see my niece, make sure she's okay."

"Well, this is one time you're not in charge, Mr. Pastor," Hollywood heckled, indignantly.

Orlando held the leather satchel handle tightly with one hand as he reached inside of it slowly with the other. He turned around to face the man behind him, the one who seemed to be in charge, the man whose voice Orlando knew.

"Hahaha," Criss-Cross chuckled, nervously, when their eyes met. He was the church intruder who caused the immense ruckus while Orlando was preaching at M.E.G.A. two weeks before.

"I never forget a voice or a face," Orlando said, calmly.

"Good for you. Now ease your hand out of the bag, nice and easy," Criss-Cross ordered.

Orlando did as he was told. He brought his hand out, with a large stack of $100 bills.

"Some now and the rest when we leave with the girl," Orlando negotiated, wisely. Then, he moved into position with his back against Nelson's, which was standard operating procedure when out-numbered in small quarters. Mosley stood to the left side of them, alone.

"Hand me the bag and take her," Criss-Cross said, reaching for the money. "I have no problems with that." He held the bundle of cash and looked it over. He wanted more. "Hand me the rest of it."

Orlando didn't blink or bend. He said,

"The girl first."

"Okay, okay. Hey, go get the girl," Criss-Cross demanded, of the thug standing next to him.

As soon as the man left, Orlando reached his hand back into satchel. "Thanks for playing this out like a gentleman. Keeping your word."

Criss-Cross narrowed his eyes. "Pastor Clay, everybody's been telling me you're such a brilliant man but I don't see it. You should have killed me when you had the chance. That nasty concrete dungeon y'all held me in was a living hell." He gave Orlando a sinister grin, which tipped his hand. "Only one of us is walking out of here alive. I'd rather die than be chained up again."

"Really? That's good to know," Orlando said, then pulled the trigger twice from the bottom of the leather bag.

Bang!

Bang!

With his hand stuck out for more money and a stupid look on his face, Criss-Cross fell dead on the floor. Orlando ruined his expensive leather bag with two bullet holes but he was one step closer to ending this violent conflict.

"What did you do?" Hollywood yelled. "Put your hands up. Wait, drop that tricky satchel *then* put your hands up."

Orlando obliged while he was facing the same gun that was taken from him.

"Watch out Hollywood, that's a hair trigger. Be careful or you're liable to shoot somebody."

"That's exactly what I'm gonna do." He pointed the barrel at Orlando's head then squeezed the trigger. It clicked but didn't fire.

He tried again.

Click. Click. Click.

"Guess I forgot to load it," Orlando informed him, then threw a right cross that toppled Hollywood to his knees.

From the other room, there was a loud gunshot. Orlando made a move to dash in there but the lone gunman was not having any of it.

"No, no. You stay here," he ordered, timidly. "Until my dude comes out of there, nobody is moving an inch."

Mosley looked at Nelson and knew immediately what he was thinking. They needed a distraction to get a jump on the gunman.

"Hey man, I'm scared and don't feel so good," Nelson whined. "I'm gonna throw up."

"I don't care what you do, just don't move," the gunman threatened, anxiously pointing the gun at Nelson. "Hey Mike! Mike, you good in there?"

Hollywood was writhing on the floor. "Why'd you bust me in the face, Preacher? That was totally uncalled for."

"But you just tried to shoot me," Orlando argued, "so stay down there dude, unless you want to join Criss-Cross."

"Mike, what's going on in there?" the gunman called out.

When he relaxed to look in the direction of the bedroom, Nelson reached out to snatch the gun away but he was too late. The gunman saw him then pulled the trigger.

Bang!

Nelson dropped to the floor like a ton of bricks.

He wasn't moving.

Orlando looked at Nelson, lying still on the floor. He had to think fast or risk catching a bullet too.

"Just calm down. Now, you're the leader," Orlando told the shooter. "Take the money and go. You can have all of it."

"And have y'all tracking me for the rest of my life. Hell naw," he declined, then aimed the gun at Orlando, deciding to shoot him next but Mosley had a plan of his own. He pulled both hands out of his pockets then threw two handfuls of sand into the man's face, then bravely placed himself between the shooter and Orlando.

The kidnapper screamed as he clutched at his eyes, burning with sand. He pointed the gun and squeezed the trigger erratically. As the gun fired, Mosley swiped at the barrel and ducked. The gun fired again just as Mosley grabbed it away using the same fancy maneuver the special agents were taught during training. The deacon had studied it on YouTube for hours since Orlando used "the" trick on him. The deacon finally got it right but Nelson laid on the floor bleeding, suffering from a gunshot wound in the chest.

Mosley trained his gun on the abductor, who was whimpering and clawing at the sand in his eyes. Orlando stepped over Hollywood's body as he sprinted into the other room to see about Jessika.

"Hollywood? Hollywood?" the last abductor standing called out, as he fell to his knees. "I can't see you, man. I can't see."

Mosley peered down to find Hollywood Harris lying still on the floor with a bullet hole in the center of his forehead.

"He can't either," Mosley told him. "Because you killed him."

"POLICE!" the kidnapper yelled. "HELP! HELP ME PLEASE, SOMEBODY!"

"Say good night, punk!" Mosley advised harshly, then slapped the groveling thug across the face with the butt of his gun to lull him to sleep.

In the front of the house, Sonny Dreadlocks stumbled out of the window with a pistol in his hand. He landed on his knees then struggled to his feet. As soon as he stepped off the curb, Grunt opened fire with this shotgun. Dreadlocks fired blindly into the darkness as Grunt walked towards him, wearing night vision goggles. Less than seven feet apart, they continued blasting at one another until, finally, Grunt pumped two hot rounds of lead into Dreadlock's chest, sending him face-first to the pavement.

Duke came strutting down the street to inspect his assistant's kill. "That's how you do it Grunt! That's how you get in a kidnapper's ass at close range!"

When there wasn't any movement from the perpetrator, Grunt lowered his heavy shotgun then removed his goggles. "Damn, I love Ebay."

Police sirens blared. Emergency vehicles raced down the street. Big Ray and Mickey Bombay walked slowly in the middle of the street, towards the cul-de-sac. Both of the big men wore fearful expressions.

Detective Vera Miles arrived on the scene with a bad feeling about what she would find in the house.

As first responders hustled in the front door, Mosley tipped out through the backyard. He disappeared through the dense bushes with a solemn look of resolve on his face and a satchel full of cash.

Inside the house, Dallas City Police officers sorted out the dead bodies and arrested the only surviving kidnapper for murder of his partner in crime, Hollywood Harris. The city cops stepped over the deceased men to attend to Nelson's wound. The bullet that entered his upper chest, exited clean through the back of his shoulder. Paramedics tried to hold him down to treat him but he wouldn't let them until he made it to the other room where Orlando had gone after Jessika. Nelson sank to the ground when his eyes saw emergency medical techs fussing with Jessika, to revive her.

Orlando stayed by Jessika's side, as they wheeled her out on a gurney. "Don't stop breathing Jessika," he said, while holding her hand all the way into the ambulance. "Don't give up honey. Don't you dare give up." As the medic closed the door, she faintly squeezed Orlando's hand. "That's it Jess. Hang in there."

"You came for me, Uncle," she whispered. "I knew you'd come."

Duke stepped into the ambulance to see about Jessika firsthand.

"Shhh, quiet," he said softly. "Go ahead and rest Lil Jay." Duke kissed her on the head as a prideful tear escaped from his eye. "I heard you blasted one of them fools then hid in the closet. I'm so proud of you, girl."

"Thanks Duke. Where's Grunt?" she asked, fighting off the need to sleep.

"He's over there, probably admiring his work, like he always does," Duke answered, as an afterthought.

Nelson watched the ambulance drive off with his best friend accompanying his niece to the hospital. St. Nick was right. Earth could be a lonely place when you didn't have family in it with you.

"Jessika's going to be fine," Nelson said, to Vera. "These idiots tried to sell her kidney to the transplant society at Medical City. When the hospital called the cops, they ran away and left the organ, chilling on ice. Jessika will probably get her own kidney back."

"The medic said you're going to pull through too," Vera teased, after the EMT bandaged Nelson's wound. "You lucky duck. All of those bullets whizzing by and you only took one in the shoulder?"

"In the chest," Nelson argued. "This kind of injury would have killed most men. Could've even blown up something I needed."

"What, like your humility gland?"

"You know, I could use one of those. Can we have drinks and talk about where to get one, Detective Miles?"

"Let's ask Orlando where he got his," she said, before reconsidering. "Never mind, his is broken half the time… and call me Vera, if you expect me to answer."

She laughed but didn't overlook how drawn she was to Nelson. Maybe it was the hole in his upper chest that made him seem more appealing.

"Call me," Vera offered, as the ambulance driver returned to fuss over Nelson's bandages.

"Nice, we'll do dinner," he said, excitedly.

"Just coffee. Don't push it."

Nelson took a lasting look at Vera's behind as she walked away.

"Okay, just coffee. Then, we'll do dinner," he said, under his breath. "All this brother from another mother needs is a chance."

"I heard that," Vera said, from the other side of the room.

Nelson smiled from ear to ear. "Ha, but you didn't say no."

After the kidnappers were bagged and tagged at Orlando's rental property, St. Nick continued to dial Orlando's cell phone. He sat in Boojie's apartment with his thugs, puzzled and pondering why the pastor wasn't picking up, then it hit him while Boojie Queen looked on impatiently.

"Turn on the news," St Nick said. "I'll bet that pretentious-ass pastor ain't picking up because he decided to handle this sticky kidnap situation his self."

Boojie sat on the sofa next to her boyfriend, watching the evening report and sipping from a champagne glass.

"Orlando said he was down with letting you manage the money drop," Boojie said innocently. "So what makes you think that?"

"Yeah, what makes you believe that preacher would say one thing then have us up in here waiting by the phone?" St. Nick's cousin asked.

"Because that's exactly what I would have done," St. Nick replied, with a soft grin. "Keep the opposition out of the way so I could set matters straight. Huh, we just got played. Well done, Orlando Clay. Next time, I'll be ready," he said, in conclusion.

"It's getting late, Nickolas," Boojie whined. "I'm hungry."

"We can get whatever you want," he answered. "We could hit the breakfast bar early and I'll even cook you something special myself."

His cell phone buzzed from the coffee table. He recognized the number. "Hold on a second. It's the restaurant calling now," he informed them, then answered it.

"Yep. Wait, slow down Chef. What? A city health inspector? Rats in the salad!" he yelled. "All of the salad? Shut the place down and throw everything out. Yes, I'm sure. Damn!" St. Nick tossed the phone on the table as steam seethed out of both nostrils.

Boojie looked on then eventually asked what everyone else was thinking.

"You think Orlando 'nem had anything to do with a health inspector finding rats in your lettuce at eleven o'clock at night?"

"Orlando's got to be the reason the city just decided to drop in and start poking around this time of night," he answered. "I'm gonna make it a point to break him if it's the last thing I do. Boojie, I'm sending Pastor Clay to be with his wife and kids. Just you wait and see. Wait and see."

Two weeks later, Big Ray and Mickey Bombay sipped Coronas from a beer hut on Miami Beach. Bishop and his sister Ophelia enjoyed a paddle boat near the shore. Duke and Grunt spent all day snorkeling and all night frequenting local strip clubs.

Mosley, Paula and their twin boys built sand castles in the sand as Grandma Gigi, spent all afternoon checking out Slim Woody's Speedo swim trunks. Two nurses doted over Jessika as her transplant wounds healed nicely beneath surgical bandages.

Orlando watched everyone having a grand time at his expense. He even talked Numbers into getting on an airplane too, as long as he was sedated and surrounded by all of the chocolate jello he could eat.

Nelson stayed in Dallas, on a stay-cation with Detective Vera Miles. She knew her days with Orlando were over, which opened up a lot of nights for her to figure out life without him. Nelson promised to do any and everything she wanted to help her forget about the pastor. *Any* and *everything*.

Carolyn declined the invitation to travel on the private jet with the crew. She blamed it on having too many boxes of tax receipts to reconcile but everyone knew she wanted her relationship with Orlando to be above board and platonic from there on out. She wanted to be absolutely necessary to him.

Orlando agreed but wouldn't commit right away. He knew there would be hell to pay, once he returned home to face St. Nick and Minister T. C. Manning's new enterprises. M.E.G.A. church was about to get torn inside out and stripped clean to the bone.

Orlando was not about sit back and watch it happen, without doing everything he could to stop it.

THE END

ABOUT THE AUTHOR

Victor McGlothin completed a Master's Degree in Human Relations & Business before penning 14 bestselling novels and three film projects. He lives near Dallas.